T4-AHF-580

The Gospels in
HARMONY

The Illustrated, Combined Accounts of the Life of Christ from Matthew, Mark, Luke, John, and Joseph Smith Translation

Compiled by: PATRICK A. BISHOP

Dedication

To my wife, Elizabeth, and my children,
John, Benjamin, Maria, Joshua, and Gabriella.
May this work strengthen your faith in Jesus the Christ.

Cover artwork: *Pondering Mary* © Jeffrey Hein. For more information, go to www.jeffreyhein.com. *Hallowed Be Thy Name* © 2010 Simon Dewey. Courtesy of Altus Fine Art. For print information, go to www.altusfineart.com. *Lovest Thou Me More Than These?* © David Lindsley For more information, go to www.davidlindsley.com. *Risen Hope* © Joseph F. Brickey. For more information, go to www.josephbrickey.com.

Jacket and book design by Christina Marcano, © 2010 Covenant Communications, Inc.

Published by Covenant Communications, Inc.
American Fork, Utah

Printed in China
First Printing: October 2010

17 16 15 14 13 12 11 10   10 9 8 7 6 5 4 3 2 1

ISBN-13: 978-1-60861-096-9

Acknowledgments

As this book is dedicated to my wife and children, I also wish to thank them for their excitement about this work. They never once complained about the time it took, but instead asked how the work was coming. My wife has been a source of strength, especially at the final hours, inspiring me on and even helping at times. My greatest hope is that this work will be a lasting testimony to my family of the love and faith I have in the Savior, Jesus Christ.

I wish to thank Shaun Athey, a former Institute student and now a Seminary teacher, for taking an interest in this project. In his extra hours he helped with some of the merging of text. His voluntary help and dedication will always be remembered.

I extend my gratitude to Phil Reschke from Covenant Communications for searching me out while teaching at BYU Education Week. He has taken an interest in many of my personal projects over the last several years. His counsel and insights have made it possible for this work to be published.

Finally, I am grateful to God our Eternal Father for the gift of His Son. I know that this gift permeates everything in my life. I am who I am because of Jesus Christ. He is my Savior and King. I am deeply humbled that I can publish something dedicated to building faith in Him.

Introduction

Studying the New Testament, and more particularly the four Gospels, should be a lifelong pursuit of every Latter-day Saint. There are no closer witnesses to the life and teaching of Jesus Christ than those of His early disciples. The Savior's beloved disciple John said that the Gospels were written "that ye might believe that Jesus is the Christ, the Son of God; and that believing ye might have life through his name" (John 20:31). One of the primary ways to come to know the Savior is by studying His word as found in these Gospels.

Many methods and study aids have been developed over the centuries as ways to study the Gospels. In reality there is no one way to study them. Every method has its benefits that reveal insights not realized by other methods. Studying each individual book separately and independently helps us see things through the eyes of each separate author of a Gospel. Further, we also learn about the intended audience that the Gospel addresses and how the teachings of Jesus apply to those specific groups of people.

Writers

The four standard Gospel writers are Matthew, Mark, Luke, and John. Most believe that Matthew was written primarily to a Jewish audience. Mark is believed to have been the first of the four Gospels written. Luke appeals to a wide audience that seems directed to Gentiles. John was written to the followers of Christ. With these different audiences, the writers of each gospel emphazied certain gospel principles and teachings over others so as to appeal to their believers and hopefully win converts.

Matthew

Before the Lord changed this Apostle's name to Matthew, he was known as Levi, the publican or tax collector (see Mark 2:14 and Luke 5:27). He was one of the original Twelve called by Jesus to follow Him and later become His Apostles. Most believe he was a Jew and that his Gospel was first written in Hebrew or Aramaic. It is evident while reading this Gospel that Matthew's purpose was to persuade his fellow Jews that Jesus of Nazareth was the promised Messiah of the Old Testament. To do this, Matthew skillfully unfolds the Old Testament prophecies that deal with the Messiah and shows their fulfillment in the life of Jesus. It was known that the promised Messiah would sit on the throne of David, so Matthew begins his Gospel with a lineage of the kings of Israel and shows that Jesus would have sat on the throne had the Jews still been in power.

Mark

"Little John Mark," as some have referred to him, was a disciple of Jesus but not one of the original Twelve. He was not with the Lord in the earliest days. Many believe that Mark was commissioned and wrote his Gospel under the direction of Peter. Therefore, Mark was able to pen with much accuracy the early accounts of the Savior's life. It is also believed that because he was asked by Peter, the chief Apostle, to write this Gospel, it was the earliest written and thus the base text used by Matthew and Luke. Mark's object was to show that Jesus was the literal Son of God born in the flesh. This is why his gospel immediately begins with the baptism of Jesus, when God's voice was heard through the veil saying, "Thou art my beloved Son."

Luke

Little is known regarding Luke's whereabouts during the Savior's entire ministry. It is possible that Luke was a member of the Seventy as he emphasizes the role of the Seventy, in his tenth chapter while the other gospels are silent on this point. Luke is first mentioned by name in Col. 4:14. It is assumed that Luke was the writer not only of his Gospel but of the book of Acts, where he refers to himself in the plural with Paul and others. Most of what we know of him is from the book of Acts, although he doesn't mention himself by name. He was a missionary companion to a few of the Apostles and his Gospel was sent to the gentile nations. His gospel seems to be written to this audience, the Gentiles. Luke emphasizes the miracles and works more than any other Gospel writer. His emphasis on healings comes from his vocation as a medical practitioner of sorts.

John

To John goes the honor of the concluding Gospel. It is unlike any of the previous synoptic Gospels, and more than 90 percent of his writings are unique to his book. As one of the chief Apostles from the beginning, John writes to those who believe in Jesus as the promised Messiah. He dwells on finer points of the gospel not familiar to non-believers. For instance, the opening lines of his work deal with pre-mortal life: "In the beginning was the Word, and the Word was with God" (John 1:1). His purpose, stated at the end of his work, is to seal the testimony in the hearts of those who already believe that Jesus is the Christ, that they "might have life through his name" (John 20:31).

Harmonies and Parallels

To try to get a more complete picture of the events and teachings in the Savior's life, scholars and historians have developed what has been termed a *Gospel harmony.* This method endeavors to bring together all that is known about the life of Jesus in a chronological time line. Because the Gospels were not written until thirty to sixty years after the events took place, some minor discrepancies occur when comparing the four Gospels. No one as yet has been able to make a perfect Gospel harmony. Nevertheless, much good can come from studying the Gospels in a harmony; often a more complete picture of the events can be seen this way.

A clarification is needed to define what a Gospel harmony actually is: "A Gospel Harmony, sometimes called a synopsis (from the Greek synoptos), endeavors to weave all the details of the Gospel tradition into a single chronological strand with one composite order or sequence. A Gospel harmony should be distinguished from another important study tool, a Gospel parallel."[1] What many of us term a *Gospel harmony* is really a *parallel*. Popular LDS titles published as harmonies that are technically gospel parallels include *Our Lord of the Gospels* by J. Rueben Clark, Jr., and Thomas M. Mumford's *Horizontal Harmony of the Four Gospels in Parallel Columns*. There are dozens of other Gospel parallels available from non-LDS authors.

A few Gospel harmonies have been created by taking the four Gospel threads and weaving them into a single cord or narrative. The earliest known attempt to do this was the *Diatessaron* (c 150–160) created by Tatian. The latest attempt at a true Gospel harmony is *The Gospels Interwoven: A Chronological Narrative of the Life of Jesus Interweaving Details from the Four Gospels* by Kermit Zarley. To date, no LDS harmony narrative has ever been published. This is the thrust of this publication.

This Work

Beginning on p. 684 of the LDS Bible Dictionary and continuing through p. 696 is a chart that provides a "Harmony of the Gospels." The headings at the top of these charts provide for a complete chronological listing of all the major events in the life of Jesus Christ as contained in the New Testament, together with the location of the event and the pertinent scriptures from Matt., Mark, Luke, and John. "As you can imagine, the development of these charts required hundreds of hours of dedicated effort."[2] The work you are about to read has taken this resource as the outline and chronology to produce the harmony narrative. All of the texts have been woven together into a single narrative. Some slight changes have been made to the headings used in the Bible Dictionary so as to avoid the overlap of text. The base text used for the narrative will be the first Gospel that deals with the event, then each additional Gospel that sheds an additional insight will be interwoven to the narrative. In most cases this means that Matthew is the base text for those events which multiple Gospels cover. Although Matthew may be the base text, this does not mean that each interwoven section will always start with Matthew. The historical timing of events is taken into account to determine which Gospel narrative will begin the section. There have also been a few changes of the verb tenses, indicated by bracketed text, to make the reading fluid. One benefit of a true Gospel harmony is that the composition does not omit any detail from any of the Gospels yet avoids repetition.

Each Gospel in this text has been given a specific font designation to aid the reader in the study process. Matthew is in black, Mark is in green, Luke is in blue, and John is in red. The Joseph Smith Translations have also been added to the run of the text. They are represented in underlined text with the corresponding colors from the books they relate to. For example, a Joseph Smith Translation from John would be underlined in red. There are at least three reasons why Joseph Smith felt inspired to make changes in the Bible text. These were to restore plain and precious truths that had been taken out, to correct mistakes made during translation

---

1   Richard Neitzel Holzapfel, Thomas A. Wayment, and Eric D. Huntsman, *Jesus Christ and the World of the New Testament* (Salt Lake City: Deseret Book Company, 2006), p. 59.

2   Daniel H. Ludlow, *Selected Writings of Daniel H. Ludlow: Gospel Scholars Series,* p. 72.

or scribing, and to give different renderings of passages for better comprehension. When either of the latter two are placed in the body of this work, the words of the original King James text have been footnoted.

This work is not intended to compete with the standard works of The Church of Jesus Christ of Latter-day Saints. It is also does not claim to be a scholarly work to stand up to the historical critics of the day. Rather it is the hope of the author that this work will be another way for Latter-day Saints to study the New Testament. This work presents to the reader a fluid reading without the repetition but with all the detail of the life of Jesus. Insights heretofore unknown will be revealed to the reader during this approach to studying the Gospels of the New Testament. One of the purposes of the Book of Mormon is to convince the "Jew and Gentile that Jesus is the Christ" (title page). By weaving together Matthew, who is to the Jew, and Luke, who is to the Gentile, along with the other Gospels, one can again read a single work that convinces both the Jew and Gentile that Jesus is the Christ.

Prologue
Matt. 1:1, Mark 1:1, Luke 1:1–4, John 1: 1–5, JST Luke 1:1, JST John 1:1–5

The beginning of the gospel of Jesus Christ, the book of the generation of Jesus Christ, the Son of God, the son of David, the son of Abraham. In the beginning was the gospel preached through the Son, and the gospel was the Word, and the Word was with the Son. And the Son was with God, and the Son was of God[3].

The same was in the beginning with God.

All things were made by him; and without him was not any thing made that was made.

In him was the gospel, and the gospel was life; and the life was the light of men.

And the light shineth in the world,[4] and the world perceiveth[5] it not.

As I [Luke] am a messenger of Jesus Christ, and knowing that[6] many have taken in hand to set forth in order a declaration of those things which are most surely believed among us,

Even as they delivered them unto us, which from the beginning were eyewitnesses, and ministers of the word;

It seemed good to me also, having had perfect understanding of all things from the very first, to write unto thee in order, most excellent Theophilus,

That thou mightest know the certainty of those things, wherein thou hast been instructed.

The Genealogies
Matt. 1:2–17, Luke 3:23–38, JST Matt. 1:16, JST Luke 3:45
*Note: the genealogies cannot be harmonized, because Matthew is the genealogy of the crown or throne of Israel, and Luke is the lineal blood line of Jesus.

Abraham begat Isaac; and Isaac begat Jacob; and Jacob begat Judas and his brethren;

And Judas begat Phares and Zara of Thamar; and Phares begat Esrom; and Esrom begat Aram;

And Aram begat Aminadab; and Aminadab begat Naasson; and Naasson begat Salmon;

And Salmon begat Booz of Rachab; and Booz begat Obed of Ruth; and Obed begat Jesse;

And Jesse begat David the king; and David the king begat Solomon of her that had been the wife of Urias;

And Solomon begat Roboam; and Roboam begat Abia; and Abia begat Asa; And Asa begat Josaphat; and Josaphat begat Joram; and Joram begat Ozias;

And Ozias begat Joatham; and Joatham begat Achaz; and Achaz begat Ezekias;

And Ezekias begat Manasses; and Manasses begat Amon; and Amon begat Josias;

And Josias begat Jechonias and his brethren, about the time they were carried away to Babylon:

---

3   John reads, "Word was God"
4   John reads, "in darkness"
5   John reads, "darkness comprehended"
6   Luke reads, "Forasmuch as"

And after they were brought to Babylon, Jechonias begat Salathiel; and Salathiel begat Zorobabel;

And Zorobabel begat Abiud; and Abiud begat Eliakim; and Eliakim begat Azor; And Azor begat Sadoc; and Sadoc begat Achim; and Achim begat Eliud;

And Eliud begat Eleazar; and Eleazar begat Matthan; and Matthan begat Jacob;

And Jacob begat Joseph the husband of Mary, of whom was born Jesus, <u>as the prophets have written,</u> who is called Christ.

So all the generations from Abraham to David are fourteen generations; and from David until the carrying away into Babylon are fourteen generations; and from the carrying away into Babylon unto Christ are fourteen generations.

And Jesus himself began to be about thirty years of age, being (as was supposed) the son of Joseph, which was the son of Heli,

Which was the son of Matthat, which was the son of Levi, which was the son of Melchi, which was the son of Janna, which was the son of Joseph,

Which was the son of Mattathias, which was the son of Amos, which was the son of Naum, which was the son of Esli, which was the son of Nagge,

Which was the son of Maath, which was the son of Mattathias, which was the son of Semei, which was the son of Joseph, which was the son of Juda,

Which was the son of Joanna, which was the son of Rhesa, which was the son of Zorobabel, which was the son of Salathiel, which was the son of Neri,

Which was the son of Melchi, which was the son of Addi, which was the son of Cosam, which was the son of Elmodam, which was the son of Er,

Which was the son of Jose, which was the son of Eliezer, which was the son of Jorim, which was the son of Matthat, which was the son of Levi,

Which was the son of Simeon, which was the son of Juda, which was the son of Joseph, which was the son of Jonan, which was the son of Eliakim,

Which was the son of Melea, which was the son of Menan, which was the son of Mattatha, which was the son of Nathan, which was the son of David,

Which was the son of Jesse, which was the son of Obed, which was the son of Booz, which was the son of Salmon, which was the son of Naasson,

Which was the son of Aminadab, which was the son of Aram, which was the son of Esrom, which was the son of Phares, which was the son of Juda,

Which was the son of Jacob, which was the son of Isaac, which was the son of Abraham, which was the son of Thara, which was the son of Nachor,

Which was the son of Saruch, which was the son of Ragau, which was the son of Phalec, which was the son of Heber, which was the son of Sala,

Which was the son of Cainan, which was the son of Arphaxad, which was the son of Sem, which was the son of Noe, which was the son of Lamech,

Which was the son of Mathusala, which was the son of Enoch, which was the son of Jared, which was the son of Maleleel, which was the son of Cainan,

Which was the son of Enos, which was the son of Seth, which was the son of Adam, <u>who was formed of God, and the first man upon the earth.</u>[7]

---

7   Luke reads, "which was the son of God."

Annunciation to Zacharias

Luke 1:5–25, JST Luke 1:8

There was in the days of Herod, the king of Judæa, a certain priest named Zacharias, of the course of Abia: and his wife was of the daughters of Aaron, and her name was Elisabeth.

And they were both righteous before God, walking in all the commandments and ordinances of the Lord blameless.

And they had no child, because that Elisabeth was barren, and they both were now well stricken in years.

And it came to pass, that while he executed the priest's office before God in the order of his <u>priesthood</u>[8],

According to the custom of the priest's office, his lot was to burn incense when he went into the temple of the Lord.

And the whole multitude of the people were praying without at the time of incense. And there appeared unto him an angel of the Lord standing on the right side of the altar of incense. And when Zacharias saw him, he was troubled, and fear fell upon him.

But the angel said unto him, Fear not, Zacharias: for thy prayer is heard; and thy wife Elisabeth shall bear thee a son, and thou shalt call his name John.

And thou shalt have joy and gladness; and many shall rejoice at his birth.

For he shall be great in the sight of the Lord, and shall drink neither wine nor strong drink; and he shall be filled with the Holy Ghost, even from his mother's womb.

And many of the children of Israel shall he turn to the Lord their God.

And he shall go before him in the spirit and power of Elias, to turn the hearts of the fathers to the children, and the disobedient to the wisdom of the just; to make ready a people prepared for the Lord.

And Zacharias said unto the angel, Whereby shall I know this? for I am an old man, and my wife well stricken in years.

And the angel answering said unto him, I am Gabriel, that stand in the presence of God; and am sent to speak unto thee, and to shew thee these glad tidings.

And, behold, thou shalt be dumb, and not able to speak, until the day that these things shall be performed, because thou believest not my words, which shall be fulfilled in their season.

And the people waited for Zacharias, and marvelled that he tarried so long in the temple.

And when he came out, he could not speak unto them: and they perceived that he had seen a vision in the temple: for he beckoned unto them, and remained speechless.

And it came to pass, that, as soon as the days of his ministration were accomplished, he departed to his own house.

---

8   Luke reads, "course"

Elisabeth's Seclusion

Luke 1:24–25

And after those days his wife Elisabeth conceived, and hid herself five months, saying,

Thus hath the Lord dealt with me in the days wherein he looked on me, to take away my reproach among men.

Annunciation to Mary

Luke 1:26–38

And in the sixth month the angel Gabriel was sent from God unto a city of Galilee, named Nazareth,

To a virgin espoused to a man whose name was Joseph, of the house of David; and the virgin's name was Mary.

And the angel came in unto her, and said, Hail, thou that art highly favoured, the Lord is with thee: blessed art thou among women.

And when she saw him, she was troubled at his saying, and cast in her mind what manner of salutation this should be.

And the angel said unto her, Fear not, Mary: for thou hast found favour with God. And, behold, thou shalt conceive in thy womb, and bring forth a son, and shalt call his name JESUS.

He shall be great, and shall be called the Son of the Highest: and the Lord God shall give unto him the throne of his father David:

And he shall reign over the house of Jacob for ever; and of his kingdom there shall be no end.

Then said Mary unto the angel, How shall this be, seeing I know not a man?

And the angel answered and said unto her, The Holy Ghost shall come upon thee, and the power of the Highest shall overshadow thee: therefore also that holy thing which shall be born of thee shall be called the Son of God.

And, behold, thy cousin Elisabeth, she hath also conceived a son in her old age: and this is the sixth month with her, who was called barren.

For with God nothing shall be impossible.

And Mary said, Behold the handmaid of the Lord; be it unto me according to thy word. And the angel departed from her.

Annunciation to Joseph

Matt. 1:18–24, JST Matt. 2:1

Now, <u>as it is written,</u> the birth of Jesus Christ was on this wise: When as his mother Mary was espoused to Joseph, before they came together, she was found with child of the Holy Ghost.

Then Joseph her husband, being a just man, and not willing to make her a publick example, was minded to put her away privily.

" . . . Fear not, Mary: for thou hast found favour with God."

But while he thought on these things, behold, the angel of the Lord appeared unto him in a dream, saying, Joseph, thou son of David, fear not to take unto thee Mary thy wife: for that which is conceived in her is of the Holy Ghost.

And she shall bring forth a son, and thou shalt call his name JESUS: for he shall save his people from their sins. Now all this was done, that it might be fulfilled which was spoken of the Lord by the prophet, saying, Behold, a virgin shall be with child, and shall bring forth a son, and they shall call his name Emmanuel, which being interpreted is, God with us.

Then Joseph being raised from sleep did as the angel of the Lord had bidden him, and took unto him his wife.

"And she shall bring forth a son, and thou shalt call his name JESUS..."

Mary Visits Elizabeth

Luke 1:39—56

And Mary arose in those days, and went into the hill country with haste, into a city of Juda;

And entered into the house of Zacharias, and saluted Elisabeth.

And it came to pass, that, when Elisabeth heard the salutation of Mary, the babe leaped in her womb; and Elisabeth was filled with the Holy Ghost:

And she spake out with a loud voice, and said, Blessed art thou among women, and blessed is the fruit of thy womb.

And whence is this to me, that the mother of my Lord should come to me?

For, lo, as soon as the voice of thy salutation sounded in mine ears, the babe leaped in my womb for joy.

And blessed is she that believed: for there shall be a performance of those things which were told her from the Lord. And Mary said, My soul doth magnify the Lord,

And my spirit hath rejoiced in God my Saviour.

For he hath regarded the low estate of his handmaiden: for, behold, from henceforth all generations shall call me blessed.

For he that is mighty hath done to me great things; and holy is his name.

And his mercy is on them that fear him from generation to generation.

He hath shewed strength with his arm; he hath scattered the proud in the imagination of their hearts.

He hath put down the mighty from their seats, and exalted them of low degree.

He hath filled the hungry with good things; and the rich he hath sent empty away.

He hath holpen his servant Israel, in remembrance of his mercy;

As he spake to our fathers, to Abraham, and to his seed for ever.

And Mary abode with her about three months, and returned to her own house.

Birth of John the Baptist
Luke 1:57–58

Now Elisabeth's full time came that she should be delivered; and she brought forth a son.

And her neighbours and her cousins heard how the Lord had shewed great mercy upon her; and they rejoiced with her.

Naming of John
Luke 1:59–66

And it came to pass, that on the eighth day they came to circumcise the child; and they called him Zacharias, after the name of his father.

And his mother answered and said, Not so; but he shall be called John.

And they said unto her, There is none of thy kindred that is called by this name.

And they made signs to his father, how he would have him called.

And he asked for a writing table, and wrote, saying, His name is John. And they marvelled all.

And his mouth was opened immediately, and his tongue loosed, and he spake, and praised God.

And fear came on all that dwelt round about them: and all these sayings were noised abroad throughout all the hill country of Judæa.

And all they that heard them laid them up in their hearts, saying, What manner of child shall this be! And the hand of the Lord was with him.

Zacharias's Prophetic Psalm
Luke 1:67–80

And his father Zacharias was filled with the Holy Ghost, and prophesied, saying,

Blessed be the Lord God of Israel; for he hath visited and redeemed his people,

And hath raised up an horn of salvation for us in the house of his servant David;

As he spake by the mouth of his holy prophets, which have been since the world began:

That we should be saved from our enemies, and from the hand of all that hate us;

To perform the mercy promised to our fathers, and to remember his holy covenant; The oath which he sware to our father Abraham,

That he would grant unto us, that we being delivered out of the hand of our enemies might serve him without fear,

In holiness and righteousness before him, all the days of our life.

And thou, child, shalt be called the prophet of the Highest: for thou shalt go before the face of the Lord to prepare his ways;

To give knowledge of salvation unto his people by the remission of their sins,

Through the tender mercy of our God; whereby the dayspring from on high hath visited us,

To give light to them that sit in darkness and in the shadow of death, to guide our feet into the way of peace.

And the child grew, and waxed strong in spirit, and was in the deserts till the day of his shewing unto Israel.

Joseph and Mary Go to Be Taxed
Luke 2:1–5

AND it came to pass in those days, that there went out a decree from Cæsar Augustus, that all the world should be taxed.

(And this taxing was first made when Cyrenius was governor of Syria.)

And all went to be taxed, every one into his own city.

And Joseph also went up from Galilee, out of the city of Nazareth, into Judæa, unto the city of David, which is called Bethlehem; (because he was of the house and lineage of David:)

To be taxed with Mary his espoused wife, being great with child.

Birth of Jesus
Luke 2:6–7, JST Luke 2:7

And so it was, that, while they were there, the days were accomplished that she should be delivered.

And she brought forth her firstborn son, and wrapped him in swaddling clothes, and laid him in a manger; because there was no room for them in the <u>inns</u>[9].

Annunciation to the Shepherds
Luke 2:8–20

And there were in the same country shepherds abiding in the field, keeping watch over their flock by night.

And, lo, the angel of the Lord came upon them, and the glory of the Lord shone round about them: and they were sore afraid.

And the angel said unto them, Fear not: for, behold, I bring you good tidings of great joy, which shall be to all people.

For unto you is born this day in the city of David a Saviour, which is Christ the Lord.

And this shall be a sign unto you; Ye shall find the babe wrapped in swaddling clothes, lying in a manger.

And suddenly there was with the angel a multitude of the heavenly host praising God, and saying,

Glory to God in the highest, and on earth peace, good will toward men.

And it came to pass, as the angels were gone away from them into heaven, the shepherds said one to another, Let us now go even unto Bethlehem, and see this thing which is come to pass, which the Lord hath made known unto us.

And they came with haste, and found Mary, and Joseph, and the babe lying in a manger.

And when they had seen it, they made known abroad the saying which was told them concerning this child.

And all they that heard it wondered at those things which were told them by the shepherds.

But Mary kept all these things, and pondered them in her heart.

And the shepherds returned, glorifying and praising God for all the things that they had heard and seen, as it was told unto them.

Naming of Jesus
Matt. 1:25, Luke 2:21

And knew her not till she had brought forth her firstborn son: And when eight days were accomplished for the circumcising of the child, he called his name JESUS, which was so named of the angel before he was conceived in the womb.

---

9   Luke reads, "inn"

Presentation in the Temple
Luke 2:22–39

And when the days of her purification according to the law of Moses were accomplished, they brought him to Jerusalem, to present him to the Lord;

(As it is written in the law of the Lord, Every male that openeth the womb shall be called holy to the Lord;)

And to offer a sacrifice according to that which is said in the law of the Lord, A pair of turtledoves, or two young pigeons.

And, behold, there was a man in Jerusalem, whose name was Simeon; and the same man was just and devout, waiting for the consolation of Israel: and the Holy Ghost was upon him.

And it was revealed unto him by the Holy Ghost, that he should not see death, before he had seen the Lord's Christ.

And he came by the Spirit into the temple: and when the parents brought in the child Jesus, to do for him after the custom of the law,

Then took he him up in his arms, and blessed God, and said,

Lord, now lettest thou thy servant depart in peace, according to thy word:

For mine eyes have seen thy salvation, Which thou hast prepared before the face of all people;

A light to lighten the Gentiles, and the glory of thy people Israel.

And Joseph and his mother marvelled at those things which were spoken of him.

And Simeon blessed them, and said unto Mary his mother, Behold, this child is set for the fall and rising again of many in Israel; and for a sign which shall be spoken against;

(Yea, a sword shall pierce through thy own soul also,) that the thoughts of many hearts may be revealed.

And there was one Anna, a prophetess, the daughter of Phanuel, of the tribe of Aser: she was of a great age, and had lived with an husband seven years from her virginity;

And she was a widow of about fourscore and four years, which departed not from the temple, but served God with fastings and prayers night and day.

And she coming in that instant gave thanks likewise unto the Lord, and spake of him to all them that looked for redemption in Jerusalem.

And when they had performed all things according to the law of the Lord, they returned into Galilee, to their own city Nazareth.

Visit of the Wise Men
Matt. 2:1–12, JST Matt. 3:2, 3:4–6

Now when Jesus was born in Bethlehem of Judæa in the days of Herod the king, behold, there came wise men from the east to Jerusalem, saying, Where is <u>the child that is born, the Messiah of the Jews?</u>[10] for we have seen his star in the east, and are come to worship him.

When Herod the king had heard these things, he was troubled, and all Jerusalem with him.

And when he had gathered all the chief priests and scribes of the people together, he demanded of them <u>saying, Where is the place that is written of by the prophets, in which Christ should be born? For he greatly feared, yet he believed not the prophets.</u>

<u>And they said unto him, It is written by the prophets, that he should be born in Bethlehem of Judea, for thus have they said,</u>

<u>The word of the Lord came unto us, saying, And thou Bethlehem, which lieth in the land of Judea, in thee shall be born a prince, which art not the least among the princes of Judea; for out of thee shall come the Messiah, who shall save my people Israel.</u>[11]

Then Herod, when he had privily called the wise men, enquired of them diligently what time the star appeared.

And he sent them to Bethlehem, and said, Go and search diligently for the young child; and when ye have found him, bring me word again, that I may come and worship him also.

When they had heard the king, they departed; and, lo, the star, which they saw in the east, went before them, till it came and stood over where the young child was.

When they saw the star, they rejoiced with exceeding great joy.

And when they were come into the house, they saw the young child with Mary his mother, and fell down, and worshipped him: and when they had opened their treasures, they presented unto him gifts; gold, and frankincense, and myrrh.

And being warned of God in a dream that they should not return to Herod, they departed into their own country another way.

Flight to Egypt
Matt. 2:13–15

And when they were departed, behold, the angel of the Lord appeareth to Joseph in a dream, saying, Arise, and take the young child and his mother, and flee into Egypt, and be thou there until I bring thee word: for Herod will seek the young child to destroy him.

When he arose, he took the young child and his mother by night, and departed into Egypt:

---

10   Matt. 2:2 says, "Where is he that is born King of the Jews?"

11   Matt. 2:4–6 says, "where Christ should be born. And they said unto him, In Bethlehem of Judæa: for thus it is written by the prophet, And thou Bethlehem, in the land of Juda, art not the least among the princes of Juda: for out of thee shall come a Governor, that shall rule my people Israel."

And was there until the death of Herod: that it might be fulfilled which was spoken of the Lord by the prophet, saying, Out of Egypt have I called my son.

Slaughter of the Infants
Matt. 2:16–18

Then Herod, when he saw that he was mocked of the wise men, was exceeding wroth, and sent forth, and slew all the children that were in Bethlehem, and in all the coasts thereof, from two years old and under, according to the time which he had diligently enquired of the wise men.

Then was fulfilled that which was spoken by Jeremy the prophet, saying,

In Rama was there a voice heard, lamentation, and weeping, and great mourning, Rachel weeping for her children, and would not be comforted, because they are not.

From Egypt to Nazareth
Matt. 2:19–23, Luke 2:39–40, JST Matt. 3:24–26

But when Herod was dead, behold, an angel of the Lord appeareth in a dream to Joseph in Egypt,

Saying, Arise, and take the young child and his mother, and go into the land of Israel: for they are dead which sought the young child's life.

And when they had performed all things according to the law of the Lord, he arose, and took the young child and his mother, and came into the land of Israel. But when he heard that Archelaus did reign in Judæa in the room of his father Herod, he was afraid to go thither: notwithstanding, being warned of God in a dream, he returned aside into the parts of Galilee, to Nazareth.

And he came and dwelt in their own city called Nazareth: that it might be fulfilled which was spoken by the prophets, He shall be called a Nazarene.

And it came to pass that the child Jesus grew up with his brethren, and waxed strong in spirit, filled with wisdom: and waited upon the Lord for the time of his ministry to come and the grace of God was upon him.

And he served under his father, and he spake not as other men, neither could he be taught; for he needed not that any man should teach him.

And after many years, the hour of his ministry drew nigh.

Visit to the Temple (Passover)
Luke 2:41–50, JST Luke 2:46

Now his parents went to Jerusalem every year at the feast of the passover.

And when he was twelve years old, they went up to Jerusalem after the custom of the feast.

And when they had fulfilled the days, as they returned, the child Jesus tarried behind in Jerusalem; and Joseph and his mother knew not of it.

But they, supposing him to have been in the company, went a day's journey; and they sought him among their kinsfolk and acquaintance.

And when they found him not, they turned back again to Jerusalem, seeking him.

And it came to pass, that after three days they found him in the temple, sitting in the midst of the doctors, <u>and they were hearing him and asking him questions.</u>[12]

And all that heard him were astonished at his understanding and answers.

And when they saw him, they were amazed: and his mother said unto him, Son, why hast thou thus dealt with us? behold, thy father and I have sought thee sorrowing.

And he said unto them, How is it that ye sought me? wist ye not that I must be about my Father's business?

And they understood not the saying which he spake unto them.

The Return to Nazareth
Luke 2:51–52

And he went down with them, and came to Nazareth, and was subject unto them: but his mother kept all these sayings in her heart.

And Jesus increased in wisdom and stature, and in favour with God and man.

---

12   Luke reads, "both hearing them, and asking them questions"

John's Prophetic Ministry
Matt. 3:1–6, Mark 1:1–6, Luke 3:1–15, JST Luke 3:4–10

Now in those days, the fifteenth year of the reign of Tiberius Cæsar, Pontius Pilate being governor of Judæa, and Herod being tetrarch of Galilee, and his brother Philip tetrarch of Ituræa and of the region of Trachonitis, and Lysanias the tetrarch of Abilene,

Annas and Caiaphas being the high priests, the word of God came unto John the Baptist, the son of Zacharias, preaching in the wilderness of Judæa,

And saying, Repent ye: for the kingdom of heaven is at hand.

For this is he that was spoken [and] written in the book of the words of Esaias the prophet, and these are the words saying, Behold, I send my messenger before thy face, which shall prepare thy way before thee.

The voice of one crying in the wilderness, Prepare ye the way of the Lord, make his paths straight.

For behold, and lo, he shall come, as it is written in the book of the prophets, to take away the sins of the world, and to bring salvation unto the heathen nations, to gather together those who are lost, who are of the sheepfold of Israel;

Yea, even the dispersed and afflicted; and also to prepare the way, and make possible the preaching of the gospel unto the Gentiles;

And to be a light unto all who sit in darkness, unto the uttermost parts of the earth; to bring to pass the resurrection from the dead, and to ascend up on high, to dwell on the right hand of the Father,

Until the fulness of time, and the law and the testimony shall be sealed, and the keys of the kingdom shall be delivered up again unto the Father;

To administer justice unto all; to come down in judgment upon all, and to convince all the ungodly of their ungodly deeds, which they have committed; and all this in the day that he shall come;

For it is a day of power; yea,

Every valley shall be filled, and every mountain and hill shall be brought low; and the crooked shall be made straight, and the rough ways shall be made smooth;

And all flesh shall see the salvation of God.

And he, John, came into all the country about Jordan, and did baptize in the wilderness, and preach the baptism of repentance for the remission of sins.

And the same John was clothed with his raiment of camel's hair, and a leathern girdle of a skin about his loins; and his meat he did eat was locusts and wild honey.

Then said he to the multitude that came forth to be baptized of him, and preached, saying, O generation of vipers, who hath warned you to flee from the wrath to come?

Bring forth therefore fruits worthy of repentance, and begin not to say within yourselves, We have Abraham to our father: for I say unto you, That God is able of these stones to raise up children unto Abraham.

And now also the axe is laid unto the root of the trees: every tree therefore which bringeth not forth good fruit is hewn down, and cast into the fire.

And the people asked him, saying, What shall we do then?

He answereth and saith unto them, He that hath two coats, let him impart to him that hath none; and he that hath meat, let him do likewise.

Then came also publicans to be baptized, and said unto him, Master, what shall we do?

And he said unto them, Exact no more than that which is appointed you.

And the soldiers likewise demanded of him, saying, And what shall we do? And he said unto them, Do violence to no man, neither accuse any falsely; and be content with your wages.

And as the people were in expectation, and all men mused in their hearts of John, whether he were the Christ, or not.

Isaiah's Prophecy of John
Matt. 3:3, Mark 1:2–3, Luke 3:4–6, John 1:23

For this is he that was spoken of by the prophet Esaias, As it is written in the book of the words of Esaias the prophet, saying, Behold, I send my messenger before thy face, which shall prepare thy way before thee.

I [John] am the voice of one crying in the wilderness, Prepare ye the way of the Lord, make his paths straight.

Every valley shall be filled, and every mountain and hill shall be brought low; and the crooked shall be made straight, and the rough ways shall be made smooth;

And all flesh shall see the salvation of God.

The Beginning of John's Ministry
Matt. 3:1, 5–6, 9, Mark 1:4, Luke 3:1–3, John 1:6–14, JST John 1:6–14

There was a man sent from God in the fifteenth year of the reign of Tiberius Cæsar, Pontius Pilate being governor of Judæa, and Herod being tetrarch of Galilee, and his brother Philip tetrarch of Ituræa and of the region of Trachonitis, and Lysanias the tetrarch of Abilene,

Annas and Caiaphas being the high priests,

There was a man sent from God, whose name was John.

The same came for a witness, to bear witness of the Light, to bear record of the

". . . in those days came John the Baptist."

gospel through the Son, unto all, that all men through him might believe. He was not that Light, but came[13] to bear witness of that Light.

Which[14] was the true Light, which lighteth every man that cometh into the world,

Even the Son of God. He who was in the world, and the world was made by him, and the world knew him not.

He came unto his own, and his own received him not.

But as many as received him, to them gave he power to become the sons of God, only[15] to them that believe on his name:

He was born,[16] not of blood, nor of the will of the flesh, nor of the will of man, but of God.

And the same Word was made flesh, and dwelt among us, (and we beheld his glory, the glory as of the only begotten of the Father,) full of grace and truth.

The word of God came unto John the son of Zacharias in the wilderness.

In those days came John the Baptist into all the country about Jordan, preaching the baptism of repentance for the remission of sins in the wilderness of Judæa.

Then went out to him Jerusalem, and all Judæa, and all the region round about Jordan,

And were baptized of him in Jordan, confessing their sins.

Warning to Pharisees and Sadducees
Matt. 3:7–9, Luke 3:7–8, JST Matt. 3:34–36, JST Luke 3:8, 13

But when he saw many of the Pharisees and Sadducees come to his baptism, he said unto the multitude that came forth to be baptized of him, O generation of vipers, who hath warned you to flee from the wrath to come?

Why is it that ye receive not the preaching of him whom God hath sent? If ye receive not this in your hearts, ye receive not me; and if ye receive not me, ye receive not him of whom I am sent to bear record; and for your sins ye have no cloak.

Repent, therefore, and

Bring forth therefore fruits meet [and] worthy for repentance: And think not to say within yourselves, We are the children of Abraham, Abraham is our father; we have kept the commandments of God, and none can inherit the promises but the children of Abraham, and we only have power to bring seed unto our father Abraham; for I say unto you, that God is able of these stones to raise up children unto Abraham.

---

13   John reads, "was sent"
14   John reads, "That"
15   John reads, "even"
16   John reads, "Which were born"

Call to Repentance

Matt. 3:10–12, Mark 1:5–8, Luke 3:10–18,
JST Matt. 3:38–40, JST Mark 1:6, JST Luke 3:19–20

And there went out unto him all the land of Judæa, and they of Jerusalem, and were all baptized of him in the river of Jordan, confessing their sins.

Then came also publicans to be baptized, and said unto him, Master, what shall we do?

And he said unto them, Exact no more than that which is appointed you. <u>For it is well known unto you, Theophilus, that after the manner of the Jews, and according to the custom of their law in receiving money into the treasury, that out of the abundance which was received, was appointed unto the poor, every man his portion;</u>

<u>And after this manner did the publicans also, wherefore John said unto them, Exact no more than that which is appointed you.</u>

And the soldiers likewise demanded of him, saying, And what shall we do? And he said unto them, Do violence to no man, neither accuse any falsely; and be content with your wages.

And John was clothed with camel's hair, and with a girdle of a skin about his loins; and he did eat locusts and wild honey; And as the people were in expectation, and all men mused in their hearts of John, whether he were the Christ, or not;

John preached, saying, There cometh one mightier than I after me, the latchet of whose shoes I am not worthy to stoop down and unloose.

I indeed baptize you with water unto repentance: <u>and when he of whom I bear record cometh, who</u> is mightier than I, whose shoes I am not worthy to bear:<u> (or whose place I am not able to fill,) as I said, I indeed baptize you before he cometh, that when he cometh</u> he shall <u>not only</u> baptize you <u>with water, but</u> with the Holy Ghost, and with fire: And now also the axe is laid unto the root of the trees: therefore every tree which bringeth not forth good fruit is hewn down, and cast into the fire. <u>And it is he of whom I shall bear record,</u>

Whose fan is in his hand, and he will throughly purge his floor, and gather his wheat into the garner; <u>but in the fulness of his own time</u> he will burn up the chaff with unquenchable fire.

<u>Thus came John, preaching and baptizing in the river of Jordan; bearing record, that he who was coming after him had power to baptize with the Holy Ghost and fire.</u>

And many other things in his exhortation preached he unto the people.

And the people asked him, saying, What shall we do then? He answereth and saith unto them, He that hath two coats, let him impart to him that hath none; and he that hath meat, let him do likewise.

Baptism of Jesus
Matt. 3:13–17, Mark 1:9–11, Luke 3:21–22, John 1:32–37, JST Matt. 3:43–46

And it came to pass in those days, that Jesus came from Nazareth from Galilee to Jordan unto John, to be baptized of him in Jordan.

But John forbad him, saying, I have need to be baptized of thee, and comest thou to me?

And Jesus answering said unto him, <u>Suffer me to be baptized of thee,</u>[17] for thus it becometh us to fulfil all righteousness. Then he suffered him.

<u>And John went down into the water and baptized him.</u> And Jesus, when he was baptized, and praying, went up straightway out of the water: <u>and John saw</u> and, lo, the heavens were opened unto him, and he saw the Spirit of God in a bodily shape descending like a dove, and lighting upon <u>Jesus:</u>

And lo a voice from heaven, saying, This is my beloved Son, in whom I am well pleased, <u>Hear ye him.</u>

And John bare record, saying, I saw the Spirit descending from heaven like a dove, and it abode upon him.

And I knew him not: but he that sent me to baptize with water, the same said unto me, Upon whom thou shalt see the Spirit descending, and remaining on him, the same is he which

17   Matthew reads, "Suffer it to be so now"

"... to fulfil all righteousness."

baptizeth with the Holy Ghost.

And I saw, and bare record that this is the Son of God.

Again the next day after John stood, and two of his disciples; And looking upon Jesus as he walked, he saith, Behold the Lamb of God!

And the two disciples heard him speak, and they followed Jesus.

Temptation of Jesus[18]
Matt. 4:1–11, Mark 1:12–13, Luke 4:1–13,
JST Matt. 4:1, JST Mark 1:10–11, JST Luke 4:2, 5

AND Jesus being full of the Holy Ghost returned from Jordan,

And immediately was Jesus led up of the Spirit into the wilderness to be with God.[19] and was with the wild beasts; and the angels ministered unto him.

And he was there in the wilderness forty days, [and] did eat nothing.

And Satan, the devil, came unto him, seeking to tempt him[20]; And when he had fasted forty days and forty nights and had communed with God, he was afterward an hungred, and was left to be tempted of the devil.

And when the tempter, the devil came to him, he said, If thou be the Son of God, command that these stones be made bread.

But he answered and said, It is written, Man shall not live by bread alone, but by every word that proceedeth out of the mouth of God.

Then Jesus was taken[21] up into Jerusalem, the holy city, and the Spirit setteth him on a pinnacle of the temple,

Then the devil came unto him and said, If thou be the Son of God, cast thyself down from hence: for it is written, He shall give his angels charge concerning thee, to keep thee: and in their hands they shall bear thee up, lest at any time thou dash thy foot against a stone.

Jesus said unto him, It is said and written again, Thou shalt not tempt the Lord thy God.

---

18   Matthew and Luke order the temptations differently.
19   Matthew reads, "tempted of the devil"
20   Mark reads, "tempted of Satan"
21   Matthew reads "the devil taketh him"

And again, Jesus was in the Spirit and it[22] taketh him up into an exceeding high mountain, and sheweth him all the kingdoms of the world, in a moment of time and the glory of them;

And the devil came unto him again, and said, All these things, and this power will I give thee, if thou wilt fall down and worship me, all shall be thine.

Then saith Jesus unto him, Get thee hence, Satan: for it is written, Thou shalt worship the Lord thy God, and him only shalt thou serve.

And when the devil had ended all the temptation,

Then the devil leaveth him, [and] departed from him for a season, and, behold, angels came and ministered unto him.

And now Jesus knew that John was cast into prison, and he sent angels, and, behold, they came and ministered unto him (John).

John the Baptist's Testimony
John 1:15–36, JST John 1:15–34

John bare witness of him, and cried, saying, This was he of whom I spake, He who[23] cometh after me is preferred before me: for he was before me.

For in the beginning was the Word, even the Son, who is made flesh, and sent unto us by the will of the Father, And as many as believe on his name shall receive of his fulness.

And of his fulness have all we received, even immortality and eternal life, through his grace.[24]

For the law was given by Moses, but life[25] and truth came by Jesus Christ.

For the law was after a carnal commandment, to the administration of death; but the gospel was after the power of an endless life, through Jesus Christ, the Only Begotten Son, who is in the bosom of the Father.

And no man hath seen God at any time; except he hath borne record of the Son; for except it is through him no man can be saved.[26] And this is the record of John, when the Jews sent priests and Levites from Jerusalem to ask him, Who art thou?

And he confessed, and denied not that he was Elias; but confessed, saying, I am not the Christ.

And they asked him, saying; How then art thou Elias? And he said, I am not that Elias who was to restore all things.[27] Art thou that prophet? And he answered, No.

Then said they unto him, Who art thou? that we may give an answer to them that sent us. What sayest thou of thyself?

He said, I am the voice of one crying in the wilderness, Make straight the way of the Lord, as said the prophet Esaias.

---

22   Matthew reads, "the devil"
23   John reads, "that"
24   John reads, "and grace for grace"
25   John reads, "grace"
26   John reads, "the only begotten Son, which is in the bosom of the Father, he hath declared him."
27   John reads, "What then? Art thou Elias? And he saith, I am not."

And they which were sent were of the Pharisees.

And they asked him, and said unto him, Why baptizest thou then, if thou be not that Christ, nor Elias <u>who was to restore all things</u>, neither that prophet?

John answered them, saying, I baptize with water: but there standeth one among you, whom ye know not;

He it is <u>of whom I bear record. He is that prophet, even Elias,</u> who coming after me is preferred before me, whose shoe's latchet I am not worthy to unloose, <u>or whose place I am not able to fill; for he shall baptize, not only with water, but with fire, and with the Holy Ghost.</u>

The next day John seeth Jesus coming unto him, and saith, Behold the Lamb of God, <u>who</u>[28] taketh away the sin of the world.

<u>And John bare record of him unto the people, saying,</u> This is he of whom I said, After me cometh a man which is preferred before me: for he was before me.

And I <u>knew him, and</u>[29] that he should be made manifest to Israel, therefore am I come baptizing with water.

And John bare record, saying, <u>When he was baptized of me,</u> I saw the Spirit descending from heaven like a dove, and it abode upon him.

And I knew <u>him;</u>[30] but he that sent me to baptize with water, the same said unto me, Upon whom thou shalt see the Spirit descending, and remaining on him, the same is he which baptizeth with the Holy Ghost.

And I saw, and bare record that this is the Son of God.

Again the next day after John stood, and two of his disciples;

And looking upon Jesus as he walked, he saith, Behold the Lamb of God!

<u>These things were done in Bethabara, beyond Jordan, where John was baptizing.</u>

John's Disciples Follow Jesus
John 1:37–51, JST John 1:42

And the two disciples heard him speak, and they followed Jesus.

Then Jesus turned, and saw them following, and saith unto them, What seek They said unto him, Rabbi, (which is to say, being interpreted, Master,) where dwellest thou?

He saith unto them, Come and see. They came and saw where he dwelt, and abode with him that day: for it was about the tenth hour.

One of the two which heard John speak, and followed him, was Andrew, Simon Peter's brother.

He first findeth his own brother Simon, and saith unto him, We have found the Messias, which is, being interpreted, the Christ.

And he brought him to Jesus. And when Jesus beheld him, he said, Thou art Simon the son of Jona: thou shalt be called Cephas, which is by interpretation, <u>a seer, or</u> a stone. <u>And they</u>

---

28   John reads, "which"
29   John reads "knew him not: but"
30   John reads, "him not"

straightway left all and followed Jesus.

The day following Jesus would go forth into Galilee, and findeth Philip, and saith unto him, Follow me.

Now Philip was of Bethsaida, the city of Andrew and Peter.

Philip findeth Nathanael, and saith unto him, We have found him, of whom Moses in the law, and the prophets, did write, Jesus of Nazareth, the son of Joseph.

And Nathanael said unto him, Can there any good thing come out of Nazareth? Philip saith unto him, Come and see.

Jesus saw Nathanael coming to him, and saith of him, Behold an Israelite indeed, in whom is no guile!

Nathanael saith unto him, Whence knowest thou me? Jesus answered and said unto him, Before that Philip called thee, when thou wast under the fig tree, I saw thee.

Nathanael answered and saith unto him, Rabbi, thou art the Son of God; thou art the King of Israel.

Jesus answered and said unto him, Because I said unto thee, I saw thee under the fig tree, believest thou? thou shalt see greater things than these.

And he saith unto him, Verily, verily, I say unto you, Hereafter ye shall see heaven open, and the angels of God ascending and descending upon the Son of man.

Marriage at Cana
John 2:1–11, JST John 2:1, 4

And the third day of the week there was a marriage in Cana of Galilee; and the mother of Jesus was there:

And both Jesus was called, and his disciples, to the marriage.

And when they wanted wine, the mother of Jesus saith unto him, They have no wine.

Jesus saith unto her, Woman, what wilt thou have me[31] to do for[32] thee? that will I do; for mine hour is not yet come.

His mother saith unto the servants, Whatsoever he saith unto you, do it.

And there were set there six waterpots of stone, after the manner of the purifying of the Jews, containing two or three firkins apiece.

Jesus saith unto them, Fill the waterpots with water. And they filled them up to the brim. And he saith unto them, Draw out now, and bear unto the governor of the feast. And they bare it.

---

31   John reads, "I"
32   John reads, "with"

When the ruler of the feast had tasted the water that was made wine, and knew not whence it was: (but the servants which drew the water knew;) the governor of the feast called the bridegroom,

And saith unto him, Every man at the beginning doth set forth good wine; and when men have well drunk, then that which is worse: but thou hast kept the good wine until now.

This beginning of miracles did Jesus in Cana of Galilee, and manifested forth his glory; and his disciples believed on him.

Visit to Capernaum
John 2:12

After this he went down to Capernaum, he, and his mother, and his brethren, and his disciples: and they continued there not many days.

First Passover
John 2:13, 23–25

And the Jews' passover was at hand, and Jesus went up to Jerusalem,

Now when he was in Jerusalem at the passover, in the feast day, many believed in his name, when they saw the miracles which he did,

But Jesus did not commit himself unto them, because he knew all men,

And needed not that any should testify of man: for he knew what was in man.

First Cleansing of the Temple
John 2:14–17

And found in the temple those that sold oxen and sheep and doves, and the changers of money sitting:

And when he had made a scourge of small cords, he drove them all out of the temple, and the sheep, and the oxen; and poured out the changers' money, and overthrew the tables;

And said unto them that sold doves, Take these things hence; make not my Father's house an house of merchandise.

And his disciples remembered that it was written, The zeal of thine house hath eaten me up.

Sign of Jonah

John 2:18–22

Then answered the Jews and said unto him, What sign shewest thou unto us, seeing that thou doest these things?

Jesus answered and said unto them, Destroy this temple, and in three days I will raise it up.

Then said the Jews, Forty and six years was this temple in building, and wilt thou rear it up in three days?

But he spake of the temple of his body.

When therefore he was risen from the dead, his disciples remembered that he had said this unto them; and they believed the scripture, and the word which Jesus had said.

Nicodemus

John 3:1–10

There was a man of the Pharisees, named Nicodemus, a ruler of the Jews:

The same came to Jesus by night, and said unto him, Rabbi, we know that thou art a teacher come from God: for no man can do these miracles that thou doest, except God be with him.

Jesus answered and said unto him, Verily, verily, I say unto thee, Except a man be born again, he cannot see the kingdom of God.

Nicodemus saith unto him, How can a man be born when he is old? can he enter the second time into his mother's womb, and be born?

Jesus answered, Verily, verily, I say unto thee, Except a man be born of water and of the Spirit, he cannot enter into the kingdom of God.

That which is born of the flesh is flesh; and that which is born of the Spirit is spirit.

Marvel not that I said unto thee, Ye must be born again.

The wind bloweth where it listeth, and thou hearest the sound thereof, but canst not tell whence it cometh, and whither it goeth: so is every one that is born of the Spirit.

Nicodemus answered and said unto him, How can these things be?

Jesus answered and said unto him, Art thou a master of Israel, and knowest not these things?

Messianic Witness to Nicodemus

John 3:11–21, JST John 3:18

Verily, verily, I say unto thee, We speak that we do know, and testify that we have seen; and ye receive not our witness.

If I have told you earthly things, and ye believe not, how shall ye believe, if I tell you of heavenly things?

And no man hath ascended up to heaven, but he that came down from heaven, even the

Son of man which is in heaven.

And as Moses lifted up the serpent in the wilderness, even so must the Son of man be lifted up:

That whosoever believeth in him should not perish, but have eternal life.

For God so loved the world, that he gave his only begotten Son, that whosoever believeth in him should not perish, but have everlasting life.

For God sent not his Son into the world to condemn the world; but that the world through him might be saved.

He that believeth on him is not condemned: but he that believeth not is condemned already, because he hath not believed in the name of the only begotten Son of God which before was preached by the mouth of the holy prophets; for they testified of me.

And this is the condemnation, that light is come into the world, and men loved darkness rather than light, because their deeds were evil.

For every one that doeth evil hateth the light, neither cometh to the light, lest his deeds should be reproved.

But he that doeth truth cometh to the light, that his deeds may be made manifest, that they are wrought in God.

Jesus' Early Ministry in Judæa
John 3:22

After these things came Jesus and his disciples into the land of Judæa; and there he tarried with them, and baptized.

John's Ministry and Testimony
John 3:23–36, JST John 3:27, 34, 36

And John also was baptizing in Ænon near to Salim, because there was much water there: and they came, and were baptized.

For John was not yet cast into prison.

Then there arose a question between some of John's disciples and the Jews about purifying.

And they came unto John, and said unto him, Rabbi, he that was with thee beyond Jordan, to whom thou barest witness, behold, the same baptizeth, and he receiveth of all people who come unto him.[33]

John answered and said, A man can receive nothing, except it be given him from heaven.

Ye yourselves bear me witness, that I said, I am not the Christ, but that I am sent before him.

He that hath the bride is the bridegroom: but the friend of the bridegroom, which standeth and heareth him, rejoiceth greatly because of the bridegroom's voice: this my joy therefore is fulfilled.

He must increase, but I must decrease.

He that cometh from above is above all: he that is of the earth is earthly, and speaketh of the earth: he that cometh from heaven is above all.

And what he hath seen and heard, that he testifieth; and no man receiveth his testimony.

He that hath received his testimony hath set to his seal that God is true.

For he whom God hath sent speaketh the words of God: for God giveth him not the Spirit by measure, for he dwelleth in him,[34] even the fulness.

The Father loveth the Son, and hath given all things into his hand.

And he who[35] believeth on the Son hath everlasting life; and shall receive of his fulness. But he who[36] believeth not the Son, shall not receive of his fulness[37]; for[38] the wrath of God is upon[39] him.

Herod Antipas Reproved by John
Matt. 14:3–5, Mark 6:17–20, Luke 3:19–20

For Herod the tetrarch had laid hold on John, being reproved by him, and bound him, and put him in prison for Herodias' sake, his brother Philip's wife, for he had married her, and for all the evils which Herod had done.

Added yet this above all, that he shut up John in prison. For John said unto him, It is not lawful for thee to have her, thy brother's wife.

Therefore Herodias had a quarrel against him, and would have killed him; but she could not:

---

33   John reads, "all men come to him."
34   John reads, "unto him"
35   John reads, "that"
36   John reads, "that"
37   John reads, "see life"
38   John reads, "but"
39   John reads, "abideth on"

For Herod feared John, knowing that he was a just man and an holy, and observed him; and when he heard him, he did many things, and heard him gladly.

And when he would have put him to death, he feared the multitude, because they counted him as a prophet.

John Imprisoned
Matt. 4:12, Mark 1:14

Now when Jesus had heard that John was cast into prison, he departed into Galilee; preaching the gospel of the kingdom of God,

Jesus Leaves Judæa for Galilee
Luke 4:14, John 4:1–3, JST John 4:1–4

When therefore the Pharisees[40] had heard that Jesus made and baptized more disciples than John,

They sought more diligently some means that they might put him to death; for many received John as a prophet, but they believed not on Jesus. When therefore the Pharisees had heard that Jesus made and baptized more disciples than John,

Now the Lord knew this, though he himself baptized not so many as his disciples;[41]

For he suffered them for an example, preferring one another. And he left Judæa,

And Jesus returned in the power of the Spirit and departed again into Galilee: and there went out a fame of him through all the region round about.

Woman at the Well
John 4:4–42, JST John 4:26, 40

And he must needs go through Samaria.

Then cometh he to a city of Samaria, which is called Sychar, near to the parcel of ground that Jacob gave to his son Joseph.

Now Jacob's well was there. Jesus therefore, being wearied with his journey, sat thus on the well: and it was about the sixth hour.

There cometh a woman of Samaria to draw water: Jesus saith unto her, Give me to drink.

(For his disciples were gone away unto the city to buy meat.)

Then saith the woman of Samaria unto him, How is it that thou, being a Jew, askest drink of me, which am a woman of Samaria? for the Jews have no dealings with the Samaritans.

Jesus answered and said unto her, If thou knewest the gift of God, and who it is that saith

---

40   John reads "When therefore the Lord knew how the Pharisees"
41   John reads, "(Though Jesus himself baptized not, but his disciples,)"

to thee, Give me to drink; thou wouldest have asked of him, and he would have given thee living water.

The woman saith unto him, Sir, thou hast nothing to draw with, and the well is deep: from whence then hast thou that living water?

Art thou greater than our father Jacob, which gave us the well, and drank thereof himself, and his children, and his cattle?

Jesus answered and said unto her, Whosoever drinketh of this water shall thirst again:

But whosoever drinketh of the water that I shall give him shall never thirst; but the water that I shall give him shall be in him a well of water springing up into everlasting life.

The woman saith unto him, Sir, give me this water, that I thirst not, neither come hither to draw.

Jesus saith unto her, Go, call thy husband, and come hither. The woman answered and said, I have no husband. Jesus said unto her, Thou hast well said, I have no husband:

For thou hast had five husbands; and he whom thou now hast is not thy husband: in that saidst thou truly.

The woman saith unto him, Sir, I perceive that thou art a prophet.

Our fathers worshipped in this mountain; and ye say, that in Jerusalem is the place where men ought to worship.

Jesus saith unto her, Woman, believe me, the hour cometh, when ye shall neither in this mountain, nor yet at Jerusalem, worship the Father.

Ye worship ye know not what: we know what we worship: for salvation is of the Jews.

But the hour cometh, and now is, when the true worshippers shall worship the Father in spirit and in truth: for the Father seeketh such to worship him.

For unto such hath God promised his Spirit[42]: and they who[43] worship him must worship him in spirit and in truth. The woman saith unto him, I know that Messias cometh, which is called Christ: when he is come, he will tell us all things.

Jesus saith unto her, I that speak unto thee am he.

And upon this came his disciples, and marvelled that he talked with the woman: yet no man said, What seekest thou? or, Why talkest thou with her?

The woman then left her waterpot, and went her way into the city, and saith to the men,

Come, see a man, which told m.e all things that ever I did: is not this the Christ?

Then they went out of the city, and came unto him.

In the mean while his disciples prayed him, saying, Master, eat.

But he said unto them, I have meat to eat that ye know not of.

Therefore said the disciples one to another, Hath any man brought him ought to eat?

Jesus saith unto them, My meat is to do the will of him that sent me, and to finish his work.

Say not ye, There are yet four months, and then cometh harvest? behold, I say unto you, Lift up your eyes, and look on the fields; for they are white already to harvest.

And he that reapeth receiveth wages, and gathereth fruit unto life eternal: that both he that soweth and he that reapeth may rejoice together.

And herein is that saying true, One soweth, and another reapeth.

I sent you to reap that whereon ye bestowed no labour: the prophets have[44] laboured, and ye are entered into their labours.

And many of the Samaritans of that city believed on him for the saying of the woman, which testified, He told me all that ever I did.

So when the Samaritans were come unto him, they besought him that he would tarry with them: and he abode there two days.

And many more believed because of his own word;

And said unto the woman, Now we believe, not because of thy saying: for we have heard him ourselves, and know that this is indeed the Christ, the Saviour of the world.

Jesus Returns to Galilee and Preaches
Matt. 4:17, Mark 1:15, Luke 4:15, John 4:43–45

Now after two days he departed thence, and went into Galilee.

For Jesus himself testified, that a prophet hath no honour in his own country.

Then when he was come into Galilee, the Galilæans received him, having seen all the things that he did at Jerusalem at the feast: for they also went unto the feast.

And he taught in their synagogues, being glorified of all.

---

42   John reads, "God is a Spirit"
43   John reads, "that"
44   John reads, "other men"

From that time Jesus began to preach, and to say, repent ye, and believe the gospel. The time is fulfilled, and the kingdom of heaven is at hand.

Healing of the Nobleman's Son
John 4:46–54

So Jesus came again into Cana of Galilee, where he made the water wine. And there was a certain nobleman, whose son was sick at Capernaum.

When he heard that Jesus was come out of Judæa into Galilee, he went unto him, and besought him that he would come down, and heal his son: for he was at the point of death.

Then said Jesus unto him, Except ye see signs and wonders, ye will not believe.

The nobleman saith unto him, Sir, come down ere my child die.

Jesus saith unto him, Go thy way; thy son liveth. And the man believed the word that Jesus had spoken unto him, and he went his way.

And as he was now going down, his servants met him, and told him, saying, Thy son liveth.

Then enquired he of them the hour when he began to amend. And they said unto him, Yesterday at the seventh hour the fever left him.

So the father knew that it was at the same hour, in the which Jesus said unto him, Thy son liveth: and himself believed, and his whole house.

This is again the second miracle that Jesus did, when he was come out of Judæa into Galilee.

Jesus Rejected at Nazareth
Matt. 4:13–16, Luke 4:16–30

And he came to Nazareth, where he had been brought up: and, as his custom was, he went into the synagogue on the sabbath day, and stood up for to read.

And there was delivered unto him the book of the prophet Esaias. And when he had opened the book, he found the place where it was written,

The Spirit of the Lord is upon me, because he hath anointed me to preach the gospel to the poor; he hath sent me to heal the brokenhearted, to preach deliverance to the captives, and recovering of sight to the blind, to set at liberty them that are bruised,

To preach the acceptable year of the Lord.

And he closed the book, and he gave it

again to the minister, and sat down. And the eyes of all them that were in the synagogue were fastened on him.

And he began to say unto them, This day is this scripture fulfilled in your ears.

And all bare him witness, and wondered at the gracious words which proceeded out of his mouth. And they said, Is not this Joseph's son?

And he said unto them, Ye will surely say unto me this proverb, Physician, heal thyself: whatsoever we have heard done in Capernaum, do also here in thy country.

And he said, Verily I say unto you, No prophet is accepted in his own country.

But I tell you of a truth, many widows were in Israel in the days of Elias, when the heaven was shut up three years and six months, when great famine was throughout all the land;

But unto none of them was Elias sent, save unto Sarepta, a city of Sidon, unto a woman that was a widow.

And many lepers were in Israel in the time of Eliseus the prophet; and none of them was cleansed, saving Naaman the Syrian.

And all they in the synagogue, when they heard these things, were filled with wrath,

And rose up, and thrust him out of the city, and led him unto the brow of the hill whereon their city was built, that they might cast him down headlong.

But he passing through the midst of them went his way,

And leaving Nazareth, he came and dwelt in Capernaum, which is upon the sea coast, in the borders of Zabulon and Nephthalim:

That it might be fulfilled which was spoken by Esaias the prophet, saying,

The land of Zabulon, and the land of Nephthalim, by the way of the sea, beyond Jordan, Galilee of the Gentiles;

The people which sat in darkness saw great light; and to them which sat in the region and shadow of death light is sprung up.

Removal to Capernaum
Matt. 4:13, Mark 1:21–22, Luke 4:31–32

And leaving Nazareth, he came down and dwelt in Capernaum, a city of Galilee which is upon the sea coast, in the borders of Zabulon and Nephthalim: and straightway taught them on the sabbath days in the synagogue.

And they were astonished at his doctrine: for his word was with power, for he taught them as one that had authority, and not as the scribes.

Casting Out an Unclean Spirit
Mark 1:23–28, Luke 4:33–37

And there was in their synagogue a man with an unclean spirit of the devil; and he cried out with a loud voice,

Saying, Let us alone; what have we to do with thee, thou Jesus of Nazareth? art thou come to destroy us? I know thee who thou art, the Holy One of God.

And Jesus rebuked him, saying, Hold thy peace, and come out of him.

And when the unclean spirit of the devil had thrown him in the midst and had torn him, and cried with a loud voice, he came out of him, and hurt him not.

And they were all amazed, insomuch that they questioned and spake among themselves, saying, What thing is this? what new doctrine or word is this? for with authority and power commandeth he even the unclean spirits, and they do obey him and come out.

And immediately his fame spread abroad throughout all the region and every place round about Galilee.

Fishermen Called to Be Fishers of Men
Matt. 4:17–22, Mark 1:16–20, JST Matt. 4:18

Now as he, Jesus, walking by the sea of Galilee, saw two brethren, Simon called Peter, and Andrew his brother, casting a net into the sea: for they were fishers.

And he saith unto them, I am he of whom it is written by the prophets; Follow me, and come ye after me, and I will make you to become fishers of men. And they straightway left and forsook their nets, and followed him.

"... come ye after me, and I will make you to become fishers of men."

Simon Dewey

And going on from thence, he saw other two brethren, James the son of Zebedee, and John his brother, who also were in a ship with Zebedee their father, mending their nets; and he called them.

And they immediately left the ship and their father Zebedee in the ship with the hired servants, and followed after him.

Proclamation of the Gospel in Galilee: The First Tour
Matt. 4:23–25, Mark 1:35–39, Luke 4:37, 42–44, JST Matt. 4:22

And in the morning, rising up a great while before day, he went out, and departed into a solitary desert place, and there prayed.

And Simon and they that were with him followed after him, and the people sought him, and came unto him, and stayed him, that he should not depart from them.

And he said unto them, I must preach the kingdom of God to other cities also: for therefore am I sent.

And when they had found him, they said unto him, All men seek for thee.

And he said unto them, Let us go into the next towns, that I may preach there also: for therefore came I forth.

And Jesus went about all Galilee, teaching in their synagogues, and preaching the gospel of the kingdom, and healing all manner of sickness and all manner of disease among the people which believed on his name.

And his fame went out into every place of the country round about all Syria: and they brought unto him all sick people that were taken with divers diseases and torments, and those which were possessed with devils, and those which were lunatick, and those that had the palsy; and he healed them.

And there followed him great multitudes of people from Galilee, and from Decapolis, and from Jerusalem, and from Judæa, and from beyond Jordan.

Discourse from the Boat
Luke 5:1–3

And it came to pass, that, as the people pressed upon him to hear the word of God, he stood by the lake of Gennesaret,

And saw two ships standing by the lake: but the fishermen were gone out of them, and were washing their nets.

And he entered into one of the ships, which was Simon's, and prayed him that he would thrust out a little from the land. And he sat down, and taught the people out of the ship.

Peter Called to Catch Men: His Heart Touched
Luke 5:4–11

Now when he had left speaking, he said unto Simon, Launch out into the deep, and let down your nets for a draught.

And Simon answering said unto him, Master, we have toiled all the night, and have taken nothing: nevertheless at thy word I will let down the net.

And when they had this done, they inclosed a great multitude of fishes: and their net brake.

And they beckoned unto their partners, which were in the other ship, that they should come and help them. And they came, and filled both the ships, so that they began to sink.

When Simon Peter saw it, he fell down at Jesus' knees, saying, Depart from me; for I am a sinful man, O Lord.

For he was astonished, and all that were with him, at the draught of the fishes which they had taken:

And so was also James, and John, the sons of Zebedee, which were partners with Simon. And Jesus said unto Simon, Fear not; from henceforth thou shalt catch men.

And when they had brought their ships to land, they forsook all, and followed him.

Healing of the Leper
Matt. 8:1–4, Mark 1:40–45, Luke 5:12–15

When he was come down from the mountain, great multitudes followed him.

And, behold, there came a leper beseeching him, who seeing Jesus fell on his face and kneeling down and worshipped him, saying, Lord, if thou wilt, thou canst make me clean.

And Jesus, moved with compassion, put forth his hand, and touched him, saying unto him, I will; be thou clean. And immediately his leprosy was cleansed and departed from him. And Jesus straitly charged him, See thou tell no man; but go thy way, shew thyself to the priest, and offer thy cleansing the gift that Moses commanded, for a testimony unto them.

But he went out, and began to publish it much, and to blaze abroad the matter, insomuch that Jesus could no more openly enter into the city, but was without in desert places: and great multitudes came together to hear him from every quarter, and to be healed by him of their infirmities.

Twelve Called and Ordained
Matt. 10:1–4, Mark 3:13–19, Luke 6:12–16

And it came to pass in those days, that he went out into a mountain to pray, and continued all night in prayer to God.

And when it was day, he called unto him whom he would, his disciples: and they came unto him: and of them he chose and ordained twelve, whom also he named apostles; that they should be with him, and that he might send them forth to preach,

And to have power to heal all manner of sicknesses, against unclean spirits and to cast out devils:

Now the names of the twelve apostles are these; The first, Simon, (whom he also named Peter,) and Andrew his brother,

And James the son of Zebedee, and John the brother of James; and he surnamed them Boanerges, which is, The sons of thunder: Philip and Bartholomew,

Matt. the publican and Thomas, James the son of Alphæus, and Lebbæus, whose surname was Thaddæus,

And Judas the brother of James, and Simon called Zelotes the Canaanite, and Judas Iscariot, which also was the traitor, who also betrayed him, and they went into an house.

Charge to the Twelve
Matt. 10:5–42, Mark 6:7–13, Luke 9:1–2; 12:2–9, 11–12, 49–53; 14:25–28,
JST Matt. 10:34, JST Luke 12:9–12, 14:26, 28

These twelve disciples Jesus called unto him together and began to send them forth by two and two; and gave them power and authority over all devils, unclean spirits; and to cure diseases.

And he sent them to preach the kingdom of God, and to heal the sick.

And commanded them, saying, Go not into the way of the Gentiles, and into any city of the Samaritans enter ye not:

But go rather to the lost sheep of the house of Israel.

And as ye go, preach, saying, The kingdom of heaven is at hand.

Heal the sick, cleanse the lepers, raise the dead, cast out devils: freely ye have received, freely give.

Take nothing for their journey, save a staff only; no scrip for your journey,

But be shod with sandals; and not put on two coats, neither shoes, nor yet staves: for the workman is worthy of his meat.

No bread, no money in their purse.

And he said unto them into whatsoever city or town or house ye shall enter, enquire who in it is worthy; and there abide till ye depart from that place and go thence.

And when ye come into an house, salute it.

And if the house be worthy, let your peace come upon it: but if it be not worthy, let your

peace return to you.

And whosoever shall not receive you, nor hear your words, when ye depart out of that house or city, shake off the dust under your feet for a testimony against them.

Verily I say unto you, It shall be more tolerable for the land of Sodom and Gomorrha in the day of judgment, than for that city.

Behold, I send you forth as sheep in the midst of wolves: be ye therefore wise as serpents, and harmless as doves. But beware of men: for they will deliver you up to the councils, and they will scourge you in their synagogues; And bring you unto the synagogues and before governors and kings and unto magistrates, and powers for my sake, for a testimony against them and the Gentiles—

But when they deliver you up, take no thought how or what ye shall answer, or what ye shall speak:

For the Holy Ghost shall teach you in the same hour what ye ought to say and it shall be given you in that same hour what ye shall speak.

For it is not ye that speak, but the Spirit of your Father which speaketh in you.

And the brother shall deliver up the brother to death, and the father the child: and the children shall rise up against their parents, and cause them to be put to death.

And ye shall be hated of all men for my name's sake: but he that endureth to the end shall be saved.

But when they persecute you in this city, flee ye into another: for verily I say unto you, Ye shall not have gone over the cities of Israel, till the Son of man be come.

The disciple is not above his master, nor the servant above his lord.

It is enough for the disciple that he be as his master, and the servant as his lord. If they have called the master of the house Beelzebub, how much more shall they call them of his household?

Fear them not therefore: for there is nothing covered, that shall not be revealed; and hid, that shall not be known.

What I tell you in darkness, that speak ye in light: and what ye hear in the ear, that preach ye upon the housetops.

Therefore whatsoever ye have spoken in darkness shall be heard in the light; and that which ye have spoken in the ear in closets shall be proclaimed upon the housetops.

And I say unto you my friends, fear not them which kill the body, but are not able to kill the soul: and after that have no more that they can do.

But I will forewarn you whom ye shall fear: Fear him, which after he hath killed hath power to cast into hell, and fear him which is able to destroy both soul and body in hell, yea, I say unto you, Fear him.

Are not two sparrows sold for a farthing? and are not five sparrows sold for two farthings? and one of them shall not fall on the ground and be forgotten before God the Father.

But the very hairs of your head are all numbered. Fear ye not therefore, ye are of more value than many sparrows.

Also I say unto you, Whosoever therefore shall confess me before men, him will I, the Son of man, confess also before the angels of God and my Father which is in heaven.

But whosoever shall deny me before men, him will I also deny before the angels of God and my Father which is in heaven.

Now his disciples knew that he said this, because they had spoken evil against him before the people; for they were afraid to confess him before men.

And they reasoned among themselves, saying, He knoweth our hearts, and he speaketh to our condemnation, and we shall not be forgiven. But he answered them, and said unto them,

Whosoever shall speak a word against the Son of man, and repenteth, it shall be forgiven him; but unto him who blasphemeth against the Holy Ghost, it shall not be forgiven him.

Think not that I am come to send peace on earth: I came not to send peace, but a sword.

For I am come to set a man at variance against his father, and the daughter against her mother, and the daughter in law against her mother in law.

I am come to send fire on the earth; and what will I, if it be already kindled?

But I have a baptism to be baptized with; and how am I straitened till it be accomplished!

Suppose ye that I am come to give peace on earth? I tell you, Nay; but rather division:

For from henceforth there shall be five in one house divided, three against two, and two against three.

And a man's foes shall be they of his own household.

The father shall be divided against the son, and the son against the father; the mother against the daughter, and the daughter against the mother; the mother in law against her daughter in law, and the daughter in law against her mother in law.

And there went great multitudes with him: and he turned, and said unto them,

He that loveth father or mother and wife, and children, and brethren, and sisters, or husband, yea, and his own life also, more than me is not worthy of me: and he that loveth son or daughter more than me, or in other words, is afraid to lay down his life for my sake is not worthy of me and cannot be my disciple.

And he that taketh not his cross, and followeth after me, is not worthy of me and cannot be my disciple.

<u>Wherefore, settle this in your hearts, that ye will do the things which I shall teach, and command you.</u>

For which of you, intending to build a tower, sitteth not down first, and counteth the cost, whether he have sufficient to finish it?

He <u>who seeketh to save</u> his life shall lose it: and he that loseth his life for my sake shall find it.

He that receiveth you receiveth me, and he that receiveth me receiveth him that sent me.

He that receiveth a prophet in the name of a prophet shall receive a prophet's reward; and he that receiveth a righteous man in the name of a righteous man shall receive a righteous man's reward.

And whosoever shall give to drink unto one of these little ones a cup of cold water only in the name of a disciple, verily I say unto you, he shall in no wise lose his reward.

And they went out, and preached that men should repent.

And they cast out many devils, and anointed with oil many that were sick, and healed them.

The Sermon on the Mount and the Sermon on the Plain
Matt. 5:1–2, Luke 6:20

AND seeing the multitudes, he went up into a mountain: and when he was set, he lifted up his eyes on his disciples and his disciples came unto him:

And he opened his mouth, and taught them, saying,

The Poor in Spirit
Matt. 5:3, Luke 6:20

Blessed are the poor in spirit: for theirs is the kingdom of God [and of] heaven.

Those Who Mourn

Matt. 5:4, Luke 6:21

Blessed are they that mourn [and] weep: for they shall be comforted [and] ye shall laugh.

The Meek

Matt. 5:5

Blessed are the meek: for they shall inherit the earth.

Hunger and Thirst After Righteousness

Matt. 5:6, Luke 6:21

Blessed are they which do hunger now and thirst after righteousness: for they shall be filled.

The Merciful

Matt. 5:7

Blessed are the merciful: for they shall obtain mercy.

The Pure in Heart

Matt. 5:8

Blessed are the pure in heart: for they shall see God.

The Peacemakers

Matt. 5:9

Blessed are the peacemakers: for they shall be called the children of God.

Persecuted by False Accusers for Righteousness

Matt. 5:10–12, Luke 6:22–26

Blessed are they which are persecuted for righteousness' sake: for theirs is the kingdom of heaven. Blessed are ye, when men shall revile you and hate you, and persecute you, and shall say all manner of evil against you falsely, and when they shall separate you from their company, and shall reproach you, and cast out your name as evil, for my, the Son of man's sake.

Rejoice, and be exceeding glad and leap for joy: for great is your reward in heaven: for in like manner did their fathers persecute they the prophets which were before you.

But woe unto you that are rich! for ye have received your consolation.

Woe unto you that are full! for ye shall hunger. Woe unto you that laugh now! for ye shall mourn and weep.

Woe unto you, when all men shall speak well of you! for so did their fathers to the false prophets.

The Salt of the Earth

Matt. 5:13, Luke 14:34–35, JST Luke 14:35–36

Then certain of them came to him, saying, Good Master, we have Moses and the prophets, and whosoever shall live by them, shall he not have life?

And Jesus answered, saying, Ye know not Moses, neither the prophets; for if ye had known them, ye would have believed on me; for to this intent they were written. For I am sent that ye might have life. Therefore I will liken it unto salt which is good;

Ye are the salt of the earth: but if the salt have lost his savour, wherewith shall it be salted and seasoned? It is neither fit for the land, nor yet for the dunghill; it is thenceforth good for nothing, but to be cast out [by] men, and to be trodden under foot of men. He that hath ears to hear, let him hear.

These things he said, signifying that which was written, verily must all be fulfilled.

"Ye Are the Light of the World"

Matt. 5:14–15, Luke 8:16, 11:33

Ye are the light of the world. A city that is set on an hill cannot be hid.

No man, when he hath lighted a candle, covereth it with a vessel, or putteth it under a bed; Neither do men light a candle, and put it under a bushel, [nor] putteth it in a secret place, but on a candlestick; and it giveth light unto all that are in the house, that they which come in may see the light.

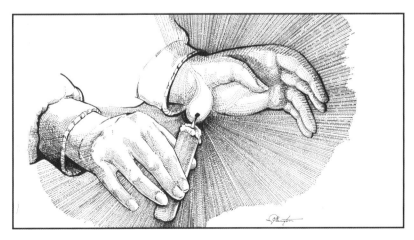

Let Your Light Shine
Matt. 5:16

Let your light so shine before men, that they may see your good works, and glorify your Father which is in heaven.

The Law Fullfilled
Matt. 5:17–20, Luke 16:17, JST Matt. 5:21

Think not that I am come to destroy the law, or the prophets: I am not come to destroy, but to fulfil.

For verily I say unto you, Till heaven and earth pass, one jot or one tittle shall in no wise pass from the law, till all be fulfilled.

It is easier for heaven and earth to pass, than one tittle of the law to fail.

Whosoever therefore shall break one of these least commandments, and shall teach men so to do, he shall in no wise be saved in the kingdom of heaven[45]: but whosoever shall do and teach these commandments of the law until it be fulfilled, the same shall be called great and shall be saved in the kingdom of heaven.

For I say unto you, That except your righteousness shall exceed the righteousness of the scribes and Pharisees, ye shall in no case enter into the kingdom of heaven.

Anger: "Thou Shalt Not Kill"
Matt. 5:21–26, Luke 12:58–59, JST Matt. 5:22

Ye have heard that it was said by them of old time, Thou shalt not kill; and whosoever shall kill shall be in danger of the judgment:

But I say unto you, That whosoever is angry with his brother[46] shall be in danger of the judgment: and whosoever shall say to his brother, Raca, shall be in danger of the council: but whosoever shall say, Thou fool, shall be in danger of hell fire.

Therefore if thou bring thy gift to the altar, and there rememberest that thy brother hath ought against thee;

Leave there thy gift before the altar, and go thy way; first be reconciled to thy brother, and then come and offer thy gift.

Agree with thine adversary quickly, When thou goest with thine adversary to the magistrate whiles thou art in the way with him give diligence that thou mayest be delivered from him; lest at any time the adversary deliver thee to the judge, and the judge deliver thee to the officer, and

---

45   Matthew reads, "be called the least in the kingdom of heaven"
46   JST deletes "without a cause"

the officer cast thee into prison.

Verily I say unto thee, Thou shalt by no means come out thence and depart thence, till thou hast paid the very last mite and the uttermost farthing.

Adultery, Lust
Matt. 5:27–30, JST Matt. 5:34

Ye have heard that it was said by them of old time, Thou shalt not commit adultery:

But I say unto you, That whosoever looketh on a woman to lust after her hath committed adultery with her already in his heart.

And if thy right eye offend thee, pluck it out, and cast it from thee: for it is profitable for thee that one of thy members should perish, and not that thy whole body should be cast into hell.

And if thy right hand offend thee, cut if off, and cast it from thee: for it is profitable for thee that one of thy members should perish, and not that thy whole body should be cast into hell. <u>And now this I speak, a parable concerning your sins; wherefore, cast them from you, that ye may not be hewn down and cast into the fire.</u>

Divorce
Matt. 5:31–32, Luke 16:18

It hath been said, Whosoever shall put away his wife, let him give her a writing of divorcement:

But I say unto you, That whosoever shall put away his wife, saving for the cause of fornication, and marrieth another, committeth adultery, and causeth her to commit adultery: and whosoever shall marry her that is divorced away from her husband committeth adultery.

Swearing an Oath: Honesty
Matt. 5:33–37

Again, ye have heard that it hath been said by them of old time, Thou shalt not forswear thyself, but shalt perform unto the Lord thine oaths:

But I say unto you, Swear not at all; neither by heaven; for it is God's throne:

Nor by the earth; for it is his footstool: neither by Jerusalem; for it is the city of the great King.

Neither shalt thou swear by thy head, because thou canst not make one hair white or black.

But let your communication be, Yea, yea; Nay, nay: for whatsoever is more than these cometh of evil.

Evil Force of Generous Service
Matt. 5:38–42

Ye have heard that it hath been said, An eye for an eye, and a tooth for a tooth:

But I say unto you, That ye resist not evil: but whosoever shall smite thee on thy right cheek, turn to him the other also.

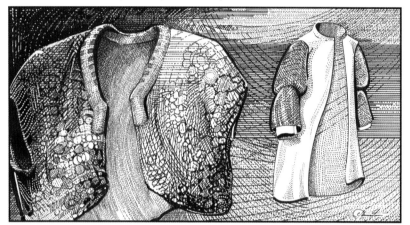

And if any man will sue thee at the law, and take away thy coat, let him have thy cloke also.

And whosoever shall compel thee to go a mile, go with him twain.

Give to him that asketh thee, and from him that would borrow of thee turn not thou away.

Love Thy Enemies
Matt. 5:43–47, Luke 6:27–36, JST Luke 6:29–30

Ye have heard that it hath been said, Thou shalt love thy neighbour, and hate thine enemy. But I say unto you which hear, Love your enemies, bless them that curse you, do good to them that hate you, and pray for them which despitefully use you, and persecute you;

And unto him that smiteth thee on the one cheek offer also the other, in other words, it is better to offer the other, than to revile again; and him that taketh away thy cloke forbid not to take thy coat also.

For it is better that thou suffer thine enemy to take these things, than to contend with him. Verily I say unto you, Your heavenly Father who seeth in secret, shall bring that wicked one into judgment. Give to every man that asketh of thee; and of him that taketh away thy goods ask them not again.

And as ye would that men should do to you, do ye also to them likewise.

For if ye love them which love you, what thank have ye? for sinners also love those that love them.

And if ye do good to them which do good to you, what thank have ye? for sinners also do even the same.

And if ye lend to them of whom ye hope to receive, what thank have ye? for sinners also lend to sinners, to receive as much again.

But love ye your enemies, and do good, and lend, hoping for nothing again; and your reward shall be great, and ye shall be the children of the Highest: for he is kind unto the unthankful and to the evil.

That ye may be the children of your Father which is in heaven: for he maketh his sun to rise on the evil and on the good, and sendeth rain on the just and on the unjust.

For if ye love them which love you, what reward have ye? do not even the publicans the same?

And if ye salute your brethren only, what do ye more than others? do not even the publicans so?

Perfect As Your Father
Matt. 5:48, Luke 6:36, JST Matt. 5:50

<u>Ye are therefore commanded to be</u>[47] perfect [and] merciful, even as your Father which is in heaven is perfect [and] merciful.

Alms: Notoriety or Generosity
Matt. 6:1–4, JST Matt. 6:1

<u>And it came to pass that, as Jesus taught his disciples, he said unto</u> them, Take heed that ye do not your alms before men, to be seen of them: otherwise ye have no reward of your Father which is in heaven.

Therefore when thou doest thine alms, do not sound a trumpet before thee, as the hypocrites do in the synagogues and in the streets, that they may have glory of men. Verily I say unto you, They have their reward.

But when thou doest alms, let not thy left hand know what thy right hand doeth: That thine alms may be in secret: and thy Father which seeth in secret himself shall reward thee openly.

Prayer: Hypocrisy or Reverence
Matt. 6:5–15, Luke 11:2–4, JST Matt. 6:14, JST Luke 11:4

And when thou prayest, thou shalt not be as the hypocrites are: for they love to pray standing in the synagogues and in the corners of the streets, that they may be seen of men. Verily I say unto you, They have their reward.

But thou, when thou prayest, enter into thy closet, and when thou hast shut thy door, pray

---

47   Matthew reads, "Be ye therefore perfect"

to thy Father which is in secret; and thy Father which seeth in secret shall reward thee openly.

But when ye pray, use not vain repetitions, as the heathen do: for they think that they shall be heard for their much speaking.

Be not ye therefore like unto them: for your Father knoweth what things ye have need of, before ye ask him.

After this manner therefore pray ye: Our Father which art in heaven, Hallowed be thy name.

Thy kingdom come. Thy will be done in earth, as it is in heaven.

Give us day by day our daily bread.

And forgive us our debts [and] sins, as we forgive our debtors.

And <u>suffer</u> us not <u>to be</u> lead <u>unto</u>[48] temptation, but deliver us from evil: For thine is the kingdom, and the power, and the glory, for ever. Amen.

For if ye forgive men their trespasses, your heavenly Father will also forgive you:

But if ye forgive not men their trespasses, neither will your Father forgive your trespasses.

Fasting: Hypocrisy or Simplicity
Matt. 6:16-18

Moreover when ye fast, be not, as the hypocrites, of a sad countenance: for they disfigure their faces, that they may appear unto men to fast. Verily I say unto you, They have their reward.

But thou, when thou fastest, anoint thine head, and wash thy face; That thou appear not unto men to fast, but unto thy Father which is in secret: and thy Father, which seeth in secret, shall reward thee openly.

Treasure on Earth or in Heaven
Matt. 6:19-34, Luke 11:34-36, 12:22-34, 16:9-13,
JST Matt. 6:22, 25-27, 34, 38, JST Luke 12:34

Sell that ye have, and give alms; provide yourselves bags which wax not old, a treasure in the heavens that faileth not,

Lay not up for yourselves treasures upon earth, where moth and rust doth corrupt, and where thieves break through and steal:

But lay up for yourselves treasures in heaven, where neither

---
48   Luke reads, "into"

moth nor rust doth corrupt, and where thieves do not break through nor steal:

For where your treasure is, there will your heart be also.

The light of the body is the eye: if therefore thine eye be single <u>to the glory of God</u>, thy whole body shall be full of light.

But if thine eye be evil, thy whole body shall be full of darkness. If therefore the light that is in thee be darkness, how great is that darkness! Take heed therefore that the light which is in thee be not darkness.

If thy whole body therefore be full of light, having no part dark, the whole shall be full of light, as when the bright shining of a candle doth give thee light.

And I say unto you, Make to yourselves friends of the mammon of unright-eousness; that, when ye fail, they may receive you into everlasting habitations.

He that is faithful in that which is least is faithful also in much: and he that is unjust in the least is unjust also in much.

If therefore ye have not been faithful in the unrighteous mammon, who will commit to your trust the true riches?

And if ye have not been faithful in that which is another man's, who shall give you that which is your own?

No man (servant) can serve two masters: for either he will hate the one, and love the other; or else he will hold to the one, and despise the other. Ye cannot serve God and mammon.

<u>And, again, I say unto you, go ye into the world, and care not for the world; for the world will hate you, and will persecute you, and will turn you out of their synagogues.</u>

<u>Nevertheless, ye shall go forth from house to house, teaching the people; and I will go before you.</u>

<u>And your heavenly Father will provide for you whatsoever things ye need for food, what ye shall eat; and for raiment, what ye shall wear or put on.</u>

Therefore I say unto you, Take no thought for your life, what ye shall eat, or what ye shall drink; nor yet for your body, what ye shall put on. Is not the life more than meat, and the body than raiment?

Behold the fowls of the air: for they sow not, neither do they reap, nor have storehouse or gather into barns; yet God your heavenly Father feedeth them. Are ye not much better than they?

Which of you by taking thought can add one cubit unto his stature?

If ye then be not able to do that thing which is least, why take ye thought for the rest?

And why take ye thought for raiment? Consider the lilies of the field, how they grow; they toil not, neither do they spin:

And yet I say unto you, That even Solomon in all his glory was not arrayed like one of these.

Wherefore, if God so clothe the grass of the field, which to day is, and to morrow is cast into the oven, how much more will he not provide for you, if ye are not of little faith.[49]

Therefore take no thought, saying, What shall we eat? or, What shall we drink? or, Wherewithal shall we be clothed? neither be ye of doubtful mind.

(For after all these things do the Gentiles, nations of the world, seek after:) for your heavenly Father knoweth that ye have need of all these things.

Wherefore, seek not the things of this world but rather seek ye to bring forth[50] the kingdom of God, and to establish his righteousness; and all these things shall be added unto you.

Fear not, little flock; for it is your Father's good pleasure to give you the kingdom.

Take therefore no thought for the morrow: for the morrow shall take thought for the things of itself. Sufficient unto the day is the evil thereof.

Judgment: Hypocritical or Helpful
Matt. 7:1–5, Luke 6:37–38, 41–42, JST Matt. 7:1

Now these are the words which Jesus taught his disciples that they should say unto the people. Judge not unrighteously, that ye shall be not judged: but judge righteous judgment.

For with what judgment ye judge, ye shall be judged: and with what measure ye mete, it shall be measured to you again.

Condemn not, and ye shall not be condemned: forgive, and ye shall be forgiven:

Give, and it shall be given unto you; good measure, pressed down, and shaken together, and running over, shall men give into your bosom. For with the same measure that ye mete withal it shall be measured to you again.

And he spake a parable unto them, Can the blind lead the blind? shall they not both fall into the ditch?

The disciple is not above his master: but every one that is perfect shall be as his master.

And why beholdest thou the mote that is in thy brother's eye, but considerest [or] perceivest not the beam that is in thine own eye?

Or how wilt thou say to thy brother, Brother, Let me pull out the mote out of thine eye; and,

49   Matthew reads, "shall he not much more clothe you, O ye of little faith?"
50   Luke reads, "first"

behold, thou thyself beholdest not the beam that is in thine own eye?

Thou hypocrite, first cast out the beam out of thine own eye; and then shalt thou see clearly to pull [and] cast out the mote out of thy brother's eye.

Holy Things Are Like Pearls
Matt. 7:6, JST Matt. 7:9–11

Go ye into the world, saying unto all, Repent, for the kingdom of heaven has come nigh unto you.

And the mysteries of the kingdom ye shall keep within yourselves; for it is not meet to give that which is holy unto the dogs, neither cast ye your pearls before swine, lest they trample them under their feet.

For the world cannot receive that which ye, yourselves, are not able to bear; wherefore ye shall not give your pearls unto them, lest they turn again and rend you.

Prayer: Ask, Seek, Knock
Matt. 7:7–12, Luke 11:9–13, JST Matt. 7:12–17, JST Luke 11:14

Say unto them, Ask of God, and it shall be given you; seek, and ye shall find; knock, and it shall be opened unto you:

For every one that asketh receiveth; and he that seeketh findeth; and to him that knocketh it shall be opened.

And then said his disciples unto him, They will say unto us, We ourselves are righteous, and need not that any man should teach us. God, we know, heard Moses and some of the prophets; but us he will not hear. And they will say, We have the law for our salvation, and that is sufficient for us.

Then Jesus answered, and said unto his disciples, Thus shall ye say unto them,

What man among you, having a son, and he shall be standing out, and shall say, Father, open thy house that I may come in and sup with thee, will not say, Come in, my son; for mine is thine, and thine is mine?

Or what man is there of you, whom if his son ask bread of any of you that is a father, will he give him a stone?

Or if he ask a fish, will he give him a serpent?

Or if he shall ask an egg, will he offer him a scorpion?

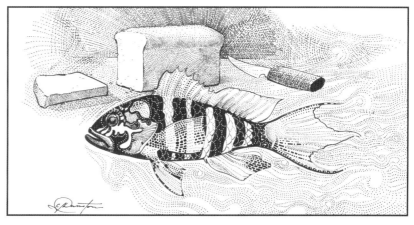

If ye then, being evil, know how to give good gifts unto your children, how much more shall your Father which is in heaven give good things and gifts, through the Holy Spirit to them that ask him?

Therefore all things whatsoever ye would that men should do to you, do ye even so to them: for this is the law and the prophets.

The Way Is Strait and Narrow
Matt. 7:13–14, Luke 13:23–24

Then said one unto him, Lord, are there few that be saved? And he said unto them, Strive to enter ye in at the strait gate: for many, I say unto you, will seek to enter in, and shall not be able. For wide is the gate, and broad is the way, that leadeth to destruction, and many there be which go in thereat: Because strait is the gate, and narrow is the way, which leadeth unto life, and few there be that find it.

False Prophets Known By Their Fruits
Matt. 7:15–20, Luke 6:43–44

Beware of false prophets, which come to you in sheep's clothing, but inwardly they are ravening wolves.

Ye shall know them by their fruits.

For every tree is known by his own fruit. Do men gather grapes of thorns, or figs of thistles? For of thorns men do not gather figs, nor of a bramble bush gather they grapes.

Even so every good tree bringeth forth good fruit; but a corrupt tree bringeth forth evil fruit.

For a good tree cannot bring forth evil [or] corrupt fruit, neither doth a corrupt tree bring forth good fruit.

Every tree that bringeth not forth good fruit is hewn down, and cast into the fire.

Wherefore by their fruits ye shall know them.

A good man out of the good treasure of his heart bringeth forth that which is good; and an evil man out of the evil treasure of his heart bringeth forth that which is evil: for of the abundance of the heart his mouth speaketh.

Do the Will of the Father
Matt. 7:21–23, Luke 6:46, JST Matt. 7:31

Not every one that saith unto me, Lord, Lord, shall enter into the kingdom of heaven; but he that doeth the will of my Father which is in heaven.

<u>For the day soon cometh, that men shall some before me to judgment, to be judged according to their works.</u>

Many will say to me in that day, Lord, Lord, have we not prophesied in thy name? and in thy name have cast out devils? and in thy name done many wonderful works?

And why call ye me, Lord, Lord, and do not the things which I say?

And then will I profess unto them, I never knew you: depart from me, ye that work iniquity.

A House Built on a Rock or on Sand
Matt. 7:24–27, Luke 6:47–49

Therefore whosoever cometh to me and heareth these sayings of mine, and doeth them, I will shew you [and] liken him unto a wise man, which built an house, and digged deep, and laid the foundation on a rock:

And the rain descended, and the floods came and arose, the stream beat vehemently upon

that house, and could not shake it, and the winds blew, and beat upon that house; and it fell not: for it was founded upon a rock.

And every one that heareth these sayings of mine, and doeth them not, shall be likened unto a foolish man, which built his house upon the sand without a foundation upon the earth; against which the stream did beat vehemently,

And the rain descended, and the floods came, and the winds blew, and beat upon that house; and it immediately fell: and great was the fall and the ruin of it.

Taught Having Authority, Not As Scribes
Matt. 7:28–29, JST Matt. 7:36–37

And it came to pass, when Jesus had ended these sayings <u>with his disciples</u>, the people were astonished at his doctrine:

For he taught them as one having authority <u>from God</u>, and not as <u>having authority from</u> the scribes.

Healing of the Centurion's Servant
Matt. 8:5–13, Luke 7: 1–10, JST Matt. 8:9

And when Jesus had ended all his sayings in the audience of the people he entered into Capernaum, and there came unto him a centurion [whose] servant was dear unto him, was sick, and ready to die.

And when he heard of Jesus, he sent unto him the elders of the Jews, beseeching him that he would come and heal his servant.

And when they came to Jesus, they besought him instantly, saying, Lord, That he was worthy for whom he should do this:

For he loveth our nation, and he hath built us a synagogue. And saying, Lord, my servant lieth at home sick of the palsy, grievously tormented.

And Jesus saith unto him, I will come and heal him.

Then Jesus went with them. And when he was now not far from the house, the centurion sent friends to him, [and] answered and said unto him, Lord, trouble not thyself, I am not worthy that thou shouldest come and enter under my roof:

Wherefore neither thought I myself worthy to come unto thee: but speak the word only, and my servant shall be healed.

For I also am a man set under authority, having soldiers under me: and I say to this man, Go, and he goeth; and to another, Come, and he cometh; and to my servant, Do this, and he doeth it.

<u>And when they that followed him, heard this, they marveled,</u> and when Jesus heard these things, he marveled at him, and turned him about, and said to them that followed him, Verily I say unto you, I have not found so great faith, no, not in Israel.

And I say unto you, That many shall come from the east and west, and shall sit down with Abraham, and Isaac, and Jacob, in the kingdom of heaven.

But the children of the kingdom shall be cast out into outer darkness: there shall be weeping and gnashing of teeth.

And Jesus said unto the centurion, Go thy way; and as thou hast believed, so be it done unto thee.

And they that were sent, returning to the house, found the servant whole that had been sick the selfsame hour.

Widow's Son Restored
Luke 7:11–17

And it came to pass the day after, that he went into a city called Nain; and many of his disciples went with him, and much people.

Now when he came nigh to the gate of the city, behold, there was a dead man carried out, the only son of his mother, and she was a widow: and much people of the city was with her.

And when the Lord saw her, he had compassion on her, and said unto her, Weep not.

And he came and touched the bier: and they that bare him stood still. And he said, Young man, I say unto thee, Arise.

And he that was dead sat up, and began to speak. And he delivered him to his mother.

And there came a fear on all: and they glorified God, saying, That a great prophet is risen up among us; and, That God hath visited his people.

And this rumour of him went forth throughout all Judæa, and throughout all the region round about.

The Mother of Peter's Wife Is Healed
Matt. 8:14–15, Mark 1:29–31, Luke 4:38–39

And when Jesus was come into Simon [Peter] and Andrew's house, with James and John, he saw his wife's mother laid, and sick of a great fever, and anon they tell him of her.

And he came [and] stood over her and he touched her hand, and lifted her up; and rebuked the fever and immediately the fever left her: and immediately she arose, and ministered unto them.

Healing in the Evening
Matt. 8:16–17, Mark 1:32–34, Luke 4:40–41

When the even was come, when the sun did set, they brought unto him many that [had] divers diseases and them that were possessed with devils.

And all the city was gathered together at the door. And he laid his hands on every one of them, and he healed all that were sick of divers diseases. And he cast out the spirits [or] many devils with his word, And devils also came out of many, crying out, and saying, Thou art Christ the Son of God. And he [rebuked] and suffered not the devils to speak, because they knew that he was the Christ.

That it might be fulfilled which was spoken by Esaias the prophet, saying, Himself took our infirmities, and bare our sicknesses.

Foxes Have Holes
Matt. 8:18–22, Luke 9:57–62

Now when Jesus saw great multitudes about him, he gave commandment to depart unto the other side.

And it came to pass, that, as they went in the way, a certain scribe came, and said unto him, Lord, Master, I will follow thee whithersoever thou goest.

And Jesus saith unto him, The foxes have holes, and the birds of the air have nests; but the Son of man hath not where to lay his head.

And he said unto another, Follow me.

And another of his disciples said unto him, Lord, suffer me first to go and bury my father.

But Jesus said unto him, Follow me; and let the dead bury their dead: but go thou and preach the kingdom of God.

And another also said, Lord, I will follow thee; but let me first go bid them farewell, which are at home at my house.

And Jesus said unto him, No man, having put his hand to the plough, and looking back, is fit for the kingdom of God.

Peace Be Still
Matt. 8:23–27, Mark 4:35–41, Luke 8:22–25, JST Luke 8:23

And now it came to pass on the same day, when the even was come, he saith unto them, Let us pass over unto the other side.

And when they had sent away the multitude, they took him even as he was in the ship. And there were also with him other little ships.

And when he was entered into a ship, his disciples followed him. And he said unto them, Let us go over unto the other side of the lake. And they launched forth.

But as they sailed he fell asleep, and, behold, there arose and came down a great storm of wind on the lake, [or] tempest in the sea, and the waves beat into the ship, insomuch that the ship was covered with the waves: so that it was now [that] they were filled with fear, and

". . . and said unto the sea,
Peace, be still."

were in danger[51].

And he was in the hinder part of the ship, asleep on a pillow.

And his disciples came to him, and awoke him, saying, Lord, Master, save us: carest thou not that we perish?

And he saith unto them, Why are ye fearful, O ye of little faith? how is it that ye have no faith? Where is your faith? Then he arose, and rebuked the winds and the raging of the water: and said unto the sea, Peace, be still. And the wind ceased, and there was a great calm.

But the men being afraid, feared exceedingly, [and] marvelled, and wondered and said one to another, What manner of man is this, for he commandeth even the winds and water, [and] the winds and the sea obey him!

Legion Enter into Swine
Matt. 8:28–34, Mark 5:1–20, Luke 8:26–39

And when he was come to the other side of the sea, into the country of the Gergesenes (Gadarenes), which is over against Galilee. And when he was come out of the ship, he went forth to land, [and] immediately there met him out of the tombs, two possessed with devils or unclean

---

51   Luke reads, "filled with water, and were in jeopardy"

spirits [for a long] time, exceeding fierce, and ware no clothes, neither abode in any house, but in the tombs, so that no man might pass by that way.

And no man could bind him, no, not with chains:

Because that he had been often bound with fetters and chains, and the chains had been plucked asunder by him, and the fetters broken in pieces: neither could any man tame him.

And always, night and day, he was in the mountains, and in the tombs, crying, and cutting himself with stones.

But when he saw Jesus afar off, he ran [and] fell down before him and worshipped him,

And, behold, they cried out, with a loud voice saying, What have we to do with thee, Jesus, thou Son of the most high God? art thou come hither to torment us before the time? I adjure thee by God, that thou torment me not.

For he said unto him, Come out of the man, thou unclean spirit.

(For oftentimes it had caught him: and he was kept bound with chains and in fetters; and he brake the bands, and was driven of the devil into the wilderness.) And he asked him, What is thy name? And he answered, saying, My name is Legion: for we are many [that are] entered into him. And he besought him much that he would not send them away out of the country [or] command them to go out into the deep. And there was a good way off from them unto the mountains a great herd of many swine feeding.

And so all the devils besought him, saying, If thou cast us out, suffer us to go away into the herd of swine, that we may enter into them. And he suffered them. And forthwith Jesus gave them leave,

And he said unto them, Go. And when they, the unclean spirits [or] devils, were come out of the man, they went into the herd of swine: and, behold, the whole herd of swine ran violently down a steep place into the sea [or] lake, (they were about two thousand;) and were choked in the sea, and perished in the waters.

And they that kept and fed the swine saw what was done, [and] they fled, and went their ways into the city, and in the country, and told every thing, and what was befallen to the possessed of the devils.

And, behold, the whole city came out to meet Jesus: and [to] see him that was possessed with the devil, and had the legion, sitting, and clothed, and in his right mind sitting at the feet of Jesus: and they were afraid.

And they also that saw it told them how it befell to him that was possessed with the devil, and also concerning the swine was healed.

Then the whole multitude of the country of the Gadarenes round about began to pray, and they besought him that he would depart from them out of their coasts; for they were taken with great fear: and he went up into the ship, and returned back again.

And when he was come into the ship, the man that had been possessed with the devil besought [and] prayed him that he might be with him.

Howbeit Jesus suffered him not [and] sent him away, saying, Go home to thy friends, and tell them how great things the Lord God hath done for thee, and hath had compassion on thee.

And he departed, and began to publish in the whole city of Decapolis how great things Jesus had done for him: and all men did marvel.

Paralytic Healed
Matt. 9:1–8, Mark 2:1–12, Luke 5:17–26, JST Matt. 9:5, JST Luke 5:23

AND he entered into a ship, and passed over, and came and again he entered into his own city, Capernaum after some days; and it was noised that he was in the house.

And straightway many were gathered together, insomuch that there was no room to receive them, no, not so much as about the door:

And it came to pass on a certain day, as he was teaching, and he preached the word unto them, the Pharisees and doctors of the law sitting by, which were come out of every town of Galilee, and Judæa, and Jerusalem: and the power of the Lord was present to heal them.

And, behold, they come unto him and brought to him a man taken and sick of the palsy, which was borne of four, lying on a bed: and they sought means to bring him in, and to lay him before him.

And when they could not come nigh unto him for the press of the multitude, they went upon the housetop, and they uncovered the roof where he was: and when they had broken it up, they let down the bed wherein the sick of the palsy lay through the tiling with his couch into the midst before Jesus.

When Jesus seeing their faith, he said unto the sick of the palsy; Son of Man, be of good cheer; thy sins be forgiven thee.

And, behold, there were certain of the scribes and Pharisees sitting there, and reasoning in their hearts, [saying] within themselves,

Who is this and why doth this man thus speak blasphemies? Who can forgive sins but God only?

And immediately when Jesus perceived in his spirit, knowing their thoughts and that they so reasoned within themselves, said, Wherefore think and reason ye evil in your hearts? <u>For is it not easier to say</u> to the sick of the palsy, Thy sins be forgiven thee;

<u>Does it require more power to forgive sins than to make the sick rise up and walk</u> and to say, Arise, and take up thy bed and walk?

But that ye may know that the Son of man hath power on earth to forgive sins, (then saith he to the sick of the palsy,) I say unto thee, Arise, take up thy couch bed, and go unto thine house. And immediately he arose up before them, and went forth before them all, and took up his bed, and departed to his house.

But when the multitudes saw it, they were all amazed, [and] they marvelled, and glorified God, and were filled with fear, saying, We never saw it on this fashion, which had given such power unto men. We have seen strange things to day.

"I say unto thee, Arise . . . "

A Feast at the House of Matthew
Matt. 9:9–13, Mark 2:13–17, Luke 5:27–32

And as Jesus passed forth from thence again by the sea side, and all the multitude resorted unto him, and he taught them.

And as he passed by he saw a publican man, named Matthew or Levi the son of Alphæus, sitting at the receipt of custom: and he saith unto him, Follow me. And he arose, and followed him.

And he left all, rose up, and followed him.

And Levi made him a great feast in his own house:

And it came to pass, as Jesus sat at meat in the house, behold, there was a great company [of] many publicans and sinners came and sat down with him, Jesus, and his disciples, for there were many, and they followed him.

And when the scribes [and] the Pharisees saw [him] eat with publicans and sinners, their scribes and Pharisees murmured against his disciples, they said unto his disciples, Why, and how is it, eateth your Master with publicans and sinners?

But when Jesus heard that, he said unto them, They that be whole need not a physician, but they that are sick.

But go ye and learn what that meaneth, I will have mercy, and not sacrifice: for I am not come to call the righteous, but sinners to repentance.

John's Disciples Ask about Fasting: Old and New (Pharisees Ask about Baptism)
Matt. 9:14–17, Mark 2:18–22, Luke 5:33–39, JST Matt. 9:18–21

And the disciples of John and of the Pharisees used to fast: Then came to him the disciples of John, saying, Why do we, the disciples of John, and likewise the disciples of the Pharisees fast oft, and make prayers, but thy disciples eat and drink [and] fast not?

And Jesus said unto them, Can the children of the bridechamber fast [or] mourn, as long as the bridegroom is with them? As long as they have the bridegroom with them, they cannot fast, but the days will come, when the bridegroom shall be taken from them, and then shall they fast in those days.

Then said the Pharisees unto him, Why will ye not receive us with our baptism, seeing we keep the whole law?

But Jesus said unto them, Ye keep not the law. If ye had kept the law, ye would have received me, for I am he who gave the law.

I receive not you with your baptism, because it profiteth you nothing.

For when that which is new is come, the old is ready to be put away. No man seweth and putteth a piece of new cloth unto an old garment, for that new piece which is put in to fill it up taketh away from the old garment, and the piece that was taken out of the new agreeth not with the old, and the rent is made worse.

Neither do men put new wine into old bottles: else the new wine doth burst the bottles [and] the bottles break, and the wine is spilled [and] runneth out, and the bottles will be marred [and] perish.

But new wine must be put into new bottles; and both are preserved. No man also having drunk old wine straightway desireth new: for he saith, The old is better.

Jairus's Daughter Raised
Matt. 9:18–19, 23–26, Mark 5:21–24, 35–43, Luke 8:40–42, 49–56

And when Jesus was passed over again by ship unto the other side, much people gathered unto him: and he was nigh unto the sea.

And it came to pass, that, when Jesus was returned, the people gladly received him: for they were all waiting for him.

And, behold while he spake these things unto them, behold, there came a man, one [of the]

certain rulers of the synagogue, Jairus by name; and when he saw him, he fell at his feet and worshipped him.

And besought him greatly that he would come into his house, saying, My only little daughter, about twelve years of age, lieth at the point of death [and] is even now dead: I pray thee, come and lay thy hand upon her, that she may be healed and she shall live.

And Jesus arose, and followed him, and so did his disciples, and much people followed him, and thronged him.

While he yet spake, there came from the ruler of the synagogue's house certain which said, Thy daughter is dead: why troublest thou the Master any further?

As soon as Jesus heard the word that was spoken, he saith unto the ruler of the synagogue, Fear not, Be not afraid, only believe and she shall be made whole.

And when he came into the house he suffered no man to follow him, save Peter, and James, and John the brother of James, and the father and the mother of the maiden.

And when Jesus came into the ruler of the synagogue's house, and saw the minstrels and the people making a noise, and the tumult, and them that wept and bewailed her greatly.

And when he was come in, he said unto them, Why make ye this ado, and weep? Give place: Weep not, for the maid is not dead, but sleepeth. And they laughed him to scorn knowing that she was dead.

But when the people were put forth all out, he taketh the father and the mother of the damsel, and them that were with him, and entereth in where the damsel was lying.

He went in, and took her, the damsel, by the hand, and said unto her, Talitha cumi; which is, being interpreted, Damsel, I say unto thee, arise.

And straightway her spirit came again and the damsel or maid arose, and he commanded to give her meat. For she was of the age of twelve years. And they, her parents, were astonished with a great astonishment.

And he charged them straitly that no man should know what was done. And the fame hereof went abroad into all that land.

Virtue (Power) Is Gone Out of Me
Matt. 9:20–22, Mark 5:25–34, Luke 8:43–48

And, behold, a certain woman, which was diseased with an issue of blood twelve years,

And had suffered many things of many physicians, and had spent all her living that she had upon physicians, neither could be healed of any, and was nothing bettered, but rather grew worse,

When she had heard of Jesus, came in the press behind him, and touched the border hem of his garment:

For she said within herself, If I may but touch his garment clothes, I shall be whole. And immediately straightway, the fountain of her issue of blood stanched [and] was dried up; and she felt in her body that she was healed of that plague.

And Jesus, immediately knowing in himself that virtue had gone out of him, turned him

about in the press, and said, Who touched my clothes?

When all denied, Peter and his disciples said unto him, Master, Thou seest the multitude thronging thee, and press[ing] thee, and sayest thou, Who touched me?

And Jesus said, Somebody hath touched me: for I perceive that virtue is gone out of me.

But he, Jesus, looked round about to see her that had done this thing. And when the woman saw that she was not hid, the woman came fearing and trembling, knowing what was done in her, came and fell down before him, she declared unto him before all the people for what cause she had touched him, and how she was healed immediately, and told him all the truth.

And he said unto her, Daughter, be of good comfort; thy faith hath made thee whole, go in peace, and be whole of thy plague. And the woman was made whole from that hour.

Two Blind Men Healed
Matt. 9:27–31

And when Jesus departed thence, two blind men followed him, crying, and saying, Thou Son of David, have mercy on us.

And when he was come into the house, the blind men came to him: and Jesus saith unto them, Believe ye that I am able to do this? They said unto him, Yea, Lord.

Then touched he their eyes, saying, According to your faith be it unto you.

And their eyes were opened; and Jesus straitly charged them, saying, See that no man know it.

But they, when they were departed, spread abroad his fame in all that country.

" . . . According to your faith be it unto you. "

Heals Demoniac: Prince of Devils
Matt. 9:32–34, Luke 11:14–15

As they went out, behold, they brought to him a dumb man possessed with a devil.

And it came to pass when the devil was cast out [and] gone, the dumb spake: and the people [and the] multitudes wondered and marvelled, saying, It was never so seen in Israel.

But the Pharisees said, He casteth out devils through Beelzebub the chief prince of the devils.

Teaching Tour in Cities of Apostles
Matt. 11:1, Luke 10:1

AND it came to pass, after these things when Jesus had made an end of commanding his twelve disciples, the Lord appointed other seventy also, and sent them two and two before his face into every city and place whither he himself would come. [And] he departed thence to teach and to preach in their cities.

John Sends Disciples to Jesus
Matt. 11:2–6, Luke 7:18–23

And the disciples of John shewed him of all these things.

Now when John had heard in the prison the works of Christ, he sent two of his disciples to Jesus, saying, Art thou he that should come? or look we for another?

When the men were come unto him, they said, John Baptist hath sent us unto thee,

And said unto him, Art thou he that should come, or do we look for another?

And in that same hour he cured many of their infirmities and plagues, and of evil spirits; and unto many that were blind he gave sight.

Then Jesus answered and said unto them, Go your way and tell [and] shew John again those things which ye do hear and see:

The blind receive their sight, and the lame walk, the lepers are cleansed, and the deaf hear, the dead are raised up, and the poor have the gospel preached to them.

And blessed is he, whosoever shall not be offended in me.

John No Greater Prophet

Matt. 11:7–19, Luke 7:24–35, 16:16, JST Matt. 11:13–15

And as they, the messengers of John were departed, Jesus began to say unto the multitudes [of] people concerning John, What went ye out into the wilderness for to see? A reed shaken with the wind?

But what went ye out for to see? A man clothed in soft raiment? behold, they that wear soft clothing which are gorgeously apparelled, and live delicately, are in kings' houses [and] courts.

But what went ye out for to see? A prophet? yea, I say unto you, and much more than a prophet.

For this is he, of whom it is written, Behold, I send my messenger before thy face, which shall prepare thy way before thee.

For verily I say unto you, Among them that are born of women there hath not risen a greater prophet than John the Baptist: notwithstanding he that is least in the kingdom of God [and] heaven is greater than he.

And all the people that heard him, and the publicans, justified God, being baptized with the baptism of John.

But the Pharisees and lawyers rejected the counsel of God against themselves, being not baptized of him.

And from the days of John the Baptist until now the kingdom of heaven suffereth violence, and the violent take it by force.

But the days will come, when the violent shall have no power; for all the prophets and the law prophesied that it should be thus until John.

Since that time the kingdom of God is preached, and every man presseth into it.

Yea, as many as have prophesied have foretold of these days.

And if ye will receive it, verily, he was the Elias, who was for to come and prepare all things.

He that hath ears to hear, let him hear.

And the Lord said, But whereunto then shall I liken this generation? and to what are they like? They are like unto children sitting in the marketplaces, and calling one to another unto their fellows,

And saying, We have piped unto you, and ye have not danced; we have mourned unto you, and ye have not wept [and] lamented.

For John the Baptist came neither eating bread nor drinking wine, and they and ye say, He hath a devil.

The Son of man came eating and drinking, and they and ye say, Behold a man gluttonous, and a winebibber, a friend of publicans and sinners. But wisdom is justified of her children.

Second Passover (Brief Trip to Judæa)
John 5:1

AFTER this there was a feast of the Jews; and Jesus went up to Jerusalem.

Healing on the Sabbath
John 5:2–16

Now there is at Jerusalem by the sheep market a pool, which is called in the Hebrew tongue Bethesda, having five porches.

In these lay a great multitude of impotent folk, of blind, halt, withered, waiting for the moving of the water.

For an angel went down at a certain season into the pool, and troubled the water: whosoever then first after the troubling of the water stepped in was made whole of whatsoever disease he had.

And a certain man was there, which had an infirmity thirty and eight years.

When Jesus saw him lie, and knew that he had been now a long time in that case, he saith unto him, Wilt thou be made whole?

The impotent man answered him, Sir, I have no man, when the water is troubled, to put me into the pool: but while I am coming, another steppeth down before me.

Jesus saith unto him, Rise, take up thy bed, and walk.

And immediately the man was made whole, and took up his bed, and walked: and on the same day was the sabbath.

The Jews therefore said unto him that was cured, It is the sabbath day: it is not lawful for thee to carry thy bed.

He answered them, He that made me whole, the same said unto me, Take up thy bed, and walk.

Then asked they him, What man is that which said unto thee, Take up thy bed, and walk?

And he that was healed wist not who it was: for Jesus had conveyed himself away, a multitude being in that place.

Afterward Jesus findeth him in the temple, and said unto him, Behold, thou art made whole: sin no more, lest a worse thing come unto thee.

The man departed, and told the Jews that it was Jesus, which had made him whole.

And therefore did the Jews persecute Jesus, and sought to slay him, because he had done these things on the sabbath day.

". . . Jesus saith unto him, Rise, take up thy bed, and walk. And immediately the man was made whole . . ."

Discourse: Witness of the Father

John 5:17–47, JST John 5:35, 37

But Jesus answered them, My Father worketh hitherto, and I work.

Therefore the Jews sought the more to kill him, because he not only had broken the sabbath, but said also that God was his Father, making himself equal with God.

Then answered Jesus and said unto them, Verily, verily, I say unto you, The Son can do nothing of himself, but what he seeth the Father do: for what things soever he doeth, these also doeth the Son likewise.

For the Father loveth the Son, and sheweth him all things that himself doeth: and he will shew him greater works than these, that ye may marvel.

For as the Father raiseth up the dead, and quickeneth them; even so the Son quickeneth whom he will.

For the Father judgeth no man, but hath committed all judgment unto the Son:

That all men should honour the Son, even as they honour the Father. He that honoureth not the Son honoureth not the Father which hath sent him.

Verily, verily, I say unto you, He that heareth my word, and believeth on him that sent me, hath everlasting life, and shall not come into condemnation; but is passed from death unto life.

Verily, verily, I say unto you, The hour is coming, and now is, when the dead shall hear the voice of the Son of God: and they that hear shall live.

For as the Father hath life in himself; so hath he given to the Son to have life in himself; And hath given him authority to execute judgment also, because he is the Son of man.

Marvel not at this: for the hour is coming, in the which all that are in the graves shall hear his voice,

And shall come forth; they that have done good, unto the resurrection of life; and they that have done evil, unto the resurrection of damnation.

I can of mine own self do nothing: as I hear, I judge: and my judgment is just; because I seek not mine own will, but the will of the Father which hath sent me.

If I bear witness of myself, my witness is not true.

There is another that beareth witness of me; and I know that the witness which he witnesseth of me is true.

Ye sent unto John, and he bare witness unto the truth.

And he received not his testimony of man, but of God, and ye yourselves say that he is a prophet, therefore ye ought to receive his testimony.[52]

These things I say, that ye might be saved.

He was a burning and a shining light: and ye were willing for a season to rejoice in his light.

But I have greater witness than the testimony of John: for the works which the Father hath given me to finish, the same works that I do, bear witness of me, that the Father hath sent me.

And the Father himself, which hath sent me, hath borne witness of me. Ye have neither heard his voice at any time, nor seen his shape.

And ye have not his word abiding in you: for whom he hath sent, him ye believe not.

Search the scriptures; for in them ye think ye have eternal life: and they are they which testify of me.

And ye will not come to me, that ye might have life.

I receive not honour from men.

But I know you, that ye have not the love of God in you.

I am come in my Father's name, and ye receive me not: if another shall come in his own name, him ye will receive.

How can ye believe, which receive honour one of another, and seek not the honour that cometh from God only?

Do not think that I will accuse you to the Father: there is one that accuseth you, even Moses, in whom ye trust.

For had ye believed Moses, ye would have believed me: for he wrote of me.

But if ye believe not his writings, how shall ye believe my words?

Proclamation of the Gospel in Galilee: Second Preaching Tour
Matt. 9:35–38, Mark 6:6

And he marvelled because of their unbelief. And Jesus went round about all the cities and villages, teaching in their synagogues, and preaching the gospel of the kingdom, and healing every sickness and every disease among the people.

But when he saw the multitudes, he was moved with compassion on them, because they fainted, and were scattered abroad, as sheep having no shepherd.

Then saith he unto his disciples, The harvest truly is plenteous, but the labourers are few;

Pray ye therefore the Lord of the harvest, that he will send forth labourers into his harvest.

---

52   John reads, "But I receive not testimony from man: but"

Third Preaching Tour
Luke 8:1–3, JST Luke 8:1

AND it came to pass afterward, that he went throughout every city and village, preaching and shewing the glad tidings of the kingdom of God: and the twelve who were ordained of him, were with him,

And certain women, which had been healed of evil spirits and infirmities, Mary called Magdalene, out of whom went seven devils,

And Joanna the wife of Chuza Herod's steward, and Susanna, and many others, which ministered unto him of their substance.

Sabbath Controversies
Matt. 12:1–21, Mark 2:23–3:12, Luke 6:1–11, JST Matt. 12:13, JST Mark 2:26–27[53]

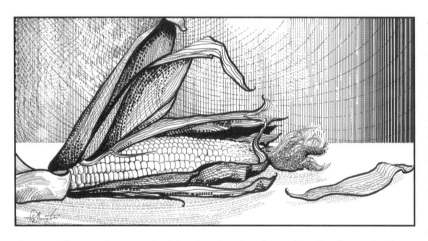

And it came to pass, at that time Jesus went on the second sabbath after the first sabbath day through the corn fields; and his disciples were an hungred, and began to pluck the ears of corn, and to eat, rubbing them in their hands.

But when certain of the Pharisees saw it, they said unto him, Behold, why do thy disciples do that which is not lawful to do upon the sabbath days?

But Jesus answering said unto them, Have ye not read so much as this, what David did, when he had need [and] was an hungred, he, and they that were with him;

How he entered into the house of God in the days of Abiathar the high priest, and did eat the shewbread, which was not lawful for him to eat, neither for them which were with him, but only for the priests?

Or have ye not read in the law, how that on the sabbath days the priests in the temple profane the sabbath, and are blameless?

But I say unto you, That in this place is one greater than the temple. But if ye had known what this meaneth, I will have mercy, and not sacrifice, ye would not have condemned the guiltless.

---

53   The JST from Mark does not add any new text when the four Gospels are merged.

And he said unto them, The sabbath was made for man, and not man for the sabbath:

For the Son of man is Lord even of the sabbath day.

And it came to pass also on another sabbath, when he was departed thence, he went into their synagogue and taught:

And, behold, there was a man which had his right hand withered. And the scribes and Pharisees watched him, whether he would heal him on the sabbath day; And they asked him, saying, Is it lawful to heal on the sabbath days? that they might accuse him.

But he knew their thoughts, and said to the man which had the withered hand, Rise up, and stand forth in the midst. And he arose and stood forth.

Then said Jesus unto them, I will ask you one thing; What man shall there be among you, that shall have one sheep, and if it fall into a pit on the sabbath day, will he not lay hold on it, and lift it out?

How much then is a man better than a sheep? Wherefore it is lawful to do well on the sabbath days, or to do evil? to save life, or to kill? But they held their peace.

And looking round about upon them all,

Then saith he to the man which had the withered hand, Stretch forth thine hand. And he stretched it forth; and it was restored whole, like as the other.

And they were filled with madness; and communed one with another what they might do to Jesus.

Then the Pharisees went out straightway, and held a council with the Herodians against him, how they might destroy him.

But Jesus knew when they took counsel, and he withdrew himself with his disciples from thence to the sea: and great multitudes from Galilee followed him, and from Judæa,

And from Jerusalem, and from Idumæa, and from beyond Jordan; and they about Tyre and Sidon, a great multitude, when they had heard what great things he did, came unto him.

And he spake to his disciples, that a small ship should wait on him because of the multitude, lest they should throng him.

For he had healed many; insomuch that they pressed upon him for to touch him, as many as had plagues, and he healed them all;

And unclean spirits, when they saw him, fell down before him, and cried, saying, Thou art the Son of God.

And he straitly charged them that they should not make him known:

That it might be fulfilled which was spoken by Esaias the prophet, saying,

Behold my servant, whom I have chosen; my beloved, in whom my soul is well pleased: I will put my spirit upon him, and he shall shew judgment to the Gentiles.

He shall not strive, nor cry; neither shall any man hear his voice in the streets.

A bruised reed shall he not break, and smoking flax shall he not quench, till he send forth judgment unto victory.

And in his name shall the Gentiles trust.

Beelzebub, Blasphemy
Matt. 12:22–37, Mark 3:22–30, Luke 6:45; 11:14–26; 12:10, JST Matt. 12:23, 26, JST Mark 3:21–25, JST Luke 11:15, 25, 26–27

Then was brought unto him one possessed with a devil, blind, and dumb: and he was casting a devil out of a man, and he was dumb, [and] healed him, And it came to pass, when the devil was gone out that the blind and dumb both spake and saw [and] the people wondered.

And all the people were amazed, and said, Is not this the son of David?

But when the Pharisees and the scribes which came down from Jerusalem heard it, some of them said, This fellow hath Beelzebub, and by Beelzebub the prince of the devils, [doth he] cast out devils.

And others, tempting him, sought of him a sign from heaven. And Jesus knew their thoughts, and he called them unto him and said unto them, Every kingdom divided against itself is brought to desolation; and every city or house divided against itself shall not stand [and] falleth:

And if Satan cast out Satan, he is divided against himself; how shall then his kingdom stand?

And if a house be divided against itself, that house cannot stand.

And if I by Beelzebub cast out devils, by whom do your children cast them out? therefore they shall be your judges.

But if I cast out devils by the Spirit [and] finger of God, no doubt then the kingdom of God is come unto you. For they also cast out devils by the Spirit of God, for unto them is given power over devils, that they may cast them out.

And if Satan rise up against himself, and be divided, he cannot stand, but hath an end.

Or else how can one enter into a strong man's house, and spoil his goods,

But when a stronger than he shall come upon him, and overcome him, and bind the strong man? He taketh from him all his armour wherein he trusted, and then he will spoil his house and divideth his spoils.

He that is not with me is against me; and he that gathereth not with me scattereth abroad.

When the unclean spirit is gone out of a man, it[54] walketh through dry places, seeking rest; and finding none, it[55] saith, I will return unto my house whence I came out. And when it cometh, it findeth the house swept and garnished.

Then goeth the evil spirit, and taketh to him seven other spirits more wicked than himself;

---

54   Luke reads, "he"
55   Luke reads, "he"

and they enter in, and dwell there: and the last state of that man is worse than the first.

Wherefore, <u>then came certain men unto him, accusing him, saying, Why do ye receive sinners, seeing thou makest thyself the Son of God.</u>

<u>But he answered them and said,</u> Verily I say unto you, All manner of sin <u>which men have committed</u> and blasphemy wherewith soever they shall blaspheme: shall be forgiven unto the men <u>**who receive me and repent [and]**</u> <u>come unto me, and do the works which they see me do.</u>: <u>for I came to preach repentance unto the sons of men.</u>

<u>But there is a sin which shall not be forgiven. He that shall</u> blaspheme against the Holy Ghost shall <u>never</u>[56] be forgiven unto men. But is in danger of <u>being cut down out of the world. And they shall inherit</u> eternal damnation:

<u>And this he said unto them</u> because they said, He hath an unclean spirit.

And whosoever speaketh a word against the Son of man, it shall be forgiven him: but whosoever speaketh against the Holy Ghost, it shall not be forgiven him, neither in this world, neither in the world to come.

Either make the tree good, and his fruit good; or else make the tree corrupt, and his fruit corrupt: for the tree is known by his fruit.

A good man out of the good treasure of his heart bringeth forth that which is good; and an evil man out of the evil treasure of his heart bringeth forth that which is evil: for of the abundance of the heart his mouth speaketh. O generation of vipers, how can ye, being evil, speak good things? for out of the abundance of the heart the mouth speaketh.

A good man out of the good treasure of the heart bringeth forth good things: and an evil man out of the evil treasure bringeth forth evil things.

But I say unto you, That every idle word that men shall speak, they shall give account thereof in the day of judgment.

For by thy words thou shalt be justified, and by thy words thou shalt be condemned.

Pharisees Asked for a Sign
Matt. 12:38, Luke 11:16

Then certain others of the scribes and of the Pharisees answered [and] tempting him, saying, Master, we would see a sign from heaven from thee.

Sign of Jonah
Matt. 12:39–45, Luke 11:29–32, JST Matt. 12:37–38

And when the people were gathered thick together, he answered and said unto them, This evil and adulterous generation seeketh after a sign; and there shall no sign be given to it, but the sign of the prophet Jonas:

---

56   Matthew reads, "not"

For as Jonas was a sign unto the Ninevites [and] was three days and three nights in the whale's belly; so shall the Son of man be to this generation [and] be three days and three nights in the heart of the earth.

The men of Nineveh shall rise in judgment with this generation, and shall condemn it: because they repented at the preaching of Jonas; and, behold, a greater than Jonas is here.

The queen of the south shall rise up in the judgment with this generation, and shall condemn it: for she came from the uttermost parts of the earth to hear the wisdom of Solomon; and, behold, a greater than Solomon is here.

Then came some of the Scribes and said unto him, Master, it is written that, Every sin shall be forgiven; but ye say, Whosoever speaketh against the Holy Ghost shall not be forgiven. And they asked him, saying, How can these things be? And he said unto them, When the unclean spirit is gone out of a man, he walketh through dry places, seeking rest, and findeth none; but when a man speaketh against the Holy Ghost, then he saith, I will return into my house from whence I came out; and when he is come, he findeth it empty, swept and garnished; for the good spirit leaveth him unto himself.

Then goeth the evil spirit[57], and taketh with himself seven other spirits more wicked than himself, and they enter in and dwell there: and the last state of that man is worse than the first. Even so shall it be also unto this wicked generation.

Jesus' Mother and Brethren
Matt. 12:46–50, Mark 3:31–35, Luke 8:19–21

While he yet talked to the people, behold, his mother and his brethren stood without, desiring to speak with him [and] calling him and could not come at him for the press.

And the multitude sat about him, [and] then [a] certain one said unto him, Behold, thy mother and thy brethren stand without, desiring to speak with thee.

But he answered and said unto him that told him, Who is my mother? and who are my brethren? And he looked round about on them which sat about him, My mother and my brethren are these which hear the word of God, and do it.

And he stretched forth his hand toward his disciples, and said, Behold my mother and my brethren!

For whosoever shall do the will of God my Father which is in heaven, the same is my brother, and sister, and mother.

57   Matthew reads, "he"

Parables:

Discourse from the Boat
Matt. 13:1–2, Mark 4:1

The same day went Jesus out of the house, and sat by the sea side. And he began again to teach by the sea side:

And great multitudes were gathered together unto him, so that he went and entered into a ship, and sat in the sea; and the whole multitude stood on the land by the sea shore.

Sower
Matt. 13:3–9, 18-23; Mark 4:2–9, 14-20; Luke 8:4–8, 11–15, JST Matt. 13:21

And when much people were gathered together, and were come to him out of every city, and he spake and taught many things unto them in parables, and said unto them in his doctrine, Hearken; Behold, a sower went forth to sow;

And it came to pass, when he sowed, some seeds fell by the way side, and it was trodden down, and the fowls of the air came and devoured them up:

Some fell upon stony places and rocks, where they had not much earth: and immediately forthwith they sprung up, because they had no deepness of earth [and] lacked moisture:

And when the sun was up, they were scorched; and because they had no root, they withered away.

And some fell among thorns; and the thorns sprung [and] grew up, and choked them: and it yielded no fruit.

But other fell into good ground, and did yield and brought forth fruit that sprang up and increased, some an hundredfold, some sixtyfold, some thirtyfold.

And he said these things unto them, He cried, He who hath ears to hear, let him hear.

Hear ye therefore the parable of the sower.

The sower soweth the word.

The seed is the word of God.

When any one heareth the word of the kingdom, and understandeth it not, then cometh immediatley the wicked one, Satan, the devil, and catcheth [and] taketh away that word which was sown in his heart lest they should believe and be saved. This is he which received seed by the way side, where the word is sown.

But he that received the seed into stony places, the same is he that heareth the word, and anon with joy [and] gladness receiveth it;

Yet hath he not root in himself, but endureth for a while: for afterward when affliction, tribulation or persecution ariseth because of the word, immediately [or] by and by he is offended, and in time of temptation fall away.

He also that received seed among the thorns is he that heareth the word; and the care of this world, and the deceitfulness of riches, and the lusts and pleasures of other things entering in, choke the word, and he becometh unfruitful and bring no fruit to perfection.

But he that received seed into the good ground is he that heareth the word which in an honest and good heart and understandeth <u>and endureth</u>; which also beareth fruit [and] having heard the word, keep it, and bring forth fruit with patience, some an hundredfold, some sixty, some thirty.

Why Parables
Matt. 13:10–17, 34–36; Mark 4:10–13; Luke 8:9–10; 10:23–24,
JST Matt. 13:10–11, JST Mark 4:9

And when he was alone <u>with the twelve, and they that believed in him</u>, [and] they that that were about him with the twelve came, and said unto him, Why speakest thou unto them in parables? [And] what might this parable be?

He answered and said unto them, Because it is given unto you to know the mysteries of the kingdom of God [and] heaven, but to them that are without it is not given, all these things are done in parables.

For whosoever <u>receiveth</u>[58], to him shall be given, and he shall have more abundance; but whosoever <u>continueth not to receive</u>[59], from him shall be taken away even that he hath.

Therefore speak I to them in parables: because they seeing, they may see, and not perceive; and hearing, they may hear, and not understand; lest at any time they should be converted, and their sins should be forgiven them.

And in them is fulfilled the prophecy of Esaias, which saith, By hearing ye shall hear, and shall not understand; and seeing ye shall see, and shall not perceive:

For this people's heart is waxed gross, and their ears are dull of hearing, and their eyes they have closed; lest at any time they should see with their eyes, and hear with their ears, and should understand with their heart, and should be converted, and I should heal them.

And he turned him unto his disciples, and said privately, But blessed are your eyes, for they

---

58   Matthew reads, "hath"
59   Matthew reads, "hath not"

see: and your ears, for they hear.

For verily I say unto you, That many prophets and kings and righteous men have desired to see those things which ye see, and have not seen them; and to hear those things which ye hear, and have not heard them.

All these things spake Jesus unto the multitude in parables; and without a parable spake he not unto them:

That it might be fulfilled which was spoken by the prophet, saying, I will open my mouth in parables; I will utter things which have been kept secret from the foundation of the world.

Then Jesus sent the multitude away, and went into the house: and his disciples came unto him, saying, Declare unto us the parable of the tares of the field.

And he said unto them, Know ye not this parable? and how then will ye know all parables?

". . . All these things spake Jesus unto the multitude in parables . . ."

Candle

Mark 4:21–25; Luke 8:16–18, JST Mark 4:20

And he said unto them, No man, when he hath lighted a candle, covereth it with a vessel. Is a candle brought to be put under a bushel, or under a bed? and not to be set on a candlestick **that they which enter in may see the light?**

For there is nothing hid, which shall not be manifested; neither was any thing kept secret, but that it should come abroad.

If any man have ears to hear, let him hear.

And he said unto them, Take heed what [and] **how** ye hear: with what measure ye mete, it shall be measured to you: and unto you that <u>continue to receive</u>[60] shall more be given.

For he that <u>receiveth</u>[61], to him shall be given: <u>but</u> he that <u>continueth</u>[62] not <u>to receive</u>, from him shall be taken even that which **he seemeth to have.**

Tares

Matt. 13:24–30; 36–43, Mark 4:26–29, JST Matt. 13:29, 39–44

Another parable put he forth unto them, saying, The kingdom of heaven is likened unto a man which sowed good seed in his field:

But while men slept, his enemy came and sowed tares among the wheat, and went his way.

And rise night and day, and the seed should spring and grow up, he knoweth not how.

For the earth bringeth forth fruit of herself; first the blade, then the ear, after that the full corn in the ear.

But when the fruit is brought forth, immediately he putteth in the sickle, because the harvest is come. But when the blade was sprung up, and brought forth fruit, then appeared the tares also.

So the servants of the householder came and said unto him, Sir, didst not thou sow good seed in thy field? from whence then hath it tares?

---

60   Mark reads, "hear"
61   Mark reads, "hath"
62   Mark reads, "hath"

He said unto them, An enemy hath done this. The servants said unto him, Wilt thou then that we go and gather them up?

But he said, Nay; lest while ye gather up the tares, ye root up also the wheat with them.

Let both grow together until the harvest: and in the time of harvest I will say to the reapers, Gather ye together first the <u>wheat</u>[63] <u>into my barn; and the tares are bound in bundles to be burned</u>. Then Jesus sent the multitude away, and went into the house: and his disciples came unto him, saying, Declare unto us the parable of the tares of the field.

He answered and said unto them, He that soweth the good seed is the Son of man;

The field is the world; the good seed are the children of the kingdom; but the tares are the children of the wicked one;

The enemy that sowed them is the devil; the harvest is the end of the world, <u>or the destruction of the wicked. The reapers are the angels, or the messengers sent of heaven.</u>

<u>As, therefore, the tares are gathered and burned in the fire, so shall it be in the end of this world, or the destruction of the wicked.</u>

<u>For in that day, before the Son of man shall come, he</u> shall send forth his angels <u>and messengers of heaven. And they shall gather out of his kingdom all things that offend, and them which do iniquity, and shall cast them</u> into a furnace of fire <u>out among the wicked; and there shall be wailing and gnashing of teeth. For the world shall be burned with fire.</u>

Then shall the righteous shine forth as the sun in the kingdom of their Father. Who hath ears to hear, let him hear.

Mustard Seed
Matt. 13:31–32, Mark 4:30–32, Luke 13:18–19

Another parable put he forth unto them, saying, Whereunto shall we liken the kingdom of God? and whereunto shall I resemble it or with what comparison shall we compare it? The kingdom of heaven is like to a grain of mustard seed, which a man took, and sowed in his garden field:

Which indeed is the least of all seeds that be in the earth: But when it is sown it groweth up, it is the greatest among herbs, and waxed [and] becometh a great tree and shooteth out great branches, so that the birds of the air come and lodge under the shadow of it, in the branches thereof.

---

63   Matthew reads "tares" first

Leaven

Matt. 13:33, Luke 13:20–21

And again, another parable spake he unto them; Whereunto shall I liken the kingdom of God? The kingdom of heaven is like unto leaven, which a woman took, and hid in three measures of meal, till the whole was leavened.

Disciples

Mark 4:33–34, JST Mark 4:26

And with many such parables spake he the word unto them, as they were able to <u>bear</u>[64] it.

But without a parable spake he not unto them: and when they were alone, he expounded all things to his disciples.

Treasure in a Field

Matt. 13:44

Again, the kingdom of heaven is like unto treasure hid in a field; the which when a man hath found, he hideth, and for joy thereof goeth and selleth all that he hath, and buyeth that field.

Pearl of Great Price

Matt. 13:45–46

Again, the kingdom of heaven is like unto a merchant man, seeking goodly pearls:

Who, when he had found one pearl of great price, went and sold all that he had, and bought it.

Net

Matt. 13:47–50, JST Matt. 13:50,51

Again, the kingdom of heaven is like unto a net, that was cast into the sea, and gathered of every kind:

Which, when it was full, they drew to shore, and sat down, and gathered the good into vessels, but cast the bad away.

So shall it be at the end of the world: <u>And the world is the children of the wicked.</u>

---

64   Mark reads, "hear"

". . . kingdom of heaven is like unto a net . . ."

The angels shall come forth, and sever the wicked from among the just, And shall cast them <u>out</u> into the <u>world to be burned</u>[65]: there shall be wailing and gnashing of teeth.

Householder
Matt. 13:51–52

Jesus saith unto them, Have ye understood all these things? They say unto him, Yea, Lord.

Then said he unto them, Therefore every scribe which is instructed unto the kingdom of heaven is like unto a man that is an householder, which bringeth forth out of his treasure things new and old.

Second Rejection at Nazareth
Matt. 13:53–58, Mark 6:1–6

And it came to pass, that when Jesus had finished these parables, he departed thence. And when he was come into his own country, his disciples follow him. And when the sabbath day was come he taught them in their synagogue, insomuch that they were astonished, and said, Whence hath this man this wisdom, and these mighty works wrought by his hands?

Is not this the carpenter's son? is not his mother called Mary? and his brethren, James, and Joses, and Simon, and Judas?

And his sisters, are they not all with us? Whence then hath this man all these things?

And they were offended in him. But Jesus said unto them, A prophet is not without honour, save in his own country, and among his own kin, and in his own house.

And he did not many mighty works there, save that he laid his hands upon a few sick folk, and healed them, because of their unbelief.

---

65   Matthew reads, "into a furnace of fire"

Herod's Fear of Jesus
Matt. 14:1–2, Mark 6:14–16, Luke 9:7–9

At that time Herod the tetrarch heard of the fame of Jesus [and] all that was done by him: and he was perplexed, for his name was spread abroad.

And said unto his servants, This is John the Baptist; he is risen from the dead; and therefore mighty works do shew forth themselves in him.

Others said, That it is Elias that had appeared. And others said, That it is one of the old prophets was risen again, or as one of the prophets.

But when Herod heard thereof, he said, John have I beheaded: but who is this, of whom I hear such things? And he desired to see him.

The Baptist's Earlier Death
Matt. 14:3–12, Mark 6:17–29, JST Mark 6:21

For Herod himself had sent forth [and] laid hold on John, and bound him, and put him in prison for Herodias' sake, his brother Philip's wife, for he had married her. For John said unto Herod, It is not lawful for thee to have thy brother's wife.

And when he would have put him to death, he feared the multitude, because they counted him as a prophet.

Therefore Herodias had a quarrel against him, and would have killed him; but she could not:

For Herod feared John, knowing that he was a holy[66] man and one who feared God and observed to worship him; and when he heard him, he did many things for him, and heard him gladly.

And when a convenient day was come, that Herod on his birthday made a supper to his lords, high captains, and chief estates of Galilee;

And when the daughter of Herodias danced before them, and pleased Herod and them that sat with him, the king said unto the damsel, Ask of me whatsoever thou wilt, and I will give it thee. Whereupon he promised with an oath to give her whatsoever she would ask, unto the half of [his] kingdom.

And she went forth, and said unto her mother, What shall I ask? And she said, The head of John the Baptist.

And she, being before instructed of her mother came in straightway with haste unto the king, saying, Give me here John Baptist's head in a charger by and by.

And the king was exceeding sorry: nevertheless for the oath's sake, and them which sat with him at meat, he would not reject her, [and] he commanded it to be given her.

And immediately the king sent an executioner, and commanded his head to be brought: and he went and beheaded John in the prison.

---

66   Mark reads, "just"

And his head was brought in a charger, and given to the damsel: and she brought it to her mother.

And when his disciples heard of it, his disciples came, and took up the body, and buried it in a tomb, and went and told Jesus.

Passover: Return of the Twelve
Matt. 14:13–15, Mark 6:30–32, Luke 9:10, John 6:1–4, JST Mark 6:32–33, JST Luke 9:10

And the apostles gathered, themselves together unto Jesus, when they were returned, and told him all things, both what they had done, and what they had taught.

When Jesus heard of it, he said unto them, Come ye yourselves apart into a solitary[67] place, and rest a while: for there were many coming and going, and they had no leisure so much as to eat.

And he took them, and they departed thence by ship, over the sea of Galilee, which is the sea of Tiberias, privately into a solitary[68] place belonging to the city called Bethsaida. And when the people had heard thereof, a great multitude followed him on foot out of the cities, because they saw  his miracles which he did on them that were diseased.

And Jesus went forth, and saw a great multitude, and was moved with compassion toward them, and he healed their sick.

And when it was evening, his disciples came to him, saying, This is a desert place, and the time is now past; send the multitude away, that they may go into the villages, and buy themselves victuals.

And Jesus went up into a mountain, and there he sat with his disciples.

And the passover, a feast of the Jews, was nigh.

---

67 Mark reads, "desert"
68 Luke reads, "desert"

Feeding the Five Thousand
Matt. 14:16–21, Mark 6:33–44, Luke 9:11–17, John 6:5–14, JST Mark 6:36

And the people, when they knew it, followed him: and he received them, and spake unto them of the kingdom of God, and healed them that had need of healing.

And when the day began to wear away, then came the twelve, and said unto him, Send the multitude away, that they may go into the towns and country round about, and lodge, and get victuals: for we are here in a solitary[69] place and now the time for our departure is come.

When Jesus then lifted up his eyes, and saw a great company come unto him, he saith unto Philip, Whence shall we buy bread, that these may eat?

And this he said to prove him: for he himself knew what he would do.

Philip answered him, Two hundred pennyworth of bread is not sufficient for them, that every one of them may take a little. But Jesus answered [and] said unto them, They need not depart; give ye them to eat.

And they say unto him, We have here but five loaves, and two fishes, except we should go and buy meat for all this people. Shall we go and buy two hundred pennyworth of bread, and give them to eat?

He saith unto them, How many loaves have ye? go and see.

One of his disciples, Andrew, Simon Peter's brother, saith unto him,

There is a lad here, which hath five barley loaves, and two small fishes: but what are they among so many?

And Jesus said, Bring them hither to me.

And he commanded them to make all the multitude to sit down by companies on the green grass. And they sat down in ranks, by hundreds, and by fifties. And they did so, and made them all sit down. And took the five loaves, and the two fishes, and looking up to heaven, he gave thanks [and] blessed them, and brake, and gave the loaves to his disciples, and the disciples to set before the multitude, and the two fishes divided he among them all.

And they did all eat, and were filled:

When they were filled, he said unto his disciples, Gather up the fragments that remain, that nothing be lost. And they took up of the fragments of the five barley loaves and of the fishes that remained twelve baskets full.

Then those men, when they had seen the miracle that Jesus did, said, This is of a truth that prophet that should come into the world.

And they that had eaten were about five thousand men, beside women and children.

". . .they had seen the miracle that Jesus did . . ."

---

69   Mark reads, "desert"

Jesus Walks on the Water

Matt. 14:22–33, Mark 6:45–52, John 6:15–21

When Jesus therefore perceived that they would come and take him by force, to make him a king, straightway Jesus constrained his disciples to get into a ship, and to go before him unto the other side unto Bethsaida, while he sent the multitudes [of] people away.

And when he had sent the multitudes away, he departed again [and] went up into a mountain himself alone, apart to pray: and when the evening was come, his disciples went down unto the sea,

And entered into a ship, and went over the sea toward Capernaum. And it was now dark, and Jesus was not come to them [for] the ship was in the midst of the sea, and he was there alone on the land.

And the sea arose by reason of a great wind that blew.

So when they had rowed about five and twenty or thirty furlongs the ship was now in the midst of the sea, tossed with waves:

And he [Jesus] saw them toiling in rowing; for the wind was contrary unto them. And in about the fourth watch of the night Jesus cometh and went unto them, walking on the sea, and would have passed by them.

And when the disciples saw him walking on the sea, and drawing nigh unto the ship: they were afraid [and] troubled, saying, It is a spirit; and they cried out for fear.

For they all saw him, and were troubled. But immediately straightway Jesus talked, [and] spake unto them, saying, Be of good cheer; it is I; be not afraid. And Peter answered him and said, Lord, if it be thou, bid me come unto thee on the water.

And he said, Come. And when Peter was come down out of the ship, he walked on the water, to go to Jesus.

But when he saw the wind boisterous, he was afraid; and beginning to sink, he cried, saying, Lord, save me.

And immediately Jesus stretched forth his hand, and caught him, and said unto him, O thou of little faith, wherefore didst thou doubt?

And he went up unto them into the ship; Then they willingly received him into the ship: And when they were come into the ship, the wind ceased, and they were sore amazed in themselves beyond measure, and wondered.

For they considered not the miracle of the loaves: for their heart was hardened.

Then they that were in the ship came and worshipped him, saying, Of a truth thou art the Son of God and immediately the ship was at the land whither they went.

Discourse: Bread of Life

John 6:22–71, JST John 6:26, 44, 65

The day following, when the people which stood on the other side of the sea saw that there was none other boat there, save that one whereinto his disciples were entered, and that Jesus went not with his disciples into the boat, but that his disciples were gone away alone;

(Howbeit there came other boats from Tiberias nigh unto the place where they did eat bread, after that the Lord had given thanks:)

When the people therefore saw that Jesus was not there, neither his disciples, they also took shipping, and came to Capernaum, seeking for Jesus.

And when they had found him on the other side of the sea, they said unto him, Rabbi, when camest thou hither?

Jesus answered them and said, Verily, verily, I say unto you, Ye seek me, not because ye desire to keep my sayings, neither because ye saw the miracles, but because ye did eat of the loaves, and were filled.

Labour not for the meat which perisheth, but for that meat which endureth unto everlasting life, which the Son of man shall give unto you: for him hath God the Father sealed.

Then said they unto him, What shall we do, that we might work the works of God?

Jesus answered and said unto them, This is the work of God, that ye believe on him whom he hath sent.

They said therefore unto him, What sign shewest thou then, that we may see, and believe thee? what dost thou work?

Our fathers did eat manna in the desert; as it is written, He gave them bread from heaven to eat.

Then Jesus said unto them, Verily, verily, I say unto you, Moses gave you not that bread from heaven; but my Father giveth you the true bread from heaven.

For the bread of God is he which cometh down from heaven, and giveth life unto the world.

Then said they unto him, Lord, evermore give us this bread.

And Jesus said unto them, I am the bread of life: he that cometh to me shall never hunger; and he that believeth on me shall never thirst.

But I said unto you, That ye also have seen me, and believe not.

All that the Father giveth me shall come to me; and him that cometh to me I will in no wise cast out.

For I came down from heaven, not to do mine own will, but the will of him that sent me.

And this is the Father's will which hath sent me, that of all which he hath given me I should lose nothing, but should raise it up again at the last day.

And this is the will of him that sent me, that every one which seeth the Son, and believeth on him, may have everlasting life: and I will raise him up at the last day.

The Jews then murmured at him, because he said, I am the bread which came down from heaven.

And they said, Is not this Jesus, the son of Joseph, whose father and mother we know? how is it then that he saith, I came down from heaven?

Jesus therefore answered and said unto them, Murmur not among yourselves.

No man can come to me, except <u>he doeth the will of my</u> Father which hath sent me.[70] <u>And this is the will of him who hath sent me, that ye receive the Son; for the Father beareth record of him; and he who receiveth the testimony, and doeth the will of him who sent me,</u> and I will raise him up <u>in the resurrection of the just.</u>[71]

It is written in the prophets, And they shall be all taught of God. Every man therefore that hath heard, and hath learned of the Father, cometh unto me.

Not that any man hath seen the Father, save he which is of God, he hath seen the Father. Verily, verily, I say unto you, He that believeth on me hath everlasting life.

I am that bread of life.

Your fathers did eat manna in the wilderness, and are dead.

This is the bread which cometh down from heaven, that a man may eat thereof, and not die.

I am the living bread which came down from heaven: if any man eat of this bread, he shall live for ever: and the bread that I will give is my flesh, which I will give for the life of the world.

The Jews therefore strove among themselves, saying, How can this man give us his flesh to eat? Then Jesus said unto them, Verily, verily, I say unto you, Except ye eat the flesh of the Son of man, and drink his blood, ye have no life in you.

Whoso eateth my flesh, and drinketh my blood, hath eternal life; and I will raise him up at the last day.

For my flesh is meat indeed, and my blood is drink indeed.

---

70   JST deletes the words "draw him" at the end of this sentence.
71   John reads, "at the last day"

He that eateth my flesh, and drinketh my blood, dwelleth in me, and I in him.

As the living Father hath sent me, and I live by the Father: so he that eateth me, even he shall live by me. This is that bread which came down from heaven: not as your fathers did eat manna, and are dead: he that eateth of this bread shall live for ever.

These things said he in the synagogue, as he taught in Capernaum.

Many therefore of his disciples, when they had heard this, said, This is an hard saying; who can hear it?

When Jesus knew in himself that his disciples murmured at it, he said unto them, Doth this offend you?

What and if ye shall see the Son of man ascend up where he was before?

It is the spirit that quickeneth; the flesh profiteth nothing: the words that I speak unto you, they are spirit, and they are life.

But there are some of you that believe not.

For Jesus knew from the beginning who they were that believed not, and who should betray him.

And he said, Therefore said I unto you, that no man can come unto me, except <u>he doeth the will of my Father who hath sent me.</u>[72]

From that time many of his disciples went back, and walked no more with him. Then said

---

72   John reads, "it were given unto him of my Father."

Jesus unto the twelve, Will ye also go away?

Then Simon Peter answered him, Lord, to whom shall we go? thou hast the words of eternal life.

And we believe and are sure that thou art that Christ, the Son of the living God.

Jesus answered them, Have not I chosen you twelve, and one of you is a devil?

He spake of Judas Iscariot the son of Simon: for he it was that should betray him, being one of the twelve.

Jesus Teaches in Galilee
John 7:1

After these things Jesus walked in Galilee: for he would not walk in Jewry, because the Jews sought to kill him.

Healings
Matt. 14:34–36, Mark 6:53–56

And when they were passed [and] gone over, they came into the land of Gennesaret, and drew to the shore.

And when they were come out of the ship, straightway they knew him, and when the men of that place had knowledge of him, they sent out into all that country round about,

And ran through that whole region round about, and began to carry about in beds those that were sick, where they heard he was, and brought unto him all that were diseased;

And whithersoever he entered, into villages, or cities, or country, they laid the sick in the streets,

And besought him that they might only touch the hem or border of his garment: and as many as touched him were made perfectly whole.

Traditions Can Defile
Matt. 15:1–20, Mark 7:1–23, JST Mark 7:10–12, 15,

Then came together to Jesus certain of the scribes and Pharisees, which were of Jerusalem,

And when they saw some of his disciples eat bread with defiled, that is to say, with un-washen, hands, they found fault, saying,

Why do thy disciples transgress the tradition of the elders? for they wash not their hands when they eat bread.

For the Pharisees, and all the Jews, except they wash their hands oft, eat not, holding the tradition of the elders.

And when they come from the market, except they wash, they eat not. And many other

things there be, which they have received to hold, as the washing of cups, and pots, brasen vessels, and of tables.

Then the Pharisees and scribes asked him, Why walk not thy disciples according to the tradition of the elders, but eat bread with unwashen hands?

But he answered and said unto them, Why do ye also transgress the commandment of God by your tradition?

Full well ye reject the commandment of God, that ye may keep your own tradition.

Full well is it written of you, by the prophets whom ye have rejected.

They testified these things of a truth, and their blood shall be upon you.

Ye have kept not the ordinances of God; For God commanded [and] Moses said, Honour thy father and mother: and, He that curseth father or mother, let him die the death of the transgressor, as it is written in your law; but ye keep not the law.

But ye say, Whosoever shall say to his father or his mother, It is Corban, that is to say, a gift, by whatsoever thou mightest be profited by me; And honour not his father or his mother, he shall be free.

And ye suffer him no more to do ought for his father or his mother;

Making the word of God of none effect through your tradition, which ye have delivered: and many such like things do ye.

Thus have ye made the commandment of God of none effect by your tradition. Ye hypocrites, well did Esaias prophesy of you, saying, as it is written; This people draweth nigh unto me with their mouth, and honoureth me with their lips; but their heart is far from me.

But in vain they do worship me, teaching for doctrines the commandments of men.

And he called the multitude, and said unto them, Hear, and understand: For laying aside the commandment of God, ye hold the tradition of men, as the washing of pots and cups: and many other such like things ye do.

And when he had called all the people unto him, he said unto them, Hearken unto me every one of you, and understand:

There is nothing from without a man, that entering into him can defile him, which is food; but the things which come out of him, those are they that defile the man, that proceedeth forth out of the heart.

Not that which goeth into the mouth defileth a man; but that which cometh out of the mouth, this defileth a man.

If any man have ears to hear, let him hear.

Then came his disciples, and said unto him, Knowest thou that the Pharisees were offended, after they heard this saying?

But he answered and said, Every plant, which my heavenly Father hath not planted, shall be rooted up.

Let them alone: they be blind leaders of the blind. And if the blind lead the blind, both shall fall into the ditch.

And when he was entered into the house from the people, his disciples [and] Peter and said unto him, Declare unto us this parable.

And Jesus saith unto them, Are ye also yet without understanding? Do not ye yet perceive [and] understand, that whatsoever thing entereth in at the mouth goeth into the belly, and is cast out into the draught? it cannot defile him;

Because it entereth not into his heart, but into the belly, and goeth out into the draught, purging all meats?

And he said, but those things which proceed out of the mouth come forth from the heart; and they defile the man.

For from within, out of the heart of men, proceed evil thoughts, murders, adulteries, fornications, thefts, false witness, blasphemies, covetousness, wickedness, deceit, lasciviousness, an evil eye, pride, foolishness:

All these are the things which come from within [and] defile a man: but to eat with unwashen hands defileth not a man.

Canaanite Daughter Healed
Matt. 15:21–28, Mark 7:24–30, JST Mark 7:22–23

Then Jesus arose [and] went thence, and departed into the coasts of Tyre and Sidon, and entered into an house, and would that no should come unto him[73]: but he could not deny them, for he had compassion upon all men[74].

And, behold, a certain woman, whose young daughter had an

unclean spirit, heard of him, and came out of the same coasts, and fell at his feet, and cried unto him, and she besought him, saying, Have mercy on me, O Lord, thou Son of David; my daughter is grievously vexed with a devil, cast forth the devil out of her.

---

73   Mark reads, "have no man know it"
74   Marks reads, "hid"

The woman was a Greek, a Syrophenician by nation, of Canaan;

But he answered her not a word. And his disciples came and besought him, saying, Send her away; for she crieth after us.

But he answered and said, I am not sent but unto the lost sheep of the house of Israel.

Then came she and worshipped him, saying, Lord, help me.

But Jesus answered and said, It is not meet to take the children's bread, and to cast it to dogs. Let the children <u>of the kingdom</u> first be filled: for it is not meet to take the children's bread, and to cast it unto the dogs.

And she answered [and] said unto him, Yes, Truth, Lord: yet the dogs under the table eat of the children's crumbs which fall from their masters' table.

Then Jesus answered and said unto her, O woman, great is thy faith: be it unto thee even as thou wilt.

For this saying go thy way; the devil is gone out of thy daughter.

And when she was come to her house, she found the devil gone out, and her daughter laid upon the bed.

And her daughter was made whole from that very hour.

Heals Lame, Blind, and Dumb
Matt. 15:29–31, Mark 7:31–37

And Jesus departed from the coasts of Tyre and Sidon, [and] he came nigh unto the sea of Galilee; through the midst of the coasts of Decapolis, and went up into a mountain, and sat down there.

And great multitudes came unto him, having with them those that were lame, blind, dumb, maimed.

And they bring unto him one that was deaf, and had an impediment in his speech; and they beseech him to put his hand upon him.

And he took him aside from the multitude, and put his fingers into his ears, and he spit, and touched his tongue;

And looking up to heaven, he sighed, and saith unto him, Ephphatha, that is, Be opened.

And straightway his ears were opened, and the string of his tongue was loosed, and he spake plain.

And he charged them that they should tell no man: but the more he charged them, so much the more a great deal they published it;

And were beyond measure astonished, saying, He hath done all things well: he maketh both the deaf to hear, and the dumb to speak.

And many others cast them down at Jesus' feet; and he healed them:

Insomuch that the multitude wondered, when they saw the dumb to speak, the maimed to be whole, the lame to walk, and the blind to see: and they glorified the God of Israel.

Four Thousand Fed
Matt. 15:32–38, Mark 8:1–9

In those days the multitude being very great, and having nothing to eat, Jesus called his disciples unto him, and said, I have compassion on the multitude, because they continue with me now three days, and have nothing to eat:

And if I send them away fasting to their own houses, they will faint by the way: for divers of them came from far. And his disciples say unto him, From whence should we have so much bread in the wilderness, as to fill so great a multitude?

And Jesus saith unto them, How many loaves have ye? And they said, Seven, and a few little small fishes.

And he commanded the multitude [of] people to sit down on the ground.

And he took the seven loaves and the fishes, and gave thanks, and brake them, and gave to his disciples to set before them, and the disciples did set them before the multitude [of] people.

And they did all eat, and were filled: and they took up of the broken meat that was left seven baskets full. And they that did eat were four thousand men, beside women and children and he sent them away.

Pharisees and Sadducees Ask a Sign
Matt. 15:39–16:4, Mark 8:10–13, Luke 12:54–57

And he sent away the multitude, And straightway he entered into a ship with his disciples, and came into the parts of Dalmanutha [and] the coasts of Magdala.

And the Pharisees also with the Sadducees came forth, and began to question with him, and tempting desired him that he would shew them a sign from heaven.

He answered and said unto them, When it is evening, ye say, It will be fair weather: for the sky is red.

And in the morning, It will be foul weather to day: for the sky is red and lowring,

And he said also to the people, When ye see a cloud rise out of the west, straightway ye say, There cometh a shower; and so it is.

And when ye see the south wind blow, ye say, There will be heat; and it cometh to pass. O ye hypocrites, ye can discern the face of the sky and of the earth; but can ye not discern the signs of the times?

Yea, and why even of yourselves judge ye not what is right?

And he sighed deeply in his spirit, and saith, Why doth this generation seek after a sign?

A wicked and adulterous generation seeketh after a sign; and there shall no sign be given unto this generation, but the sign of the prophet Jonas. And he left them, and entering into the ship again departed to the other side.

Leaven of the Pharisees and Sadducees
Matt. 16:5–12, Mark 8:14–21, Luke 12:1, JST Matt. 16:9

And when his disciples were come to the other side, they had forgotten to take bread, neither had they in the ship with them more than one loaf. Then Jesus charged them [and] said unto them, Take heed and beware of the leaven of the Pharisees and of the Sadducees and of the leaven of Herod.

And they reasoned among themselves, saying, It is because we have taken no bread.

And when they reasoned among themselves, Jesus perceived it,[75] [and] he said unto them, O ye of little faith, why reason ye among yourselves, because ye have brought no bread? perceive ye not yet, neither understand? have ye your heart yet hardened?

Having eyes, see ye not? and having ears, hear ye not? and do ye not remember?

Do ye not yet understand, neither remember when I brake the five loaves of the five thousand, and how many baskets full of fragments ye took up? They say unto him, Twelve.

Neither the seven loaves of the four thousand, and how many baskets full of fragments ye took up? And they said, Seven.

And he said unto them, How is it that ye do not understand that I spake it not to you concerning bread, that ye should beware of the leaven of the Pharisees and of the Sadducees?

Then understood they how that he bade them not beware of the leaven of bread, but of the doctrine of the Pharisees and of the Sadducees. In the mean time, when there were gathered together an innumerable multitude of people, insomuch that they trode one upon another, he began to say unto his disciples first of all, Beware ye of the leaven of the Pharisees, which is hypocrisy.

Jesus Calms the Storm
Luke 8:22–26

Now it came to pass on a certain day, that he went into a ship with his disciples: and he said unto them, Let us go over unto the other side of the lake. And they launched forth.

But as they sailed he fell asleep: and there came down a storm of wind on the lake; and they were filled with water, and were in jeopardy.

And they came to him, and awoke him, saying, Master, master, we perish. Then he arose, and rebuked the wind and the raging of the water: and they ceased, and there was a calm.

---

75   Matthew reads, "which when Jesus perceived"

And he said unto them, Where is your faith? And they being afraid wondered, saying one to another, What manner of man is this! for he commandeth even the winds and water, and they obey him. And they arrived at the country of the Gadarenes, which is over against Galilee.

Testimony of Peter and Sealing Keys of the Kingdom Promised

Matt. 16:13–20, Mark 8:27–30, Luke 9:18–21

And Jesus went out, and his disciples, into the towns [and] the coasts of Cæsarea Philippi:

And it came to pass, as he was alone praying, his disciples were with him: he asked his disciples, saying unto them, Whom do men say that I the Son of man am?

And they answered [and] said, Some say that thou art John the Baptist: but some say, Elias; and others, Jeremias, or one of the old prophets [is] risen again.

And he saith unto them, But whom say ye that I am? And Simon Peter answered and said, Thou art the Christ, the Son of the living God.

And Jesus answered and said unto him, Blessed art thou, Simon Bar-jona: for flesh and blood hath not revealed it unto thee, but my Father which is in heaven.

And I say also unto thee, That thou art Peter, and upon this rock I will build my church; and the gates of hell shall not prevail against it.

And I will give unto thee the keys of the kingdom of heaven: and whatsoever thou shalt bind on earth shall be bound in heaven: and whatsoever thou shalt loose on earth shall be loosed in heaven.

Then charged them and commanded he his disciples that they should tell no man that he was Jesus the Christ.

Prophecy of Death and Resurrection
Matt. 16:21, Mark 8:31, Luke 9:22

From that time forth began Jesus to teach [and] shew unto his disciples, how that he, the Son of man, must go unto Jerusalem, and suffer many things, and be rejected of the elders and chief priests and scribes, and be slain [and] killed, and be raised again the third day.

Peter Rebuked
Matt. 16:22–23, Mark 8:32–33

And he spake that saying openly.

Then Peter took him, and began to rebuke him, saying, Be it far from thee, Lord: this shall not be unto thee.

But when he turned about and looked on his disciples, he rebuked, and said unto Peter, saying, Get thee behind me, Satan: thou art an offence unto me: for thou savourest not the things that be of God, but those things that be of men.

Take Up a Cross
Matt. 16:24–27, Mark 8:34–9:1, Luke 9:23–26,
JST Matt. 16:26, JST Mark 8:37–38, 42–43, JST Luke 9:24–25, 26

Then said Jesus unto all his disciples, when he had called the people unto him with his disciples also, If any man will come after me, let him deny himself, and take up his cross daily, and follow me.

And now for a man to take up his cross, is to deny himself of all ungodliness, and every worldly lust, and keep my commandments.

For whosoever will save his life shall lose it: or whosoever will save his life, shall and must be willing to lay it down for my sake; and if he is not willing to lay it down for my sake, he shall lose it.

But whosoever will lose his life for my sake and the gospel, the same shall save it and find it.

For what is a man profited [or] advantaged, if he shall gain the whole world, and yet he receive him not whom God hath ordained, and lose his own soul [or be] cast away? or what shall a man give in exchange for his soul?

Therefore deny yourselves of these, and be not ashamed of me.

Whosoever therefore shall be ashamed of me and of my words in this adulterous and sinful generation; of him also shall the Son of man be ashamed, when he cometh in his own kingdom[76], clothed in the glory of his Father with the holy angels.

For the Son of man shall come in the glory of his Father with his angels; and then he shall reward every man according to his works.

And they shall not have part in that resurrection when he cometh.

For verily I say unto you, That he shall come; and he that layeth down his life for my sake and the gospel's, shall come with him, and shall be clothed with his glory in the cloud, on the right hand of the Son of man.

Some Not to Taste Death
Matt. 16:28, Mark 9:1, Luke 9:27

And he said unto them, verily I say unto you, [and] tell you of a truth, that there be some them that [are] standing here, which shall not taste of death, till they see the kingdom of God [and] the Son of man coming with power in his kingdom.

Transfiguration: Sealing Keys Committed
Matt. 17:1–13, Mark 9:2–13, Luke 9:28–36, JST Mark 9:1 ,3 ,10, 11, JST Luke 9:31

And after six days [or] eight days Jesus taketh Peter, James, and John his brother, who asked him many questions concerning his sayings, and Jesus leadeth and bringeth them up into an

high mountain apart by themselves to pray.

And as he prayed, the fashion of his countenance was altered, and was transfigured before them: and his face did shine as the sun, and his raiment became shining [and] was white as the light, exceeding white as snow and glistering, so as no fuller on earth can white them.

And, behold, there appeared unto them Moses and Elias or in other words, John the Baptist and Moses.

Who appeared in glory, and spake of his

---

76   Luke reads, "glory"

death, and also his resurrection[77], which he should accomplish at Jerusalem. And they were talking with him Jesus.

But Peter and they that were with him were heavy with sleep: and when they were awake, they saw his glory, and the two men that stood with him.

And it came to pass, as they departed from him, Peter said unto Jesus, Lord, Master, it is good for us to be here: if thou wilt, let us make here three tabernacles; one for thee, and one for Moses, and one for Elias not knowing what he said.

For he wist not what to say; for they were sore afraid.

While he yet spake, behold, there came a bright cloud overshadowed them: and they feared as they entered into the cloud. And behold a voice out of the cloud, which said, This is my beloved Son, in whom I am well pleased; hear ye him.

And when the disciples heard it, they fell on their face, and were sore afraid.

And Jesus came and touched them, and said, Arise, and be not afraid. And suddenly when they had lifted up their eyes, [and] when they had looked round about they saw no man any more, save Jesus only with themselves.

And as they came down from the mountain, Jesus charged them, saying, Tell the vision to no man, until the Son of man be risen again from the dead.

And they kept it close, and told no man in those days any of those things which they had seen.

And his disciples asked him, saying, Why then say the scribes that Elias must first come?

And Jesus answered and said unto them, Elias truly shall first come, and prepareth and restore all things and teacheth you of the prophets.

But I say unto you, That Elias is come already, and they knew him not, but have done unto him whatsoever they listed as it is written of him and he bore record of me, and they received him not. Verily this was Elias.

Then the disciples understood that he spake unto them of John the Baptist.

Likewise it is also written that the Son of man must suffer many things of them and be set at nought.

Heals Demoniac Child: Fasting and Prayer
Matt. 17:14–21, Mark 9:14–29, Luke 9:37–43

And it came to pass, that on the next day, when he came down from the hill to his disciples, he saw a great multitude [of] much people about them met him, and the scribes questioning with them.

And straightway all the people, when they beheld him, were greatly amazed and, running to him saluted him.

And he asked the scribes, What question ye with them?

And when they were come to the multitude, there came to him a certain man of the company [or] multitude, kneeling down to him, and cried out, saying,

---

77   Luke reads, "decease"

Lord Master, I beseech thee, I have brought unto thee my son, which hath a dumb spirit; look upon my son: for he is mine only child, have mercy on my son: for he is lunatick, and sore vexed:

And, lo, wheresoever a spirit taketh him, and he suddenly crieth out; he teareth him: and he foameth again, and gnasheth with his teeth, and pineth away: and bruising him hardly departeth from him. And I spake [and] brought him to thy disciples, that they should cast him out; and they could not cure him.

Then Jesus answered [him] and said, O faithless and perverse generation, how long shall I be with you? how long shall I suffer you? bring him hither to me.

And they brought him unto him: and when he saw him, straightway the spirit tare and threw him down; and he fell on the ground, and wallowed foaming.

And he asked his father, How long is it ago since this came unto him? And he said, Of a child.

And ofttimes it hath cast him into the fire, and into the waters, to destroy him: but if thou canst do any thing, have compassion on us, and help us.

Jesus said unto him, If thou canst believe, all things are possible to him that believeth.

And straightway the father of the child cried out, and said with tears, Lord, I believe; help thou mine unbelief.

When Jesus saw that the people came running together, And Jesus rebuked the foul, unclean, devil spirit; and healed the child, saying unto him, Thou dumb and deaf spirit, I charge thee, come out of him, and enter no more into him.

And the spirit cried, and rent him sore, and he departed out of him: and he was as one dead; insomuch that many said, He is dead.

But Jesus took him by the hand, and lifted him up; and delivered him again to his father, and he arose, and the child was cured from that very hour.

And when he was come into the house, then came the disciples to Jesus apart, and his disciples asked him privately, Why could not we cast him out?

And Jesus said unto them, Because of your unbelief: for verily I say unto you, This kind can come forth by nothing, but by prayer and fasting. If ye have faith as a grain of mustard seed, ye shall say unto this mountain, Remove hence to yonder place; and it shall remove; and nothing shall be impossible unto you.

Howbeit this kind goeth not out but by prayer and fasting.

Prophecy of Death and Resurrection
Matt. 17:22–23, Mark 9:30–32, Luke 9:43–45

And they departed thence, and passed through Galilee; and he would not that any man should know it.

And while they abode in Galilee, they were all amazed at the mighty power of God. But while they wondered every one at all things which Jesus did, he said unto his disciples,

Let these sayings sink down into your ears: for Jesus said unto them, The Son of man shall be betrayed [and] delivered into the hands of men:

And they shall kill him, and after that he is killed, the third day he shall be raised again.

But they understood not that saying, and it was hid from them, that they perceived it not: and were afraid to ask him. And they were exceeding sorry.

Tribute Coin in the Mouth of a Fish
Matt. 17:24–27

And when they were come to Capernaum, they that received tribute money came to Peter,  and said, Doth not your master pay tribute?

He saith, Yes. And when he was come into the house, Jesus prevented him, saying, What thinkest thou, Simon? of whom do the kings of the earth take custom or tribute? of their own children, or of strangers?

Peter saith unto him, Of strangers. Jesus saith unto him, Then are the children free.

Notwithstanding, lest we should offend them, go thou to the sea, and cast an hook, and take up the fish that first cometh up; and when thou hast opened his mouth, thou shalt find a piece of money: that take, and give unto them for me and thee.

Who Is the Greatest in the Kingdom
Matt. 18:1–6, Mark 9:33–37, Luke 9:46–48, JST Mark 9:34–35

And he came to Capernaum: and being in the house he asked them, What was it that ye disputed among yourselves by the way?

But they held their peace: for by the way there arose a reasoning among them, [and] they had disputed among themselves, who should be the greatest.

And he sat down, and called the twelve, at the same time came the disciples unto Jesus, saying, Who is the greatest in the kingdom of heaven?

And saith unto them, If any man desire to be first, the same shall be last of all, and servant of all.

And Jesus perceiving the thought of their heart, called and he took a little child unto him, and set him in the midst of them: and when he had taken him in his arms, he said unto them,

Verily I say unto you, Except ye be converted, and become as little children, ye shall not enter into the kingdom of heaven. Whosoever shall humble himself like one of these children,

Del Parson

and receiveth me, ye shall receive my name.

And whoso shall receive one of such children in my name, receiveth me: and whosoever shall receive me, receiveth not me only, but him that sent me even the Father. Whosoever therefore shall humble himself as this little child, the same is greatest in the kingdom of heaven for he that is least among you all, the same shall be great.

But whoso shall offend one of these little ones which believe in me, it were better for him that a millstone were hanged about his neck, and that he were drowned in the depth of the sea.

Discourse: Offenses and Forgiveness. Parable: Lost Sheep (Coin, Prodigal Son), Sealing Keys to Be Used. Parable: Unmerciful Servant

Matt. 18:7–35, Mark 9:38–50, Luke 17:1–4, 15:1–32, John 20:23, JST Matt. 18:9, 11, JST Mark 9:40–48, JST Luke 15:4

And John answered him, saying, Master, we saw one casting out devils in thy name, and he followeth not us: and we forbad him, because he followeth not us.

But Jesus said, Forbid him not: for there is no man which shall do a miracle in my name, that can lightly speak evil of me.

For he that is not against us is on our part. Then said he unto the disciples,

Woe unto the world because of offences! It is impossible but that offences will come: for it must needs be that offences come; but woe to that man by whom the offence cometh!

Wherefore if thy hand or thy foot offend thee, cut them off, and cast them from thee: it is better for thee to enter into life halt or maimed, rather than having two hands or two feet to be cast into hell [and] everlasting fire that never shall be quenched:

Where their worm dieth not, and the fire is not quenched.

And if thine eye offend thee, pluck it out, and cast it from thee: it is better for thee to enter into life [and] the kingdom of God with one eye, rather than having two eyes to be cast into hell fire.

Where their worm dieth not, and the fire is not quenched.

And a man's hand is his friend, and his foot, also; and a man's eye, are they of his own household.

For every one shall be salted with fire, and every sacrifice shall be salted with salt.

Salt is good: but if the salt have lost his saltness, wherewith will ye season it? Have salt in yourselves, and have peace one with another.

For whosoever shall give you a cup of water to drink in my name, because ye belong to Christ, verily I say unto you, he shall not lose his reward.

For he that is not against us is on our part. Take heed that ye despise [or] offend not one of these little ones that believe on me; [for] whosoever shall offend one of these little ones that believe in me, it is better for him that a millstone were hanged about his neck, and he were cast into the sea than that he should offend one of these little ones.

Even so it is not the will of your Father which is in heaven, that one of these little ones should perish.

For I say unto you, That in heaven their angels do always behold the face of my Father which is in heaven.

For the Son of man is come to save that which was lost and to call sinners to repentance; but these little ones have no need of repentance, and I will save them.

Then drew near unto him all the publicans and sinners for to hear him.

And the Pharisees and scribes murmured, saying, This man receiveth sinners, and eateth with them.

And he spake this parable unto them, saying, How think ye? What man of you, if a man have an hundred sheep, and one of them be gone astray, doth he not leave the ninety and nine and go into the wildreness, and goeth into the mountains, and seeketh that which is lost [and] gone astray, until he find it?

And if so be that he find it, verily I say unto you, he layeth it on his shoulders [and] rejoiceth more of that sheep, than of the ninety and nine which went not astray.

And when he cometh home, he calleth together his friends and neighbours, saying unto them, Rejoice with me; for I have found my sheep which was lost.

I say unto you, that likewise joy shall be in heaven over one sinner that repenteth, more than over ninety and nine just persons, which need no repentance.

Either what woman having ten pieces of silver, if she lose one piece, doth not light a candle, and sweep the house, and seek diligently till she find it?

And when she hath found it, she calleth her friends and her neighbours together, saying, Rejoice with me; for I have found the piece which I had lost.

Likewise, I say unto you, there is joy in the presence of the angels of God over one sinner that repenteth.

And he said, A certain man had two sons:

And the younger of them said to his father, Father, give me the portion of goods that falleth to me. And he divided unto them his living. And not many days after the younger son gathered all together, and took his journey into a far country, and there wasted his substance with riotous living.

And when he had spent all, there arose a mighty famine in that land; and he began to be in want.

And he went and joined himself to a citizen of that country; and he sent him into his fields to feed swine.

And he would fain have filled his belly with the husks that the swine did eat: and no man gave unto him.

And when he came to himself, he said, How many hired servants of my father's have bread enough and to spare, and I perish with hunger!

I will arise and go to my father, and will say unto him, Father, I have sinned against heaven, and before thee,

And am no more worthy to be called thy son: make me as one of thy hired servants.

And he arose, and came to his father. But when he was yet a great way off, his father saw him, and had compassion, and ran, and fell on his neck, and kissed him.

And the son said unto him, Father, I have sinned against heaven, and in thy sight, and am no more worthy to be called thy son.

But the father said to his servants, Bring forth the best robe, and put it on him; and put a ring on his hand, and shoes on his feet:

And bring hither the fatted calf, and kill it; and let us eat, and be merry:

For this my son was dead, and is alive again; he was lost, and is found. And they began to be merry.

Now his elder son was in the field: and as he came and drew nigh to the house, he heard musick and dancing.

And he called one of the servants, and asked what these things meant.

". . . his father saw him, and had compassion, and ran, . . . and kissed him."

And he said unto him, Thy brother is come; and thy father hath killed the fatted calf, because he hath received him safe and sound.

And he was angry, and would not go in: therefore came his father out, and intreated him.

And he answering said to his father, Lo, these many years do I serve thee, neither transgressed I at any time thy commandment: and yet thou never gavest me a kid, that I might make merry with my friends: But as soon as this thy son was come, which hath devoured thy living with harlots, thou hast killed for him the fatted calf.

And he said unto him, Son, thou art ever with me, and all that I have is thine.

It was meet that we should make merry, and be glad: for this thy brother was dead, and is alive again; and was lost, and is found.

Moreover, take heed to yourselves: if thy brother shall trespass against thee, rebuke [and] go and tell him his fault between thee and him alone: if he shall hear thee and repent, forgive him [and] thou hast gained thy brother.

But if he will not hear thee, then take with thee one or two more, that in the mouth of two or three witnesses every word may be established.

And if he shall neglect to hear them, tell it unto the church: but if he neglect to hear the church, let him be unto thee as an heathen man and a publican.

Verily I say unto you, Whatsoever ye shall bind on earth shall be bound in heaven: and whatsoever ye shall loose on earth shall be loosed in heaven.

Again I say unto you, That if two of you shall agree on earth as touching any thing that they shall ask, it shall be done for them of my Father which is in heaven.

For where two or three are gathered together in my name, there am I in the midst of them.

And if he trespass against thee seven times in a day, and seven times in a day turn again to thee, saying, I repent; thou shalt forgive him.

Then came Peter to him, and said, Lord, how oft shall my brother sin against me, and I forgive him? till seven times?

Jesus saith unto him, I say not unto thee, Until seven times: but, Until seventy times seven.

Whose soever sins ye remit, they are remitted unto them; and whose soever sins ye retain, they are retained.

Therefore is the kingdom of heaven likened unto a certain king, which would take account of his servants.

And when he had begun to

". . . Lord, have patience with me . . ."

reckon, one was brought unto him, which owed him ten thousand talents.

But forasmuch as he had not to pay, his lord commanded him to be sold, and his wife, and children, and all that he had, and payment to be made.

The servant therefore fell down, and worshipped him, saying, Lord, have patience with me, and I will pay thee all.

Then the lord of that servant was moved with compassion, and loosed him, and forgave him the debt.

But the same servant went out, and found one of his fellowservants, which owed him an hundred pence: and he laid hands on him, and took him by the throat, saying, Pay me that thou owest.

And his fellowservant fell down at his feet, and besought him, saying, Have patience with me, and I will pay thee all.

And he would not: but went and cast him into prison, till he should pay the debt. So when his fellowservants saw what was done, they were very sorry, and came and told unto their lord all that was done.

Then his lord, after that he had called him, said unto him, O thou wicked servant, I forgave thee all that debt, because thou desiredst me:

Shouldest not thou also have had compassion on thy fellowservant, even as I had pity on thee?

And his lord was wroth, and delivered him to the tormentors, till he should pay all that was due unto him.

So likewise shall my heavenly Father do also unto you, if ye from your hearts forgive not every one his brother their trespasses.

Time of the Feast of Tabernacles
Mark 3:20–21, John 7:2–9

And the multitude cometh together again, so that they could not so much as eat bread.

And when his friends heard of it, they went out to lay hold on him: for they said, He is beside himself.

Now the Jews' feast of tabernacles was at hand.

His brethren therefore said unto him, Depart hence, and go into Judæa, that thy disciples also may see the works that thou doest.

For there is no man that doeth any thing in secret, and he himself seeketh to be known openly. If thou do these things, shew thyself to the world.

For neither did his brethren believe in him.

Then Jesus said unto them, My time is not yet come: but your time is alway ready.

The world cannot hate you; but me it hateth, because I testify of it, that the works thereof are evil.

Go ye up unto this feast: I go not up yet unto this feast; for my time is not yet full come.

When he had said these words unto them, he abode still in Galilee.

Leaves Galilee (Luke's "Travel Narrative")
Matt. 19:1, Luke 9:51

And it came to pass, that when Jesus had finished these sayings, when the time was come that he should be received up, he departed from Galilee, and stedfastly set his face to go to Jerusalem, [and] came into the coasts of Judæa beyond Jordan.

Messengers Sent into Samaria
Luke 9:52–53

And sent messengers before his face: and they went, and entered into a village of the Samaritans, to make ready for him.

And they did not receive him, because his face was as though he would go to Jerusalem.

Samaritan Village Rejects the Apostles
Luke 9:54–56

And when his disciples James and John saw this, they said, Lord, wilt thou that we command fire to come down from heaven, and consume them, even as Elias did?

But he turned, and rebuked them, and said, Ye know not what manner of spirit ye are of.

For the Son of man is not come to destroy men's lives, but to save them. And they went to another village.

Seventy Appointed
Luke 10:1

AFTER these things the Lord appointed other seventy also, and sent them two and two before his face into every city and place, whither he himself would come.

Seventy Charged, Sent
Luke 10:2–12

Therefore said he unto them, The harvest truly is great, but the labourers are few: pray ye therefore the Lord of the harvest, that he would send forth labourers into his harvest.

Go your ways: behold, I send you forth as lambs among wolves.

Carry neither purse, nor scrip, nor shoes: and salute no man by the way.

And into whatsoever house ye enter, first say, Peace be to this house. And if the son of peace be there, your peace shall rest upon it: if not, it shall turn to you again.

And in the same house remain, eating and drinking such things as they give: for the labourer is worthy of his hire. Go not from house to house.

And into whatsoever city ye enter, and they receive you, eat such things as are set before you:

And heal the sick that are therein, and say unto them, The kingdom of God is come nigh unto you.

But into whatsoever city ye enter, and they receive you not, go your ways out into the streets of the same, and say,

Even the very dust of your city, which cleaveth on us, we do wipe off against you: notwithstanding be ye sure of this, that the kingdom of God is come nigh unto you.

But I say unto you, that it shall be more tolerable in that day for Sodom, than for that city.

Jesus Upbraids Capernaum, Bethsaida, and Chorazin
Matt. 11:20–24, Luke 10:13–16, JST Luke 10:16

Then began he to upbraid the cities wherein most of his mighty works were done, because they repented not:

Woe unto thee, Chorazin! woe unto thee, Bethsaida! for if the mighty works, which were done in you, had been done in Tyre and Sidon, they would have repented long ago in sackcloth and ashes.

But I say unto you, It shall be more tolerable for Tyre and Sidon at the day of judgment, than for you.

And thou, Capernaum, which art exalted unto heaven, shalt be brought [or] thrust down to hell: for if the mighty works, which have been done in thee, had been done in Sodom, it would have remained until this day.

But I say unto you, That it shall be more tolerable for the land of Sodom in the day of judgment, than for thee.

<u>And he said unto his disciples,</u> He that heareth you heareth me; and he that despiseth you despiseth me; and he that despiseth me despiseth him that sent me.

Seventy Return, Authority Confirmed
Luke 10:17–20

And the seventy returned again with joy, saying, Lord, even the devils are subject unto us through thy name. And he said unto them, I beheld Satan as lightning fall from heaven. Behold, I give unto you power to tread on serpents and scorpions, and over all the power of the enemy: and nothing shall by any means hurt you. Notwithstanding in this rejoice not, that the spirits are subject unto you; but rather rejoice, because your names are written in heaven.

Jesus' Prayer and Gratitude
Matt. 11:25–26, Luke 10:21, <u>JST Luke 10:21</u>

In that hour Jesus rejoiced in spirit, and answered and said, I thank thee, O Father, Lord of heaven and earth, because thou hast hid these things from <u>them who think they are</u> wise and prudent, and hast revealed them unto babes.

Even so, Father: for so it seemed good in thy sight.

Jesus' Promised Rest
Matt. 11:27–30, Luke 10:22, <u>JST Matt. 11:28</u>, <u>JST Luke 10:22</u>

All things are delivered unto me of my Father: and no man knoweth <u>that</u>[78] the Son is <u>the Father, and the Father is the Son, but him to whom the Son will reveal</u> himself; they shall see the Father also.

---

78   Luke reads, "who"

Come unto me, all ye that labour and are heavy laden, and I will give you rest.

Take my yoke upon you, and learn of me; for I am meek and lowly in heart: and ye shall find rest unto your souls.

For my yoke is easy, and my burden is light.

Parable: The Good Samaritan
Luke 10:25–37

And, behold, a certain lawyer stood up, and tempted him, saying, Master, what shall I do to inherit eternal life?

He said unto him, What is written in the law? how readest thou?

And he answering said, Thou shalt love the Lord thy God with all thy heart, and with all thy soul, and with all thy strength, and with all thy mind; and thy neighbour as thyself.

And he said unto him, Thou hast answered right: this do, and thou shalt live.

But he, willing to justify himself, said unto Jesus, And who is my neighbour?

And Jesus answering said, A certain man went down from Jerusalem to Jericho, and fell among thieves, which stripped him of his raiment, and wounded him, and departed, leaving him half dead.

And by chance there came down a certain priest that way: and when he saw him, he passed by on the other side.

And likewise a Levite, when he was at the place, came and looked on him, and passed by on the other side.

But a certain Samaritan, as he journeyed, came where he was: and when he saw him, he had compassion on him,

And went to him, and bound up his wounds, pouring in oil and wine, and set him on his own beast, and brought him to an inn, and took care of him.

And on the morrow when he departed, he took out two pence, and gave them to the host, and said unto him, Take care of him; and whatsoever thou spendest more, when I come again, I will repay thee.

Which now of these three, thinkest thou, was neighbour unto him that fell among the thieves?

And he said, He that shewed mercy on him. Then said Jesus unto him, Go, and do thou likewise.

". . . said Jesus unto him, Go, and do thou likewise. . . ."

Mary, Martha: One Thing Needful
Luke 10:38–42

Now it came to pass, as they went, that he entered into a certain village: and a certain woman named Martha received him into her house.

And she had a sister called Mary, which also sat at Jesus' feet, and heard his word.

But Martha was cumbered about much serving, and came to him, and said, Lord, dost thou not care that my sister hath left me to serve alone? bid her therefore that she help me.

And Jesus answered and said unto her, Martha, Martha, thou art careful and troubled about many things:

But one thing is needful: and Mary hath chosen that good part, which shall not be taken away from her.

"But one thing is needful:
and Mary hath chosen that good part. . . ."

Friend at Midnight
Luke 11:1, 5–8, JST Luke 11:5–6

And it came to pass, that, as he was praying in a certain place, when he ceased, one of his disciples said unto him, Lord, teach us to pray, as John also taught his disciples.

And he said unto them, <u>Your heavenly Father will not fail to give unto you whatsoever ye ask of him. And he spake a parable, saying,</u> Which of you shall have a friend, and shall go unto him at midnight, and say unto him, Friend, lend me three loaves;

For a friend of mine in his journey is come to me, and I have nothing to set before him?

And he from within shall answer and say, Trouble me not: the door is now shut, and my children are with me in bed; I cannot rise and give thee.

I say unto you, Though he will not rise and give him, because he is his friend, yet because of his importunity he will rise and give him as many as he needeth.

Hear, Keep the Word
Luke 11:27–28

And it came to pass, as he spake these things, a certain woman of the company lifted up her voice, and said unto him, Blessed is the womb that bare thee, and the paps which thou hast sucked.

But he said, Yea rather, blessed are they that hear the word of God, and keep it.

Covetousness
Luke 12:13–21

And one of the company said unto him, Master, speak to my brother, that he divide the inheritance with me.

And he said unto him, Man, who made me a judge or a divider over you?

And he said unto them, Take heed, and beware of covetousness: for a man's life consisteth not in the abundance of the things which he possesseth.

And he spake a parable unto them, saying, The ground of a certain rich man brought forth plentifully:

And he thought within himself, saying, What shall I do, because I have no room where to bestow my fruits?

And he said, This will I do: I will pull down my barns, and build greater; and there will I bestow all my fruits and my goods.

And I will say to my soul, Soul, thou hast much goods laid up for many years; take thine ease, eat, drink, and be merry.

But God said unto him, Thou fool, this night thy soul shall be required of thee: then whose shall those things be, which thou hast provided? So is he that layeth up treasure for himself, and is not rich toward God.

Repentance

Luke 13:1—5

THERE were present at that season some that told him of the Galilæans, whose blood Pilate had mingled with their sacrifices.

And Jesus answering said unto them, Suppose ye that these Galilæans were sinners above all the Galilæans, because they suffered such things?

I tell you, Nay: but, except ye repent, ye shall all likewise perish.

Or those eighteen, upon whom the tower in Siloam fell, and slew them, think ye that they were sinners above all men that dwelt in Jerusalem?

I tell you, Nay: but, except ye repent, ye shall all likewise perish.

Woman Healed on Sabbath

Luke 13:10—17

And he was teaching in one of the synagogues on the sabbath.

And, behold, there was a woman which had a spirit of infirmity eighteen years, and was bowed together, and could in no wise lift up herself.

And when Jesus saw her, he called her to him, and said unto her, Woman, thou art loosed from thine infirmity.

And he laid his hands on her: and immediately she was made straight, and glorified God.

And the ruler of the synagogue answered with indignation, because that Jesus had healed on the sabbath day, and said unto the people, There are six days in which men ought to work: in them therefore come and be healed, and not on the sabbath day.

The Lord then answered him, and said, Thou hypocrite, doth not each one of you on the sabbath loose his ox or his ass from the stall, and lead him away to watering?

And ought not this woman, being a daughter of Abraham, whom Satan hath bound, lo, these eighteen years, be loosed from this bond on the sabbath day?

And when he had said these things, all his adversaries were ashamed: and all the people rejoiced for all the glorious things that were done by him.

*". . . and immediately she
was made straight,
and glorified God."*

Toward Jerusalem
Luke 13:22

And he went through the cities and villages, teaching, and journeying toward Jerusalem.

"Tell That Fox"
Luke 13:31–33, JST Luke 13:34

The same day there came certain of the Pharisees, saying unto him, Get thee out, and depart hence: for Herod will kill thee.

And he said unto them, Go ye, and tell that fox, Behold, I cast out devils, and I do cures to day and to morrow, and the third day I shall be perfected.

Nevertheless I must walk to day, and to morrow, and the day following: for it cannot be that a prophet perish out of Jerusalem. <u>This he spake, signifying of his death. And in this very hour he began to weep over Jerusalem.</u>

Counting the Cost
Luke 14:28–33, JST Luke 14:30

For which of you, intending to build a tower, sitteth not down first, and counteth the cost, whether he have sufficient to finish it?

Lest haply, after he hath laid the foundation, and is not able to finish it, all that behold it begin to mock him,

Saying, This man began to build, and was not able to finish. <u>And this he said, signifying there should not any man follow him, unless he was able to continue; saying,</u>

What king, going to make war against another king, sitteth not down first, and consulteth whether he be able with ten thousand to meet him that cometh against him with twenty thousand?

Or else, while the other is yet a great way off, he sendeth an ambassage, and desireth conditions of peace.

So likewise, whosoever he be of you that forsaketh not all that he hath, he cannot be my disciple.

Parable: The Unjust Steward
Luke 16:1–8

And he said also unto his disciples, There was a certain rich man, which had a steward; and the same was accused unto him that he had wasted his goods.

And he called him, and said unto him, How is it that I hear this of thee? give an account of thy stewardship; for thou mayest be no longer steward.

Then the steward said within himself, What shall I do? for my lord taketh away from me the stewardship: I cannot dig; to beg I am ashamed.

I am resolved what to do, that, when I am put out of the stewardship, they may receive me into their houses. So he called every one of his lord's debtors unto him, and said unto the first, How much owest thou unto my lord?

And he said, An hundred measures of oil. And he said unto him, Take thy bill, and sit down quickly, and write fifty.

Then said he to another, And how much owest thou? And he said, An hundred measures of wheat. And he said unto him, Take thy bill, and write fourscore.

And the lord commended the unjust steward, because he had done wisely: for the children of this world are in their generation wiser than the children of light.

Parable: Lazarus and the Rich Man
Luke 16:14–15, 19–31

And the Pharisees also, who were covetous, heard all these things: and they derided him.

And he said unto them, Ye are they which justify yourselves before men; but God knoweth your hearts: for that which is highly esteemed among men is abomination in the sight of God.

There was a certain rich man, which was clothed in purple and fine linen, and fared sumptuously every day:

And there was a certain beggar named Lazarus, which was laid at his gate, full of sores,

And desiring to be fed with the crumbs which fell from the rich man's table: moreover the dogs came and licked his sores.

And it came to pass, that the beggar died, and was carried by the angels into Abraham's bosom: the rich man also died, and was buried;

And in hell he lift up his eyes, being in torments, and seeth Abraham afar off, and Lazarus in his bosom.

And he cried and said, Father Abraham, have mercy on me, and send Lazarus, that he may dip the tip of his finger in water, and cool my tongue; for I am tormented in this flame.

But Abraham said, Son, remember that thou in thy lifetime receivedst thy good things, and likewise Lazarus evil things: but now he is comforted, and thou art tormented.

And beside all this, between us and you there is a great gulf fixed: so that they which would pass from hence to you cannot; neither can they pass to us, that would come from thence. Then he said, I pray thee therefore, father, that thou wouldest send him to my father's house:

For I have five brethren; that he may testify unto them, lest they also come into this place of torment.

Abraham saith unto him, They have Moses and the prophets; let them hear them.

And he said, Nay, father Abraham: but if one went unto them from the dead, they will repent.

And he said unto him, If they hear not Moses and the prophets, neither will they be persuaded, though one rose from the dead.

Ten Lepers Healed

Luke 17:11–19

And it came to pass, as he went to Jerusalem, that he passed through the midst of Samaria and Galilee.

And as he entered into a certain village, there met him ten men that were lepers, which stood afar off:

And they lifted up their voices, and said, Jesus, Master, have mercy on us.

And when he saw them, he said unto them, Go shew yourselves unto the priests. And it came to pass, that, as they went, they were cleansed.

And one of them, when he saw that he was healed, turned back, and with a loud voice glorified God,

And fell down on his face at his feet, giving him thanks: and he was a Samaritan.

And Jesus answering said, Were there not ten cleansed? but where are the nine?

There are not found that returned to give glory to God, save this stranger. And he said unto him, Arise, go thy way: thy faith hath made thee whole.

". . . he was healed, turned back, and with a loud voice glorified God. . . ."

Parable: The Unjust Judge
Luke 18:1–8, JST Luke 18:8

AND he spake a parable unto them to this end, that men ought always to pray, and not to faint;

Saying, There was in a city a judge, which feared not God, neither regarded man:

And there was a widow in that city; and she came unto him, saying, Avenge me of mine adversary.

And he would not for a while: but afterward he said within himself, Though I fear not God, nor regard man;

Yet because this widow troubleth me, I will avenge her, lest by her continual coming she weary me.

And the Lord said, Hear what the unjust judge saith.

And shall not God avenge his own elect, which cry day and night unto him, though he bear long with them?

I tell you that he will <u>come, and when he does come, he will</u> avenge <u>his saints</u>[79] speedily. Nevertheless when the Son of man cometh, shall he find faith on the earth?

Jesus Enters Perea
Matt. 19:1, Mark 10:1

And it came to pass, that when Jesus had finished these sayings, he arose from thence, and he departed from Galilee, and came into the coasts of Judæa beyond Jordan: and the people resort unto him again; and, as he was wont, he taught them again.

Healing in Perea
Matt. 19:2

And great multitudes followed him; and he healed them there.

Jesus Attends Feast of Tabernacles
John 7:10–13

But when his brethren were gone up, then went he also up unto the feast, not openly, but as it were in secret.

Then the Jews sought him at the feast, and said, Where is he?

And there was much murmuring among the people concerning him: for some said, He is a good man: others said, Nay; but he deceiveth the people. Howbeit no man spake openly of him for fear of the Jews.

---

79   Luke reads, "them"

The Doctrine of the Father

John 7:14–36, JST John 7:24

Now about the midst of the feast Jesus went up into the temple, and taught.

And the Jews marvelled, saying, How knoweth this man letters, having never learned?

Jesus answered them, and said, My doctrine is not mine, but his that sent me.

If any man will do his will, he shall know of the doctrine, whether it be of God, or whether I speak of myself.

He that speaketh of himself seeketh his own glory: but he that seeketh his glory that sent him, the same is true, and no unrighteousness is in him.

Did not Moses give you the law, and yet none of you keepeth the law? Why go ye about to kill me?

The people answered and said, Thou hast a devil: who goeth about to kill thee?

Jesus answered and said unto them, I have done one work, and ye all marvel.

Moses therefore gave unto you circumcision; (not because it is of Moses, but of the fathers;) and ye on the sabbath day circumcise a man.

If a man on the sabbath day receive circumcision, that the law of Moses should not be broken; are ye angry at me, because I have made a man every whit whole on the sabbath day?

Judge not according to your traditions[80], but judge righteous judgment.

Then said some of them of Jerusalem, Is not this he, whom they seek to kill?

But, lo, he speaketh boldly, and they say nothing unto him. Do the rulers know indeed that this is the very Christ?

Howbeit we know this man whence he is: but when Christ cometh, no man knoweth whence he is.

Then cried Jesus in the temple as he taught, saying, Ye both know me, and ye know whence I am: and I am not come of myself, but he that sent me is true, whom ye know not.

But I know him: for I am from him, and he hath sent me.

Then they sought to take him: but no man laid hands on him, because his hour was not yet come.

And many of the people believed on him, and said, When Christ cometh, will he do more miracles than these which this man hath done?

The Pharisees heard that the people murmured such things concerning him; and the Pharisees

---

80   John reads, "the appearance"

and the chief priests sent officers to take him.

Then said Jesus unto them, Yet a little while am I with you, and then I go unto him that sent me.

Ye shall seek me, and shall not find me: and where I am, thither ye cannot come. Then said the Jews among themselves, Whither will he go, that we shall not find him? will he go unto the dispersed among the Gentiles, and teach the Gentiles?

What manner of saying is this that he said, Ye shall seek me, and shall not find me: and where I am, thither ye cannot come?

The Spirit Testifies of Jesus' Ministry
John 7:37–53, JST John 7:39

In the last day, that great day of the feast, Jesus stood and cried, saying, If any man thirst, let him come unto me, and drink.

He that believeth on me, as the scripture hath said, out of his belly shall flow rivers of living water.

(But this spake he of the Spirit, which they that believe on him should receive: for the Holy Ghost was promised unto them who believe, and after[81] that Jesus was glorified[82].)

Many of the people therefore, when they heard this saying, said, Of a truth this is the Prophet.

Others said, This is the Christ. But some said, Shall Christ come out of Galilee?

Hath not the scripture said, That Christ cometh of the seed of David, and out of the town of Bethlehem, where David was?

So there was a division among the people because of him.

And some of them would have taken him; but no man laid hands on him.

Then came the officers to the chief priests and Pharisees; and they said unto them, Why have ye not brought him?

The officers answered, Never man spake like this man.

Then answered them the Pharisees, Are ye also deceived?

Have any of the rulers or of the Pharisees believed on him?

But this people who knoweth not the law are cursed.

Nicodemus saith unto them, (he that came to Jesus by night, being one of them,) Doth our law judge any man, before it hear him, and know what he doeth?

They answered and said unto him, Art thou also of Galilee? Search, and look: for out of Galilee ariseth no prophet. And every man went unto his own house.

---

81 John reads, "not yet given; because"
82 John reads, "that Jesus was not yet glorified." The JST deletes the words "not yet"

The Adulterous Woman

John 8:1–11

Jesus went unto the mount of Olives.

And early in the morning he came again into the temple, and all the people came unto him; and he sat down, and taught them.

And the scribes and Pharisees brought unto him a woman taken in adultery; and when they had set her in the midst,

They say unto him, Master, this woman was taken in adultery, in the very act.

Now Moses in the law commanded us, that such should be stoned: but what sayest thou?

This they said, tempting him, that they might have to accuse him. But Jesus stooped down, and with his finger wrote on the ground, as though he heard them not.

So when they continued asking him, he lifted up himself, and said unto them, He that is without sin among you, let him first cast a stone at her.

And again he stooped down, and wrote on the ground.

And they which heard it, being convicted by their own conscience, went out one by one, beginning at the eldest, even unto the last: and Jesus was left alone, and the woman standing in the midst.

When Jesus had lifted up himself, and saw none but the woman, he said unto her, Woman, where are those thine accusers? hath no man condemned thee?

She said, No man, Lord. And Jesus said unto her, Neither do I condemn thee: go, and sin no more.

The Light of the World

John 8:12–59, JST John 8:43, 47

Then spake Jesus again unto them, saying, I am the light of the world: he that followeth me shall not walk in darkness, but shall have the light of life.

The Pharisees therefore said unto him, Thou bearest record of thyself; thy record is not true.

Jesus answered and said unto them, Though I bear record of myself, yet my record is true: for I know whence I came, and whither I go; but ye cannot tell whence I come, and whither I go.

Ye judge after the flesh; I judge no man.

And yet if I judge, my judgment is true: for I am not alone, but I and the Father that sent me.

It is also written in your law, that the testimony of two men is true.

I am one that bear witness of myself, and the Father that sent me beareth witness of me.

Then said they unto him, Where is thy Father? Jesus answered, Ye neither know me, nor my Father: if ye had known me, ye should have known my Father also.

These words spake Jesus in the treasury, as he taught in the temple: and no man laid hands on him; for his hour was not yet come.

Then said Jesus again unto them, I go my way, and ye shall seek me, and shall die in your sins: whither I go, ye cannot come.

Then said the Jews, Will he kill himself? because he saith, Whither I go, ye cannot come.

And he said unto them, Ye are from beneath; I am from above: ye are of this world; I am not of this world.

I said therefore unto you, that ye shall die in your sins: for if ye believe not that I am he, ye shall die in your sins.

Then said they unto him, Who art thou? And Jesus saith unto them, Even the same that I said unto you from the beginning.

I have many things to say and to judge of you: but he that sent me is true; and I speak to the world those things which I have heard of him.

They understood not that he spake to them of the Father. Then said Jesus unto them, When ye have lifted up the Son of man, then shall ye know that I am he, and that I do nothing of myself; but as my Father hath taught me, I speak these things.

And he that sent me is with me: the Father hath not left me alone; for I do always those things that please him.

As he spake these words, many believed on him.

Then said Jesus to those Jews which believed on him, If ye continue in my word, then are ye my disciples indeed;

And ye shall know the truth, and the truth shall make you free.

They answered him, We be Abraham's seed, and were never in bondage to any man: how sayest thou, Ye shall be made free?

Jesus answered them, Verily, verily, I say unto you, Whosoever committeth sin is the servant of sin.

And the servant abideth not in the house for ever: but the Son abideth ever.

If the Son therefore shall make you free, ye shall be free indeed.

I know that ye are Abraham's seed; but ye seek to kill me, because my word hath no place in you.

I speak that which I have seen with my Father: and ye do that which ye have seen with your father.

They answered and said unto him, Abraham is our father. Jesus saith unto them, If ye were Abraham's children, ye would do the works of Abraham.

But now ye seek to kill me, a man that hath told you the truth, which I have heard of God: this did not Abraham.

Ye do the deeds of your father. Then said they to him, We be not born of fornication; we have one Father, even God.

Jesus said unto them, If God were your Father, ye would love me: for I proceeded forth and came from God; neither came I of myself, but he sent me.

Why do ye not understand my speech? even because ye cannot <u>bear</u>[83] my word.

Ye are of your father the devil, and the lusts of your father ye will do. He was a murderer from the beginning, and abode not in the truth, because there is no truth in him. When he speaketh a lie, he speaketh of his own: for he is a liar, and the father of it.

And because I tell you the truth, ye believe me not.

Which of you convinceth me of sin? And if I say the truth, why do ye not believe me? He that is of God <u>receiveth</u>[84] God's words: ye therefore <u>receive</u>[85] them not, because ye are not of God.

Then answered the Jews, and said unto him, Say we not well that thou art a Samaritan, and hast a devil?

Jesus answered, I have not a devil; but I honour my Father, and ye do dishonour me.

And I seek not mine own glory: there is one that seeketh and judgeth.

Verily, verily, I say unto you, If a man keep my saying, he shall never see death.

Then said the Jews unto him, Now we know that thou hast a devil. Abraham is dead, and the prophets; and thou sayest, If a man keep my saying, he shall never taste of death.

Art thou greater than our father Abraham, which is dead? and the prophets are dead: whom makest thou thyself?

Jesus answered, If I honour myself, my honour is nothing: it is my Father that honoureth me; of whom ye say, that he is your God:

Yet ye have not known him; but I know him: and if I should say, I know him not, I shall be a liar like unto you: but I know him, and keep his saying.

Your father Abraham rejoiced to see my day: and he saw it, and was glad.

Then said the Jews unto him, Thou art not yet fifty years old, and hast thou seen Abraham?

Jesus said unto them, Verily, verily, I say unto you, Before Abraham was, I am.

Then took they up stones to cast at him: but Jesus hid himself, and went out of the temple, going through the midst of them, and so passed by.

---

83 John reads, "hear"
84 John reads, "heareth"
85 John reads, "hear"

Blind Man Healed on the Sabbath

John 9:1–41, JST John 9:4, 32

AND as Jesus passed by, he saw a man which was blind from his birth.

And his disciples asked him, saying, Master, who did sin, this man, or his parents, that he was born blind?

Jesus answered, Neither hath this man sinned, nor his parents: but that the works of God should be made manifest in him.

I must work the works of him that sent me, while <u>I am with you; the time cometh when I shall have finished my work then I go unto the Father.</u>[86]

As long as I am in the world, I am the light of the world.

When he had thus spoken, he spat on the ground, and made clay of the spittle, and he anointed the eyes of the blind man with the clay,

And said unto him, Go, wash in the pool of Siloam, (which is by interpretation, Sent.) He went his way therefore, and washed, and came seeing.

The neighbours therefore, and they which before had seen him that he was blind, said, Is not this he that sat and begged?

Some said, This is he: others said, He is like him: but he said, I am he.

Therefore said they unto him, How were thine eyes opened?

He answered and said, A man that is called Jesus made clay, and anointed mine eyes, and said unto me, Go to the pool of Siloam, and wash: and I went and washed, and I received sight.

Then said they unto him, Where is he? He said, I know not.

They brought to the Pharisees him that aforetime was blind.

And it was the sabbath day when Jesus made the clay, and opened his eyes.

Then again the Pharisees also asked him how he had received his sight. He said unto them, He put clay upon mine eyes, and I washed, and do see.

Therefore said some of the Pharisees, This man is not of God, because he keepeth not the sabbath day. Others said, How can a man that is a sinner do such miracles? And there was a division among them.

They say unto the blind man again, What sayest thou of him, that he hath opened thine eyes? He said, He is a prophet.

But the Jews did not believe concerning him, that he had been blind, and received his sight, until they called the parents of him that had received his sight.

---

86   John reads, "it is day: the night cometh, when no man can work."

And they asked them, saying, Is this your son, who ye say was born blind? how then doth he now see?

His parents answered them and said, We know that this is our son, and that he was born blind:

But by what means he now seeth, we know not; or who hath opened his eyes, we know not: he is of age; ask him: he shall speak for himself.

These words spake his parents, because they feared the Jews: for the Jews had agreed already, that if any man did confess that he was Christ, he should be put out of the synagogue.

Therefore said his parents, He is of age; ask him.

Then again called they the man that was blind, and said unto him, Give God the praise: we know that this man is a sinner. He answered and said, Whether he be a sinner or no, I know not: one thing I know, that, whereas I was blind, now I see.

Then said they to him again, What did he to thee? how opened he thine eyes?

He answered them, I have told you already, and ye did not hear: wherefore would ye hear it again? will ye also be his disciples?

Then they reviled him, and said, Thou art his disciple; but we are Moses' disciples.

We know that God spake unto Moses: as for this fellow, we know not from whence he is.

The man answered and said unto them, Why herein is a marvellous thing, that ye know not from whence he is, and yet he hath opened mine eyes.

Now we know that God heareth not sinners: but if any man be a worshipper of God, and doeth his will, him he heareth.

Since the world began was it not heard that any man opened the eyes of one that was born blind except he be of God.

If this man were not of God, he could do nothing. They answered and said unto him, Thou wast altogether born in sins, and dost thou teach us? And they cast him out.

Jesus heard that they had cast him out; and when he had found him, he said unto him, Dost thou believe on the Son of God? He answered and said, Who is he, Lord, that I might believe on him?

And Jesus said unto him, Thou hast both seen him, and it is he that talketh with thee.

And he said, Lord, I believe. And he worshipped him.

And Jesus said, For judgment I am come into this world, that they which see not might see; and that they which see might be made blind.

And some of the Pharisees which were with him heard these words, and said unto him, Are we blind also?

Jesus said unto them, If ye were blind, ye should have no sin: but now ye say, We see; therefore your sin remaineth.

Parable: The Good Shepherd

John 10:1–21, JST John 10:8

Verily, verily, I say unto you, He that entereth not by the door into the sheepfold, but climbeth up some other way, the same is a thief and a robber.

But he that entereth in by the door is the shepherd of the sheep.

To him the porter openeth; and the sheep hear his voice: and he calleth his own sheep by name, and leadeth them out.

And when he putteth forth his own sheep, he goeth before them, and the sheep follow him: for they know his voice.

And a stranger will they not follow, but will flee from him: for they know not the voice of strangers.

This parable spake Jesus unto them: but they understood not what things they were which he spake unto them.

Then said Jesus unto them again, Verily, verily, I say unto you, I am the door of the sheep.

All that ever came before me who testified not of me are thieves and robbers: but the sheep did not hear them.

I am the door: by me if any man enter in, he shall be saved, and shall go in and out, and find pasture.

" . . . I am the good shepherd . . ."

Simon Dewey

The thief cometh not, but for to steal, and to kill, and to destroy: I am come that they might have life, and that they might have it more abundantly.

I am the good shepherd: the good shepherd giveth his life for the sheep.

But he that is an hireling, and not the shepherd, whose own the sheep are not, seeth the wolf coming, and leaveth the sheep, and fleeth: and the wolf catcheth them, and scattereth the sheep.

The hireling fleeth, because he is an hireling, and careth not for the sheep.

I am the good shepherd, and know my sheep, and am known of mine.

As the Father knoweth me, even so know I the Father: and I lay down my life for the sheep.

And other sheep I have, which are not of this fold: them also I must bring, and they shall hear my voice; and there shall be one fold, and one shepherd.

Therefore doth my Father love me, because I lay down my life, that I might take it again.

No man taketh it from me, but I lay it down of myself. I have power to lay it down, and I have power to take it again. This commandment have I received of my Father.

There was a division therefore again among the Jews for these sayings.

And many of them said, He hath a devil, and is mad; why hear ye him?

Others said, These are not the words of him that hath a devil. Can a devil open the eyes of the blind?

Pharisees Ask about Divorce
Matt. 19:3–12, Mark 10:2–12

The Pharisees also came unto him, tempting him, and asked saying unto him, Is it lawful for a man to put away his wife for every cause?

And he answered and said unto them, What did Moses command you?

And they said, Moses suffered to write a bill of divorcement, and to put her away.

But, have ye not read, that he which made them at the beginning made them male and female,

And said, For this cause shall a man leave father and mother, and shall cleave to his wife: and they twain shall be one flesh?

Wherefore they are no more twain, but one flesh. What therefore God hath joined together, let not man put asunder.

They say unto him, Why did Moses then command to give a writing of divorcement, and to put her away?

He saith unto them, Moses because of the hardness of your hearts suffered you to put away your wives: but from the beginning it was not so.

And I say unto you, Whosoever shall put away his wife, except it be for fornication, and shall marry another, committeth adultery against her: and whoso marrieth her which is put away doth commit adultery.

And if a woman shall put away her husband, and be married to another, she committeth adultery.

His disciples say unto him, If the case of the man be so with his wife, it is not good to marry. But he said unto them, All men cannot receive this saying, save they to whom it is given.

For there are some eunuchs, which were so born from their mother's womb: and there are some eunuchs, which were made eunuchs of men: and there be eunuchs, which have made themselves eunuchs for the kingdom of heaven's sake. He that is able to receive it , let him receive it.

Suffer Little Children
Matt. 19:13–15, Mark 10:13–16, Luke 18:15–17, JST Matt. 19:13

Then were there brought unto him infants, [and] little children, that he should touch them, [and] put his hands on them, and pray: and the disciples rebuked those that brought them, <u>saying, There is no need, for Jesus hath said, Such shall be saved.</u>

But when Jesus saw it, he was much displeased, and said unto them, Suffer the little children, and forbid them not, to come unto me: for of such is the kingdom of God [and] heaven.

Verily I say unto you, Whosoever shall not receive the kingdom of God as a little child, he shall not enter therein.

And he took them up in his arms, and he laid his hands on them, and blessed them, and departed thence.

Rich Young Ruler
Matt. 19:16–26, Mark 10:17–27, Luke 18:18–27,
JST Matt. 19:26, JST Mark 10:26, JST Luke 18:27

And, behold, when he was gone forth into the way, there came a certain ruler, running and kneeled to him, and said unto him, Good Master, what good thing shall I do, that I may inherit eternal life?

And he said unto him, Why callest thou me good? there is none good save one, that is, God: but if thou wilt enter into life, keep the commandments.

He saith unto him, Which? Jesus said, Thou knowest the commandments, Thou shalt do no murder, Thou shalt not commit adultery, Thou shalt not steal, Thou shalt not bear false witness, Defraud not,

Honour thy father and thy mother: and, Thou shalt love thy neighbour as thyself.

The young man saith unto him, All these things have I kept from my youth up: what lack I yet?

Then Jesus beholding him loved him, [and] said unto him, Yet one thing thou lackest: If thou wilt be perfect, go thy way and sell whatsoever thou hast, and give to the poor, and thou shalt have treasure in heaven: and come, take up the cross, and follow me.

But when the young man heard that saying, he went away sorrowful, [and] grieved: for he had great possessions, for he was very rich.

And Jesus looked round about, and then said Jesus unto his disciples, Verily I say unto you, That a rich man shall hardly enter into the kingdom of heaven.

And the disciples were astonished at his words. But Jesus answereth again, and saith unto them, Children, how hard is it for them that trust in riches to enter into the kingdom of God!

And again I say unto you, It is easier for a camel to go through the eye of a needle, than for a rich man to enter into the kingdom of God.

When his disciples heard it, they were exceedingly amazed, saying among themselves, Who then can be saved?

But Jesus looking upon them beheld their thoughts,[87] and said unto them, With men that trust in riches, this is impossible to enter into the kingdom of God, but not impossible with men who trust in God and leave all things of this world for my sake: for if they will forsake all things for my sake, whatsoever things I speak[88] are possible with God that he should enter in.

The Twelve to Judge the Tribes of Israel
Matt. 19:27–30, Mark 10:28–31, Luke 18:28–30; 22:28–30, JST Matt. 19:28, JST Mark 10:30–31

Then answered Peter and said unto him, Behold, we have forsaken all, and followed thee; what shall we have therefore?

And Jesus said unto them, Verily I say unto you, That ye are they which have continued with me in my temptations [and] have followed me,

And I appoint unto you a kingdom, as my Father hath appointed unto me;

That ye may eat and drink at my table in my kingdom, and in the resurrection,[89] when the Son of man shall sit in the throne of his glory, ye also shall sit upon twelve thrones, judging the

---

87   Matthew reads, "them"
88   Matthew reads, "all things"
89   Matthew reads, "regeneration"

twelve tribes of Israel.

And every one that hath forsaken houses, or brethren, or sisters, or father, or mother, or wife, or children, or lands, for my name's sake, [and] the kingdom of God's sake, shall receive an hundredfold, and shall inherit everlasting life.

But he shall receive an hundredfold now in this present time, houses, and brethren, and sisters, and mothers, and children, and lands, with persecutions; and in the world to come eternal life.

But many that make themselves first, that shall be last; and the last shall be first. This he said rebuking Peter.

Parable: Laborers in Vineyard
Matt. 20:1–16

For the kingdom of heaven is like unto a man that is an householder, which went out early in the morning to hire labourers into his vineyard.

And when he had agreed with the labourers for a penny a day, he sent them into his vineyard.

And he went out about the third hour, and saw others standing idle in the marketplace,

And said unto them; Go ye also into the vineyard, and whatsoever is right I will give you. And they went their way.

Again he went out about the sixth and ninth hour, and did likewise.

And about the eleventh hour he went out, and found others standing idle, and saith unto them, Why stand ye here all the day idle?

They say unto him, Because no man hath hired us. He saith unto them, Go ye also into the vineyard; and whatsoever is right, that shall ye receive.

So when even was come, the lord of the vineyard saith unto his steward, Call the labourers, and give them their hire, beginning from the last unto the first.

And when they came that were hired about the eleventh hour, they received every man a penny.

But when the first came, they supposed that they should have received more; and they likewise received every man a penny.

And when they had received it, they murmured against the goodman of the house,

Saying, These last have wrought but one hour, and thou hast made them equal unto us, which have borne the burden and heat of the day.

But he answered one of them, and said, Friend, I do thee no wrong: didst not thou agree with me for a penny?

Take that thine is, and go thy way: I will give unto this

last, even as unto thee.

Is it not lawful for me to do what I will with mine own? Is thine eye evil, because I am good?

So the last shall be first, and the first last: for many be called, but few chosen.

The Feast of Dedication
John 10:22–39

And it was at Jerusalem the feast of the dedication, and it was winter.

And Jesus walked in the temple in Solomon's porch.

Then came the Jews round about him, and said unto him, How long dost thou make us to doubt? If thou be the Christ, tell us plainly.

Jesus answered them, I told you, and ye believed not: the works that I do in my Father's name, they bear witness of me.

But ye believe not, because ye are not of my sheep, as I said unto you.

My sheep hear my voice, and I know them, and they follow me:

And I give unto them eternal life; and they shall never perish, neither shall any man pluck them out of my hand.

My Father, which gave them me, is greater than all; and no man is able to pluck them out of my Father's hand.

I and my Father are one.

Then the Jews took up stones again to stone him.

Jesus answered them, Many good works have I shewed you from my Father; for which of those works do ye stone me?

The Jews answered him, saying, For a good work we stone thee not; but for blasphemy; and because that thou, being a man, makest thyself God.

Jesus answered them, Is it not written in your law, I said, Ye are gods?

If he called them gods, unto whom the word of God came, and the scripture cannot be broken;

Say ye of him, whom the Father hath sanctified, and sent into the world, Thou blasphemest; because I said, I am the Son of God?

If I do not the works of my Father, believe me not.

But if I do, though ye believe not me, believe the works: that ye may know, and believe, that the Father is in me, and I in him.

Therefore they sought again to take him: but he escaped out of their hand,

Admirers of the Baptist Believe
John 10:40–42

And went away again beyond Jordan into the place where John at first baptized; and there he abode.

And many resorted unto him, and said, John did no miracle: but all things that John spake of this man were true.

And many believed on him there.

Summoned to Lazarus
John 11:1–7, JST John 11:2

Now a certain man was sick, named Lazarus, of Bethany, the town of Mary and her sister Martha.

And Mary, his sister, who[90] anointed the Lord with ointment, and wiped his feet with her hair, lived with her sister Martha, in whose house her brother Lazarus was sick.

Therefore his sisters sent unto him, saying, Lord, behold, he whom thou lovest is sick.

When Jesus heard that, he said, This sickness is not unto death, but for the glory of God, that the Son of God might be glorified thereby.

Now Jesus loved Martha, and her sister, and Lazarus.

When he had heard therefore that he was sick, he abode two days still in the same place where he was.

Then after that saith he to his disciples, Let us go into Judæa again.

---

90   John reads, "It was that Mary which"

Prophecy of Death and Resurrection
Matt. 20:17–19, Mark 10:32–34, Luke 18:31–34

And they were in the way going up to Jerusalem; and Jesus went before them: and they were amazed; and as they followed, they were afraid. And he took again the twelve, and began to tell them what things should happen unto him, and said unto them,

Behold, we go up to Jerusalem, and all things that are written by the prophets concerning the Son of man shall be accomplished; and the Son of man shall be betrayed, and shall be delivered unto the chief priests and unto the scribes, and they shall condemn him to death,

And shall deliver him to the Gentiles to mock him, and spitefully entreat [him], and scourge him, and shall spit upon him, and to crucify him: and the third day he shall rise again.

And they understood none of these things: and this saying was hid from them, neither knew they the things which were spoken.

The Greatest Is to Minister
Matt. 20:20–28, Mark 10:35–45, Luke 22:24–27

Then came to him the mother of Zebedee's children with her sons, James and John, worshipping him, and desiring a certain thing of him, saying, Master, we would that thou shouldest do for us whatsoever we shall desire.

And he said unto her, What wilt thou that I should do for you? She saith unto him, Grant that these my two sons may sit, the one on thy right hand, and the other on the left, in thy glory, in thy kingdom.

But Jesus answered and said, Ye know not what ye ask. Are ye able to drink of the cup that I shall drink of, and to be baptized with the baptism that I am baptized with? They say unto him, We are able.

And he saith unto them, Ye shall drink indeed of the cup that I drink of, and be baptized with the baptism that I am baptized with: but to sit on my right hand, and on my left, is not mine to give, but it shall be given to them for whom it is prepared of my Father. And when the ten heard it, they were much displeased [and] moved with indignation against James and John.

And there was also a strife among them, which of them should be accounted the greatest,

But Jesus called them unto him, and said unto them, Ye know that the princes, kings, of the Gentiles exercise dominion, [and] lordship, over them, and they that are great exercise authority upon them, [and] are called benefactors.

But it shall not be so among you: but whosoever will be great among you, let him be as the younger; let him be your minister;

And whosoever will be chief among you, let him be your servant:

For whether is greater, he that sitteth at meat, or he that serveth? is not he that sitteth at meat? but I am among you as he that serveth.

For even as the Son of man came not to be ministered unto, but to minister, and to give his life a ransom for many.

Two Blind Men Healed (Bartimæus)
Matt. 20:29–34, Mark 10:46–52, Luke 18:35–43

And as they departed from Jericho, a great multitude followed him. And, behold, two blind men, [one named] Bartimæus, the son of Timæus sitting by the highway side begging.

And hearing the multitude pass by, he asked what it meant.

And they told him, that Jesus of Nazareth passeth by.

When they heard that Jesus of Nazareth passed by, cried out, saying, Have mercy on us, O Lord, Jesus, thou Son of David.

And the multitude rebuked them, because they should hold their peace: but they cried the more, saying, Have mercy on us, O Lord, thou Son of David.

And Jesus stood still, and commanded him to be called. And they call the blind man, saying unto him, Be of good comfort, rise; he calleth thee.

And he, casting away his garment, rose, and came to Jesus.

And Jesus answered and said unto him, What will ye that I shall do unto you?

They say unto him, Lord, that our eyes may be opened, that I might receive my sight.

So Jesus had compassion on them, and touched their eyes,

And Jesus said unto him, Go thy way; thy faith hath made thee whole: and immediately their eyes received sight, and they followed him in the way, glorifying God: and all the people, when they saw it, gave praise unto God.

". . .that our eyes may be opened. . . ."

". . .And he sought to see Jesus. . . ."

Salvation Comes to the House of Zacchæus
Luke 19:1–10

And Jesus entered and passed through Jericho.

And, behold, there was a man named Zacchæus, which was the chief among the publicans, and he was rich.

And he sought to see Jesus who he was; and could not for the press, because he was little of stature.

And he ran before, and climbed up into a sycomore tree to see him: for he was to pass that way.

And when Jesus came to the place, he looked up, and saw him, and said unto him, Zacchæus, make haste, and come down; for to day I must abide at thy house.

And he made haste, and came down, and received him joyfully.

And when they saw it, they all murmured, saying, That he was gone to be guest with a man that is a sinner.

And Zacchæus stood, and said unto the Lord; Behold, Lord, the half of my goods I give to the poor; and if I have taken any thing from any man by false accusation, I restore him fourfold.

And Jesus said unto him, This day is salvation come to this house, forsomuch as he also is a son of Abraham.

For the Son of man is come to seek and to save that which was lost.

Parable of the Pounds
Luke 19:11–27, JST Luke 19:25

And as they heard these things, he added and spake a parable, because he was nigh to Jerusalem, and because they thought that the kingdom of God should immediately appear.

He said therefore, A certain nobleman went into a far country to receive for himself a kingdom, and to return.

And he called his ten servants, and delivered them ten pounds, and said unto them, Occupy till I come.

But his citizens hated him, and sent a message after him, saying, We will not have this man to reign over us.

And it came to pass, that when he was returned, having received the kingdom, then he commanded these servants to be called unto him, to whom he had given the money, that he might know how much every man had gained by trading.

Then came the first, saying, Lord, thy pound hath gained ten pounds.

And he said unto him, Well, thou good servant: because thou hast been faithful in a very little, have thou authority over ten cities.

And the second came, saying, Lord, thy pound hath gained five pounds.

And he said likewise to him, Be thou also over five cities.

And another came, saying, Lord, behold, here is thy pound, which I have kept laid up in a napkin:

For I feared thee, because thou art an austere man: thou takest up that thou layedst not down, and reapest that thou didst not sow.

And he saith unto him, Out of thine own mouth will I judge thee, thou wicked servant. Thou knewest that I was an austere man, taking up that I laid not down, and reaping that I did not sow:

Wherefore then gavest not thou my money into the bank, that at my coming I might have required mine own with usury?

And he said unto them that stood by, Take from him the pound, and give it to him that hath ten pounds.

(And they said unto him, Lord, he hath ten pounds.)

For I say unto you, That unto every one <u>who occupieth,</u> shall be given; and from him that <u>occupieth</u>[91] not, even that he hath <u>received</u> shall be taken away from him.

But those mine enemies, which would not that I should reign over them, bring hither, and slay them before me.

---

91   Luke reads, "hath"

Lazarus Restored
Luke 19:28, John 11:8–53, JST John 11:16–17

And when he had thus spoken, he went before, ascending up to Jerusalem.

His disciples say unto him, Master, the Jews of late sought to stone thee; and goest thou thither again?

Jesus answered, Are there not twelve hours in the day? If any man walk in the day, he stumbleth not, because he seeth the light of this world.

But if a man walk in the night, he stumbleth, because there is no light in him.

These things said he: and after that he saith unto them, Our friend Lazarus sleepeth; but I go, that I may awake him out of sleep.

Then said his disciples, Lord, if he sleep, he shall do well.

Howbeit Jesus spake of his death: but they thought that he had spoken of taking of rest in sleep.

Then said Jesus unto them plainly, Lazarus is dead.

And I am glad for your sakes that I was not there, to the intent ye may believe; nevertheless let us go unto him.

Then said Thomas, which is called Didymus, unto his fellow disciples, Let us also go, that we may die with him for they feared lest the Jews should take Jesus and put him to death, for as yet they did not understand the power of God.

Then when Jesus came to Bethany to Martha's house, Lazarus had already been in the grave[92] four days already.

Now Bethany was nigh unto Jerusalem, about fifteen furlongs off:

And many of the Jews came to Martha and Mary, to comfort them concerning their brother.

Then Martha, as soon as she heard that Jesus was coming, went and met him: but Mary sat still in the house.

Then said Martha unto Jesus, Lord, if thou hadst been here, my brother had not died.

But I know, that even now, whatsoever thou wilt ask of God, God will give it thee. Jesus saith unto her, Thy brother shall rise again. Martha saith unto him, I know that he shall rise again in the resurrection at the last day.

Jesus said unto her, I am the resurrection, and the life: he that believeth in me, though he were dead, yet shall he live:

And whosoever liveth and believeth in me shall never die. Believest thou this?

She saith unto him, Yea, Lord: I believe that thou art the Christ, the Son of God, which should come into the world.

And when she had so said, she went her way, and called Mary her sister secretly, saying, The Master is come, and calleth for thee.

As soon as she heard that, she arose quickly, and came unto him.

Now Jesus was not yet come into the town, but was in that place where Martha met him.

The Jews then which were with her in the house, and comforted her, when they saw Mary, that she rose up hastily and went out, followed her, saying, She goeth unto the grave to weep there.

---

92   John reads, "he found that he had lain in the grave"

Then when Mary was come where Jesus was, and saw him, she fell down at his feet, saying unto him, Lord, if thou hadst been here, my brother had not died.

When Jesus therefore saw her weeping, and the Jews also weeping which came with her, he groaned in the spirit, and was troubled,

And said, Where have ye laid him? They said unto him, Lord, come and see.

Jesus wept.

Then said the Jews, Behold how he loved him!

And some of them said, Could not this man, which opened the eyes of the blind, have caused that even this man should not have died?

Jesus therefore again groaning in himself cometh to the grave. It was a cave, and a stone lay upon it.

Jesus said, Take ye away the stone. Martha, the sister of him that was dead, saith unto him, Lord, by this time he stinketh: for he hath been dead four days.

Jesus saith unto her, Said I not unto thee, that, if thou wouldest believe, thou shouldest see the glory of God?

Then they took away the stone from the place where the dead was laid. And Jesus lifted up his eyes, and said, Father, I thank thee that thou hast heard me.

And I knew that thou hearest me always: but because of the people which stand by I said it, that they may believe that thou hast sent me.

And when he thus had spoken, he cried with a loud voice, Lazarus, come forth.

And he that was dead came forth, bound hand and foot with graveclothes: and his face was

bound about with a napkin. Jesus saith unto them, Loose him, and let him go.

Then many of the Jews which came to Mary, and had seen the things which Jesus did, believed on him.

But some of them went their ways to the Pharisees, and told them what things Jesus had done.

Then gathered the chief priests and the Pharisees a council, and said, What do we? for this man doeth many miracles.

If we let him thus alone, all men will believe on him: and the Romans shall come and take away both our place and nation.

And one of them, named Caiaphas, being the high priest that same year, said unto them, Ye know nothing at all,

Nor consider that it is expedient for us, that one man should die for the people, and that the whole nation perish not.

And this spake he not of himself: but being high priest that year, he prophesied that Jesus should die for that nation;

And not for that nation only, but that also he should gather together in one the children of God that were scattered abroad.

Then from that day forth they took counsel together for to put him to death.

Retires to Ephraim
Luke 19:28

And when he had thus spoken, he went before, ascending up to Jerusalem.

To Jerusalem for Passover
John 11:55–57

And the Jews' passover was nigh at hand: and many went out of the country up to Jerusalem before the passover, to purify themselves.

Then sought they for Jesus, and spake among themselves, as they stood in the temple, What think ye, that he will not come to the feast?

Now both the chief priests and the Pharisees had given a commandment, that, if any man knew where he were, he should shew it, that they might take him.

The Sixth Day Before Passover
John 12:1

Then Jesus six days before the passover came to Bethany, where Lazarus was which had been dead, whom he raised from the dead.

A Supper at Martha's and Mary's
John 12:2

There they made him a supper; and Martha served: but Lazarus was one of them that sat at the table with him.

Jesus Anointed by Mary
John 12:3

Then took Mary a pound of ointment of spikenard, very costly, and anointed the feet of Jesus, and wiped his feet with her hair: and the house was filled with the odour of the ointment.

Judas's Protest
John 12:4–8, JST John 12:7

Then saith one of his disciples, Judas Iscariot, Simon's son, which should betray him,

Why was not this ointment sold for three hundred pence, and given to the poor?

This he said, not that he cared for the poor; but because he was a thief, and had the bag, and bare what was put therein.

Then said Jesus, Let her alone: <u>for she hath preserved this ointment until now, that she might anoint me in token of my burial.</u>[93]

For the poor always ye have with you; but me ye have not always.

People Gather to Jesus, Lazarus
John 12:9

Much people of the Jews therefore knew that he was there: and they came not for Jesus' sake only, but that they might see Lazarus also, whom he had raised from the dead.

---

93   John reads, "against the day of my burying hath she kept this."

Conspiracy Against Lazarus
John 12:10—11

But the chief priests consulted that they might put Lazarus also to death;

Because that by reason of him many of the Jews went away, and believed on Jesus.

The Fifth Day Before Passover
John 12:12

On the next day much people that were come to the feast, when they heard that Jesus was coming to Jerusalem.

Prophecy Fulfilled
Matt. 21:1—5, Mark 11:1—6, Luke 19:28—34

And when they drew nigh unto Jerusalem, and were come to Bethphage and Bethany, unto the mount, called the mount of Olives, then sent Jesus two disciples,

Saying unto them, Go your way into the village over against you, and straightway ye shall find an ass tied, and a colt with her, whereon never man sat; loose them, and bring them unto me.

And if any man say unto you, Why do ye this? ye shall say, The Lord hath need of them; and straightway he will send them hither.

And they that were sent went their way, and found even as he had said unto them, the colt tied by the door without in a place where two ways met; and they loose him.

And certain of them, the owners, that stood there said unto them, What do ye, loosing the colt?

And they said unto them, The Lord hath need of him, even as Jesus had commanded: and they let them go.

All this was done, that it might be fulfilled which was spoken by the prophet, saying,

Tell ye the daughter of Sion, Behold, thy King cometh unto thee, meek, and sitting upon an ass, and a colt the foal of an ass.

Triumphal Entry

Matt. 21:6–11, Mark 11:7–11,
Luke 19:35–38, John 12:12–18,
JST Matt. 21:5, JST Mark 11:11–12

And the disciples went, and did as Jesus commanded them,

And brought the <u>colt</u>[94], and put on <u>it</u>[95] their clothes, <u>and Jesus took the colt and sat thereon, and they followed him.</u>[96]

And as he went, a very great multitude spread their garments in the way; and others cut down branches from the trees, and strawed them in the way.

And when he was come nigh, even now at the descent of the mount of Olives, the whole multitude of the disciples began to rejoice and praise God with a loud voice for all the mighty works that they had seen;

And the multitudes that went before, and they that followed, cried, saying, Hosanna to the Son of David: Blessed be the King that cometh in the name of the Lord; <u>that bringeth the kingdom of our father David; Blessed is he that cometh in the name of the Lord.</u> Peace in heaven, and glory in the highest. Hosanna in the highest.

And when he was come into Jerusalem, and into the temple: all the city was moved, saying, Who is this?

And the multitude said, This is Jesus the prophet of Nazareth of Galilee. And when he had looked round about upon all things, and now the eventide was come, he went out unto Bethany with the twelve.

Pharisees Disapprove

Luke 19:39–40, John 12:19

The Pharisees therefore said among themselves, Perceive ye how ye prevail nothing? behold, the world is gone after him.

And some of the Pharisees from among the multitude said unto him, Master, rebuke thy disciples.

And he answered and said unto them, I tell you that, if these should hold their peace, the stones would immediately cry out.

---

94   Matthew reads, "ass, and the colt,"
95   Matthew reads, "them"
96   Matthew reads, "and they set him thereon"

Jesus Weeps Over Jerusalem
Luke 19:41–44

And when he was come near, he beheld the city, and wept over it,

Saying, If thou hadst known, even thou, at least in this thy day, the things which belong unto thy peace! but now they are hid from thine eyes.

For the days shall come upon thee, that thine enemies shall cast a trench about thee, and compass thee round, and keep thee in on every side,

And shall lay thee even with the ground, and thy children within thee; and they shall not leave in thee one stone upon another; because thou knewest not the time of thy visitation.

Greeks Wish to See Jesus
John 12:20–22

And there were certain Greeks among them that came up to worship at the feast:

The same came therefore to Philip, which was of Bethsaida of Galilee, and desired him, saying, Sir, we would see Jesus.

Philip cometh and telleth Andrew: and again Andrew and Philip tell Jesus.

Discourse: Jesus Sent by the Father
John 12:23–50

And Jesus answered them, saying, The hour is come, that the Son of man should be glorified. Verily, verily, I say unto you, Except a corn of wheat fall into the ground and die, it abideth alone: but if it die, it bringeth forth much fruit.

He that loveth his life shall lose it; and he that hateth his life in this world shall keep it unto life eternal.

If any man serve me, let him follow me; and where I am, there shall also my servant be: if any man serve me, him will my Father honour. Now is my soul troubled; and what shall I say? Father, save me from this hour: but for this cause came I unto this hour.

Father, glorify thy name. Then came there a voice from heaven, saying, I have both glorified it, and will glorify it again.

The people therefore, that stood by, and heard it, said that it thundered: others said, An angel spake to him.

Jesus answered and said, This voice came not because of me, but for your sakes. Now is the judgment of this world: now shall the prince of this world be cast out.

And I, if I be lifted up from the earth, will draw all men unto me.

This he said, signifying what death he should die.

The people answered him, We have heard out of the law that Christ abideth for ever: and how sayest thou, The Son of man must be lifted up? who is this Son of man?

Then Jesus said unto them, Yet a little while is the light with you. Walk while ye have the light, lest darkness come upon you: for he that walketh in darkness knoweth not whither he goeth.

While ye have light, believe in the light, that ye may be the children of light.

These things spake Jesus, and departed, and did hide himself from them.

But though he had done so many miracles before them, yet they believed not on him:

That the saying of Esaias the prophet might be fulfilled, which he spake, Lord, who hath believed our report? and to whom hath the arm of the Lord been revealed?

Therefore they could not believe, because that Esaias said again,

He hath blinded their eyes, and hardened their heart; that they should not see with their eyes, nor understand with their heart, and be converted, and I should heal them.

These things said Esaias, when he saw his glory, and spake of him.

Nevertheless among the chief rulers also many believed on him; but because of the Pharisees they did not confess him, lest they should be put out of the synagogue:

For they loved the praise of men more than the praise of God.

Jesus cried and said, He that believeth on me, believeth not on me, but on him that sent me.

And he that seeth me seeth him that sent me. I am come a light into the world, that whosoever believeth on me should not abide in darkness.

And if any man hear my words, and believe not, I judge him not: for I came not to judge the world, but to save the world.

He that rejecteth me, and receiveth not my words, hath one that judgeth him: the word that I have spoken, the same shall judge him in the last day.

For I have not spoken of myself; but the Father which sent me, he gave me a commandment, what I should say, and what I should speak.

And I know that his commandment is life everlasting: whatsoever I speak therefore, even as the Father said unto me, so I speak.

Money Changers Cast Out
Matt. 21:12–16, Mark 11:15–19, Luke 19:45–48, JST Matt. 21:15

And they come to Jerusalem: And Jesus went into the temple of God, and began to cast out all them that sold and bought in the temple, and overthrew the tables of the moneychangers, and the seats of them that sold doves,

And would not suffer that any man should carry any vessel through the temple.

And he taught and said unto them, It is written, My house shall be called of all nations the house of prayer; but ye have made it a den of thieves.

And he taught daily in the temple. But the chief priests and the scribes and the chief of the people sought to destroy him,

And could not find what they might do: for all the people were very attentive to hear him.

And the blind and the lame came to him in the temple; and he healed them.

And when the chief priests and scribes saw the wonderful things that he did, and the children of the kingdom crying in the temple, and saying, Hosanna to the Son of David; they were sore displeased, and sought how they might destroy him: for they feared him, because all the people was astonished at his doctrine.

And said unto him, Hearest thou what these say? And Jesus saith unto them, Yea; have ye never read, Out of the mouth of babes and sucklings thou hast perfected praise?

And when even was come, he went out of the city.

The Fourth Day Before Passover
Matt. 21:17–18, Mark 11:12

And he left them, and went out of the city into Bethany; and he lodged there.

Now in the morning, when they were come from Bethany, as he returned into the city, he hungered.

Fig Tree Cursed, Withers
Matt. 21:18–22, Mark 11:12–14, 20–26, Luke 13:6–9

Now in the morning, when they were come from Bethany as he returned into the city, he hungered.

And when he saw a fig tree afar off in the way having leaves, he came to it, if haply he might find any thing thereon: and when he came to it, he found nothing thereon, but leaves only; for the time of figs was not yet.

And Jesus answered and said unto it, Let no fruit grow on thee henceforward for ever, [and] No man eat fruit of thee hereafter for ever. And his disciples heard it. And presently the fig tree withered away.

And in the morning, as they passed by, they saw the fig tree dried up from the roots.

And Peter calling to remembrance saith unto him, Master, behold, the fig tree which thou cursedst is withered away.

And when the disciples saw it, they marvelled, saying, How soon is the fig tree withered away!

Jesus answered and said unto them, Verily I say unto you, If ye have faith in God, and doubt not, ye shall not only do this which is done to the fig tree, but also if ye shall say unto this mountain, Be thou removed, and be thou cast into the sea; and shall not doubt in his heart, but shall believe that those things which he saith shall come to pass; he shall have whatsoever he saith. Therefore I say unto you, What things soever ye desire, when ye pray, believe that ye receive them, and ye shall have them.

And all things, whatsoever ye shall ask in prayer, believing, ye shall receive.

And when ye stand praying, forgive, if ye have ought against any: that your Father also which is in heaven may forgive you your trespasses.

But if ye do not forgive, neither will your Father which is in heaven forgive your trespasses.

He spake also this parable; A certain man had a fig tree planted in his vineyard; and he came and sought fruit thereon, and found none. Then said he unto the dresser of his vineyard, Behold, these three years I come seeking fruit on this fig tree, and find none: cut it down; why cumbereth it the ground?

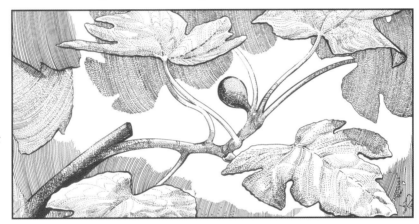

And he answering said unto him, Lord, let it alone this year also, till I shall dig about it, and dung it: And if it bear fruit, well: and if not, then after that thou shalt cut it down.

Priests Challenge Jesus' Authority
Matt. 21:23–27, Mark 11:27–33, Luke 20:1–8, JST Matt. 21:32-34

And they come again to Jerusalem: And when he was come walking into the temple, the chief priests and the scribes, and the elders of the people came unto him as he was teaching the people in the temple, and preached the gospel, and said, By what authority doest thou these things? and who gave thee this authority to do these things? or who is he that gave thee this authority?

And Jesus answered and said unto them, I also will ask you one thing, which if ye tell me, I in like wise will tell you by what authority I do these things.

The baptism of John, whence was it? from heaven, or of men? answer me. And they reasoned with themselves, saying, If we shall say, From heaven; he will say unto us, Why did ye not then believe him?

But if we shall say, Of men; we fear the people will stone us; for all hold that he, John, was a prophet indeed.

And they answered Jesus, and said, We cannot tell whence it was. And Jesus said unto them, Neither tell I you by what authority I do these things.

The baptism of John, whence was it? from heaven, or of men? And they reasoned with themselves, saying, If we shall say, From heaven; he will say unto us, Why did ye not then believe him?

But if we shall say, Of men; we fear the people; for all hold John as a prophet.

And they answered Jesus, and said, We cannot tell. And he said unto them, Neither tell I you by what authority I do these things.

Parable: Two Sons
Matt. 21:28–32

But what think ye? A certain man had two sons; and he came to the first, and said, Son, go work to day in my vineyard.

He answered and said, I will not: but afterward he repented, and went.

And he came to the second, and said likewise. And he answered and said, I go, sir: and went not.

Whether of them twain did the will of his father? They say unto him, The first. Jesus saith unto them, Verily I say unto you, That the publicans and the harlots go into the kingdom of God before you.

For John came unto you in the way of righteousness, and ye believed him not: but the publicans and the harlots believed him: and ye, when ye had seen it, repented not afterward, that ye might believe him.

Parable: Wicked Husbandmen
Matt. 21:33–46, Mark 12:1–12, Luke 20:9–20, JST Matt. 21:47–56

And then he began to speak unto the people, Hear another parable: There was a certain householder, which planted a vineyard, and hedged it round about, and digged a place for the winefat, a winepress, in it, and built a tower, and let it out to husbandmen, and went into a far country for a long time.

And when the time, season, of the fruit drew near, he sent his servants to the husbandmen, that they might receive the fruits of the vineyard [and] give him of the fruit of the vineyard.

And the husbandmen caught his servants, and beat one, and sent him away empty.

Again, he sent unto them other servants more than the first: and they did unto them likewise and sent him away empty.

And again he sent unto them another third servant; and at him they cast stones, and wounded him in the head, and sent him away shamefully handled and cast him out.

And again he sent another; and him they killed, and many others; beating some, and killing some.

Then said the lord of the vineyard, What shall I do? But last of all having yet therefore one son, his wellbeloved, he sent unto them his son, saying, They will reverence my son when they see him.

But when the husbandmen saw the son, they said and reasoned among themselves, This is the heir; come, let us kill him, and let us seize on his inheritance, that the inheritance may be ours.

And they caught him, and cast him out of the vineyard, and slew him.

When the lord therefore of the vineyard cometh, What shall therefore the lord of the vineyard do unto those husbandmen?

They say unto him, He will come and miserably destroy those wicked husbandmen, and will let out his vineyard unto other husbandmen, which shall render him the fruits in their seasons.

And when they heard it, they said, God forbid. And Jesus beheld them [and] saith unto them, What is this then that is written, Did ye never read in the scriptures, The stone which the builders rejected, the same is become the head of the corner: this is the Lord's doing, and it is marvellous in our eyes?

Therefore say I unto you, The kingdom of God shall be taken from you, and given to a nation bringing forth the fruits thereof.

And whosoever shall fall on this stone shall be broken: but on whomsoever it shall fall, it will grind him to powder.

And when the chief priests and Pharisees had heard his parables, they perceived that he spake the parable against them the same hour sought to lay hands on him.

And they said among themselves, Shall this man think that he alone can spoil this great kingdom? And they were angry with him.

But when they sought to lay hands on him, they feared the multitude [of] the people because they learned that the multitude took him for a prophet: and they left him, and went their way.

And they watched him, and sent forth spies, which should feign themselves just men, that they might take hold of his words, so that they might deliver him unto the power and authority of the governor.

And now his disciples came to him, and Jesus said unto them, Marvel ye at the words of the parable which I spake unto them?

Verily, I say unto you, I am the stone, and those wicked ones reject me.

I am the head of the corner. These Jews shall fall upon me, and shall be broken.

And the kingdom of God shall be taken from them, and shall be given to a nation bringing forth the fruits thereof; (meaning the Gentiles.)

Wherefore, on whomsoever this stone shall fall, it shall grind him to powder. And when the Lord therefore of the vineyard cometh, he will destroy those miserable, wicked men, and

will let again his vineyard unto other husbandmen, even in the last days, who shall render him the fruits in their seasons.

And then understood they the parable which he spake unto them, that the Gentiles should be destroyed also, when the Lord should descend out of heaven to reign in his vineyard, which is the earth and the inhabitants thereof.

Parable: Wedding of King's Son
Matt. 22:1–14, Luke 14:1–24, JST Matt. 22:14

And it came to pass, as he went into the house of one of the chief Pharisees to eat bread on the sabbath day, that they watched him.

And, behold, there was a certain man before him which had the dropsy.

And Jesus answering spake unto the lawyers and Pharisees, saying, Is it lawful to heal on the sabbath day?

And they held their peace. And he took him, and healed him, and let him go;

And answered them, saying, Which of you shall have an ass or an ox fallen into a pit, and will not straightway pull him out on the sabbath day?

And they could not answer him again to these things.

And he put forth a parable to those which were bidden, when he marked how they chose out the chief rooms; saying unto them,

When thou art bidden of any man to a wedding, sit not down in the highest room; lest a more honourable man than thou be bidden of him;

And he that bade thee and him come and say to thee, Give this man place; and thou begin with shame to take the lowest room.

But when thou art bidden, go and sit down in the lowest room; that when he that bade thee cometh, he may say unto thee, Friend, go up higher: then shalt thou have worship in the presence of them that sit at meat with thee.

For whosoever exalteth himself shall be abased; and he that humbleth himself shall be exalted.

Then said he also to him that bade him, When thou makest a dinner or a supper, call not thy friends, nor thy brethren, neither thy kinsmen, nor thy rich neighbours; lest they also bid thee again, and a recompence be made thee.

But when thou makest a feast, call the poor, the maimed, the lame, the blind:

And thou shalt be blessed; for they cannot recompense thee: for thou shalt be recompensed at the resurrection of the just.

And when one of them that sat at meat with him heard these things, he said unto him, Blessed is he that shall eat bread in the kingdom of God.

And Jesus answered and spake unto them again by parables, and said,

The kingdom of heaven is like unto a certain king, which made a marriage supper for his son, and bade many,

And sent forth his servants at supper time to call them that were bidden to the wedding: Come; for all things are now ready. and they all with one consent began to make excuse and would not come.

Again, he sent forth other servants, saying, Tell them which are bidden, Behold, I have prepared my dinner: my oxen and my fatlings are killed, and all things are ready: come unto the marriage.

But they made light of it, and went their ways, The first said unto him, I have bought a piece of ground, and I must needs go and see it: I pray thee have me excused.

And another said, I have bought five yoke of oxen, and I go to prove them: I pray thee have me excused.

And another said, I have married a wife, and therefore I cannot come. [The] one to his farm, another to his merchandise:

And the remnant took his servants, and entreated them spitefully, and slew them.

So that servant came, and shewed his lord these things.

But when the king, the master of the house, heard thereof he was wroth: and he sent forth his armies, and destroyed those murderers, and burned up their city.

Then saith he to his servants, The wedding is ready, but they which were bidden were not worthy.

Go ye out quickly therefore into the highways and into the streets and lanes of the city, [and] as many as ye shall find, bid to the marriage; bring in hither the poor, and the maimed, and the halt, and the blind.

So those servants went out into the highways, and gathered together all as many as they found, both bad and good: and the wedding was furnished with guests.

And the servant said, Lord, it is done as thou hast commanded, and yet there is room.

And the lord said unto the servant, Go out into the highways and hedges, and compel them to come in, that my house may be filled.

For I say unto you, That none of those men which were bidden shall taste of my supper.

And when the king came in to see the guests, he saw there a man which had not on a wedding garment:

And he saith unto him, Friend, how camest thou in hither not having a wedding garment? And he was speechless.

Then said the king to the servants, Bind him hand and foot, and take him away, and cast him into outer darkness; there shall be weeping and gnashing of teeth.

For many are called, but few are chosen wherefore all do not have on the wedding garment.

Tribute to Caesar: Pharisees and Herodians
Matt. 22:15–22, Mark 12:13–17, Luke 20:21–26

Then went the Pharisees, and took counsel how they might entangle him in his talk.

And they sent out unto him their disciples with the Herodians,

And when they were come, they say unto him, Master, we know that thou art true, and teachest the way of God in truth, neither carest thou for any man: for thou regardest not the person of men.

Tell us therefore, What thinkest thou? Is it lawful to give tribute unto Cæsar, or not?

Shall we give, or shall we not give? But Jesus, knowing their hypocrisy, perceived their wickedness and craftiness, and said, Why tempt ye me, ye hypocrites?

Shew me a penny, the tribute money. And they brought unto him a penny.

And he saith unto them, Whose is this image and superscription?

And they say unto him, Cæsar's. Then Jesus answering said unto them, Render therefore unto Cæsar the things which are Cæsar's; and unto God the things that are God's.

When they had heard these words, they could not take hold of his words before the people: and they marvelled at his answer. And left him, and went their way, [and] held their peace.

Marriage, Seven Husbands: Sadducees
Matt. 22:23–33, Mark 12:18–27, Luke 20:27–38, JST Mark 12:28,32, JST Luke 20:35

The same day came to him the Sadducees, which say that there is no resurrection, and asked him,

Saying, Master, Moses wrote unto us [and] said, If a man's brother die, and leave his wife behind him, and having no children, that his brother shall marry his wife, and raise up seed unto his brother.

Now there were with us seven brethren: and the first, when he had married a wife, deceased, having no issue or seed, left his wife unto his brother:

And the second took her, and died, neither left he any seed: and the third likewise. And the

seven had her, and left no seed:

And last of all the woman died also.

Therefore in the resurrection, when they shall rise, whose wife shall she be of the seven? for they all seven had her to wife.

Jesus answered and said unto them, Ye do err therefore, because ye know not, and understand not the scriptures, nor the power of God.

The children of this world marry, and are given in marriage:

But they which shall be accounted worthy to obtain that world, through the resurrection, when they shall rise from the dead, they neither marry, nor are given in marriage,

Neither can they die any more: but are as the angels of God in heaven, and are the children of God, being the children of the resurrection.

But as touching the resurrection of the dead, have ye not read in the book of Moses, that which was spoken unto you by God in the bush, saying,

I am the God of Abraham, and the God of Isaac, and the God of Jacob? God is not therefore the God of the dead, but of the living: for all live unto him for he raiseth them up out of their graves. Ye therefore do greatly err.

And when the multitude heard this, they were astonished at his doctrine.

Great Commandment: Pharisees
Matt. 22:34–40, Mark 12:28–31, Luke 10:25–37

But when the Pharisees had heard that he had put the Sadducees to silence, they were gathered together. Then one of them, one of the scribes, which was a lawyer, and having heard them reasoning together, and perceiving that he had answered them well, asked him a question, tempting him, and saying,

Master, which is the first great commandment of all in the law?

And Jesus said unto him, The first of all the commandments is, Hear, O Israel; The Lord our God is one Lord:

And thou shalt love the Lord thy God with all thy heart, and with all thy soul, and with all thy mind.

This is the first and great commandment.

And the second is like unto it, namely this, Thou shalt love thy neighbour as thyself. There is none other commandment greater than these.

On these two commandments hang all the law and the prophets.

And, behold, a certain lawyer stood up, and tempted him, saying, Master, what shall I do to inherit eternal life?

He said unto him, What is written in the law? how readest thou?

And he answering said, Thou shalt love the Lord thy God with all thy heart, and with all thy soul, and with all thy strength, and with all thy mind; and thy neighbour as thyself.

And he said unto him, Thou hast answered right: this do, and thou shalt live.

But he, willing to justify himself, said unto Jesus, And who is my neighbour?

And Jesus answering said, A certain man went down from Jerusalem to Jericho, and fell among thieves, which stripped him of his raiment, and wounded him, and departed, leaving him half dead.

And by chance there came down a certain priest that way: and when he saw him, he passed by on the other side.

And likewise a Levite, when he was at the place, came and looked on him, and passed by on the other side.

But a certain Samaritan, as he journeyed, came where he was: and when he saw him, he had compassion on him,

And went to him, and bound up his wounds, pouring in oil and wine, and set him on his own beast, and brought him to an inn, and took care of him.

And on the morrow when he departed, he took out two pence, and gave them to the host, and said unto him, Take care of him; and whatsoever thou spendest more, when I come again, I will repay thee.

Which now of these three, thinkest thou, was neighbour unto him that fell among the thieves? And he said, He that shewed mercy on him. Then said Jesus unto him, Go, and do thou likewise.

Pharisees Put to Silence
Matt. 22:41–46, Mark 12:35–37, Luke 20:39–44

Then certain of the scribes answering said, Master, thou hast well said.

And after that they durst not ask him any question at all. While the Pharisees were gathered together, Jesus asked them, while he taught in the temple,

Saying, What think ye of Christ? whose son is he? They say unto him, The Son of David.

And Jesus answered and said, How say the scribes that Christ is the Son of David? How then doth David in spirit call him Lord,

For David himself said by the Holy Ghost, in the book of Psalms,

The LORD said unto my Lord, Sit thou on my right hand, till I make thine enemies thy footstool?

If David then call him Lord, how is he and whence is he then his son? And the common people heard him gladly.

And no man was able to answer him a word, neither durst any man from that day forth ask him any more questions.

"but she . . . did cast in all that she had. . . ."

Widow's Mite

Mark 12:41–44, Luke 21:1–4

And Jesus sat over against the treasury, **And he looked up,** and beheld how the people cast money into the treasury: and many that were rich cast in much.

    And there came a certain poor widow, and she threw in two mites, which make a farthing.

    And he called unto him his disciples, and saith unto them, Verily, **of a truth** I say unto you, That this poor widow hath cast more in, than all they which have cast into the treasury: For all they did cast in of their abundance **unto the offerings of God**; but she of her want, **penury,** did cast in all that she had, even all her living.

Denunciation of Hypocrisy
Matt. 23:1–36, Mark 12:38–40, Luke 11:37–54, 18:9–14, 20:45–47,
JST Matt. 23:6–7, 21, 34–35, JST Luke 11:42, 53

Then in the audience or multitude of all the people, Jesus said unto his disciples, in his doctrine,

Saying, The scribes and the Pharisees, love to go in long clothing, [and] sit in Moses' seat:

All therefore whatsoever they bid you observe, that observe and do; but do not ye after their works: for they say, and do not.

For they bind heavy burdens and grievous to be borne, and lay them on men's shoulders; but they themselves will not move them with one of their fingers.

But all their works they do for to be seen of men: they make broad their phylacteries, and enlarge the borders of their garments,

And love the uppermost rooms at feasts, and the chief seats in the synagogues,

And greetings in the markets, and to be called of men, Rabbi, Rabbi.

But be not ye called Rabbi: for one is your Master, even Christ; and all ye are brethren.

And call no one your creator upon the earth, or your heavenly Father; for one is your creator and heavenly Father, even he who is in heaven.[97]

Neither be ye called masters: for one is your Master, even he whom your heavenly Father sent, which is Christ; for he hath sent him among you that ye might have life.

But he that is greatest among you shall be your servant.

And whosoever shall exalt himself shall be abased; and he that shall humble himself shall be exalted.

And as he spake, a certain Pharisee besought him to dine with him: and he went in, and sat down to meat.

And when the Pharisee saw it, he marvelled that he had not first washed before dinner.

And the Lord said unto him, woe unto you, scribes and Pharisees, hypocrites! for ye shut up the kingdom of heaven against men: for ye neither go in yourselves, neither suffer ye them that are entering to go in.

Woe unto you, scribes and Pharisees, hypocrites! for ye devour widows' houses, and for a pretence, and for a shew, make long prayer: therefore ye shall receive the greater damnation.

Woe unto you, scribes and Pharisees, hypocrites! for ye compass sea and land to make one proselyte, and when he is made, ye make him twofold more the child of hell than yourselves.

Woe unto you, ye blind guides, which say, Whosoever shall swear by the temple, it is nothing; but whosoever shall swear by the gold of the temple, he is a debtor!

Ye fools and blind: for whether is greater, the gold, or the temple that sanctifieth the gold?

And, Whosoever shall swear by the altar, it is nothing; but whosoever sweareth by the gift that is upon it, he is guilty.

Ye fools and blind: for whether is greater, the gift, or the altar that sanctifieth the gift?

Whoso therefore shall swear by the altar, sweareth by it, and by all things thereon.

---

97   Matthew reads, "man your father upon the earth: for one is your Father, which is in heaven."

"... for one is your Master, even Christ."

And whoso shall swear by the temple, sweareth by it, and by him that dwelleth therein.

And he that shall swear by heaven, sweareth by the throne of God, and by him that sitteth thereon.

Woe unto you, scribes and Pharisees, hypocrites! for ye pay tithe of mint and rue and all manner of herbs and anise and cummin, and have omitted the weightier matters of the law, judgment, the love of God, mercy, and faith: these ought ye to have done, and not to leave the other undone. Ye blind guides, which strain at a gnat, and swallow a camel who make yourselves appear unto men that ye would not commit the least sin, and yet ye yourselves, transgress the whole law. Woe unto you, scribes and Pharisees, hypocrites! for ye make clean the outside of the cup and of the platter, but within they are full of extortion, excess, ravening and wickedness.

Ye fools, did not he that made that which is without make that which is within also?

But if ye would rather give alms of such things as ye have; and observe to do all things which I have commanded you, then would your inward parts be clean also.[98]

Thou blind Pharisee, cleanse first that which is within the cup and platter, that the outside of them may be clean also.

Woe unto you, scribes and Pharisees, hypocrites! for ye are like unto whited sepulchres, which indeed appear beautiful outward, but are within full of dead men's bones, and of all uncleanness.

Even so ye also outwardly appear righteous unto men, but within ye are full of hypocrisy and iniquity.

Woe unto you, scribes and Pharisees, hypocrites! for ye are as graves which appear not, and the men that walk over them are not aware of them. Then answered one of the lawyers, and said unto him, Master, thus saying thou reproachest us also.

And he said, Woe unto you, scribes and Pharisees [and] lawyers, hypocrites! for ye lade men with burdens grievous to be borne, and ye yourselves touch not the burdens with one of your fingers.

Woe unto you! for because ye build the tombs of the prophets, and garnish the sepulchres of the righteous,

And say, If we had been in the days of our fathers, we would not have been partakers with them in the blood of the prophets.

Wherefore ye be witnesses unto yourselves, that ye are the children of them which killed the prophets.

Fill ye up then the measure of your fathers.

Ye serpents, ye generation of vipers, how can ye escape the damnation of hell?

Wherefore, behold, I send unto you prophets and apostles, and wise men, and scribes: and some of them ye shall slay, persecute, kill and crucify; and some of them shall ye scourge in your synagogues, and persecute them from city to city:

That upon you may come all the righteous blood shed upon the earth, shed from the foundation of the world, from the blood of righteous Abel unto the blood of Zacharias son of Barachias, whom ye slew between the temple and the altar.

Verily I say unto you, All these things shall come upon this generation. Ye bear testimony

---

98   Luke reads, "behold, all things are clean unto you."

against your fathers, when ye, yourselves, are partakers of the same wickedness. Behold your fathers did it through ignorance, but ye do not; wherefore, their sins shall be upon your heads. Woe unto you, lawyers! for ye have taken away the key of knowledge, the fulness of the scriptures; ye entered not in yourselves to the kingdom, and those that[99] were entering in ye hindered.

And as he said these things unto them, the scribes and the Pharisees began to urge him vehemently, and to provoke him to speak of many things:

Laying wait for him, and seeking to catch something out of his mouth, that they might accuse him.

And he spake this parable unto certain which trusted in themselves that they were righteous, and despised others:

Two men went up into the temple to pray; the one a Pharisee, and the other a publican.

The Pharisee stood and prayed thus with himself, God, I thank thee, that I am not as other men are, extortioners, unjust, adulterers, or even as this publican.

I fast twice in the week, I give tithes of all that I possess.

And the publican, standing afar off, would not lift up so much as his eyes unto heaven, but smote upon his breast, saying, God be merciful to me a sinner.

I tell you, this man went down to his house justified rather than the other: for every one that exalteth himself shall be abased; and he that humbleth himself shall be exalted.

Jesus' Lament over Jerusalem
Matt. 23:37–39, Luke 13:34–35, JST Luke 13:34

O Jerusalem, Jerusalem, thou that killest the prophets, and stonest them which are sent unto thee, how often would I have gathered thy children together, even as a hen gathereth her chickens under her wings, and ye would not!

Behold, your house is left unto you desolate.

For verily I say unto you, Ye shall not know[100] me henceforth, until ye have received from the hand of the Lord a just recompense for all your sins; till the time come when ye shall say, Blessed is he that cometh in the name of the Lord.

---

99   Luke reads, "them that"
100   Luke reads, "see"

Discourse: Signs of the Second Coming

Matt. 24:1–51, Mark 13:1–37, Luke 12:37–48, 17:20–37, 21:5–38,
JST Luke 12:21, 41–57, 21:24

And when he was demanded of the Pharisees, when the kingdom of God should come, he answered them and said, The kingdom of God cometh not with observation:

Neither shall they say, Lo here! or, lo there! for, behold, the kingdom of God has already come unto you[101].

And Jesus went out, and departed from the temple: and his disciples came to him for to shew him the buildings of the temple, and one of his disciples saith unto him, Master, see what manner of stones and what buildings are here!

And Jesus said unto them, See ye not all these things? Seest thou these great buildings? verily I say unto you, There shall not be left here one stone upon another, that shall not be thrown down.

And as he sat upon the mount of Olives over against the temple, the disciples, Peter and James and John and Andrew came unto him privately, saying, Tell us, when shall these things be? and what shall be the sign of thy coming, the sign when all these things shall be fulfilled and of the end of the world?

And Jesus answered and said unto them, The days will come, when ye shall desire to see one of the days of the Son of man, and ye shall not see it.

And they shall say to you, See here; or, see there: go not after them, nor follow them. Take heed that no man deceive you.

For many shall come in my name, saying, I am Christ; and shall deceive many.

And when ye shall hear of wars and rumours of wars: see that ye be not troubled: for all these things must come to pass, but the end is not yet.

For nation shall rise against nation, and kingdom against kingdom: and there shall be famines and troubles, and pestilences, and earthquakes, in divers places.

All these are the beginning of sorrows.

But take heed to yourselves: Then shall they deliver you up to councils; to be afflicted, and shall kill you: and ye shall be hated of all nations for my name's sake; and in the synagogues ye shall be beaten: and ye shall be brought before rulers and kings for my sake, for a testimony against them.

And then shall many be offended, and shall betray one another, and shall hate one another.

And many false prophets shall rise, and shall deceive many.

And because iniquity shall abound, the love of many shall wax cold.

But he that shall endure unto the end, the same shall be saved.

And this gospel of the kingdom must first be preached in all the world for a witness unto all nations;

But when they shall lead you, and deliver you up, take no thought beforehand what ye shall speak, neither do ye premeditate: but whatsoever shall be given you in that hour, that speak ye:

---

101   Luke reads, "is within you"

for it is not ye that speak, but the Holy Ghost.

Now the brother shall betray the brother to death, and the father the son; and children shall rise up against their parents, and shall cause them to be put to death. And ye shall be hated of all men for my name's sake: but he that shall endure unto the end, the same shall be saved, and then shall the end come.

When ye therefore shall see the abomination of desolation, spoken of by Daniel the prophet, standing in the holy place where it ought not, (whoso readeth, let him understand:)

Then let them which be in Judæa flee into the mountains:

Let him which is on the housetop not come down to take anything out of his house:

Neither let him which is in the field return back to take his clothes. And woe unto them that are with child, and to them that give suck in those days! for there shall be great distress in the land, and wrath upon this people.

And they sall fall by the edge of the sword, and shall be led away captive into all nations: and Jerusalem shall be trodden down of the Gentiles, until the times of the Gentiles be fulfilled.

But pray ye that your flight be not in the winter, neither on the sabbath day:

For in those days then shall be great tribulation, such as was not since the beginning of the creation which God created, the world to this time, no, nor ever shall be.

And except that the Lord had shortened those, there should no flesh be saved: but for the elect's sake, whom he hath chosen, those days shall be shortened.

Then if any man shall say unto you, Lo, here is Christ, or lo, there; believe it not.

For there shall arise false Christs, and false prophets, and shall shew great signs and wonders to seduce; insomuch that, if it were possible, they shall deceive the very elect.

But take ye heed: Behold, I have told you before all things.

Wherefore if they shall say unto you, Behold, he is in the desert; go not forth: behold, he is in the secret chambers; believe it not.

For as the lightning cometh out of the east, and shineth even unto the west [and], that lighteneth out of the one part under heaven, and shineth unto the other part under heaven; so shall also the coming of the Son of man be in his day. And they answered and said unto him, Where, Lord? And he said unto them, For wheresoever the carcase is, there will the eagles be gathered together.

But first must he suffer many things, and be rejected of this generation.

Immediately after the tribulation of those days shall the sun be darkened, and the moon shall not give her light, and the stars shall fall from heaven, and the powers of the heavens shall be shaken:

And then shall appear the sign of the Son

of man in heaven: and then shall all the tribes of the earth mourn, and they shall see the Son of man coming in the clouds of heaven with power and great glory.

And he then shall send his angels with a great sound of a trumpet, and they shall gather together his elect from the four winds, from one end of heaven to the other, from the uttermost part of the earth to the uttermost part of heaven.

Now learn a parable of the fig tree; When his branch is yet tender, and putteth forth leaves, ye know that summer is nigh:

So likewise ye, when ye shall see all these things come to pass, know that it is near, even at the doors.

Verily I say unto you, that this generation, the generation when the times of the Gentiles, shall not pass away till all be fulfilled.

Heaven and earth shall pass away, but my words shall not pass away.

But of that day and hour knoweth no man, no, not the angels of heaven, neither the Son, but my Father only.

Take ye heed, watch and pray: for ye know not when the time is.

For the Son of man is as a man taking a far journey, who left his house, and gave authority to his servants, and to every man his work, and commanded the porter to watch.

Watch ye therefore, and pray always, and keep my commandments, that ye may be accounted worthy to escape all these things that shall come to pass, and to stand before the Son of man when he shall come clothed in the glory of his Father.

For ye know not when the master of the house cometh, at even, or at midnight, or at the cockcrowing, or in the morning:

Lest coming suddenly he find you sleeping.

And what I say unto you I say unto all, Watch.

But as it was in the days of Noe were, so shall also the coming of the Son of man be.

For as in the days that were before the flood they were eating and drinking, marrying wives and giving in marriage, until the day that Noe entered into the ark,

And knew not until the flood came, and took them all away and destroyed them all; so shall also the coming of the Son of man be.

Likewise also as it was in the days of Lot; they did eat, they drank, they bought, they sold, they planted, they builded; But the same day that Lot went out of Sodom it rained fire and brimstone from heaven, and destroyed them all.

Even thus shall it be in the day when the Son of man is revealed.

In that day, he which shall be upon the housetop, and his stuff in the house, let him not come down to take it away: and he that is in the field, let him likewise not return back.

Remember Lot's wife.

Whosoever shall seek to save his life shall lose it; and whosoever shall lose his life shall preserve it. I tell you, in that night there shall be two men in one bed; the one shall be taken, and the other shall be left. Then shall two men be in the field; the one shall be taken, and the other left.

Two women shall be grinding together at the mill; the one shall be taken, and the other left. Blessed are those servants, whom the lord when he cometh shall find watching: verily I say unto you, that he shall gird himself, and make them to sit down to meat, and will come forth and serve them.

For, behold, he cometh in the first watch of the night, and he shall also come in the second watch, and again he shall come in the third watch.

And verily I say unto you, He hath already come, as it is written of him; and again when he shall come in the second watch, or come in the third watch, and find them so doing, blessed are those servants when he cometh.

For the Lord of those servants shall gird himself, and make them to sit down to meat, and will come forth and serve them.

And now, verily I say these things unto you, that ye may know this, that the coming of the Lord is as a thief in the night.

And it is like unto a man who is an householder, who, if he watcheth not his goods, the thief cometh in an hour of which he is not aware, and taketh his goods, and divideth them among his fellows.

And they said among themselves, If the good man of the house had known what hour the thief would come, he would have watched, and not have suffered his house to be broken through and the loss of his goods.

And he said unto them, Verily I say unto you, be ye therefore ready also; for the Son of man cometh at an hour when ye think not.

Then Peter said unto him, Lord, speakest thou this parable unto us, or unto all?

And the Lord said, I speak unto those whom the Lord shall make rulers over his household, to give his children their portion of meat in due season.

And they said, Who then is that faithful and wise servant?

And the Lord said unto them, It is that servant who watcheth, to impart his portion of meat in due season.

Blessed be that servant whom his Lord shall find, when he cometh, so doing.

Of a truth I say unto you, that he will make him ruler over all that he hath.

But the evil servant is he who is not found watching. And if that servant is not found watching, he will say in his heart, My Lord delayeth his coming; and shall begin to beat the menservants, and the maidens, and to eat, and drink, and to be drunken.

The Lord of that servant will come in a day he looketh not for, and at an hour when he is not aware, and will cut him down, and will appoint him his portion with the unbelievers and there shall be weeping and gnashing of teeth.

And that servant, which knew his lord's will, and prepared not for his Lord's coming, neither did according to his will, shall be beaten with many stripes.

But he that knew not his Lord's will, and did commit things worthy of stripes, shall be beaten with few stripes. For unto whomsoever much is given, of him shall be much required: and to whom the Lord have committed much, of him will men ask the more.

Parable: Ten Virgins
Matt. 25:1–13, Luke 12:35–36, JST Matt. 25:1

And then, at that day, before the Son of Man comes, shall the kingdom of heaven be likened unto ten virgins, which took their lamps, and went forth to meet the bridegroom.

And five of them were wise, and five were foolish.

They that were foolish took their lamps, and took no oil with them:

But the wise took oil in their vessels with their lamps.

While the bridegroom tarried, they all slumbered and slept.

And at midnight there was a cry made, Behold, the bridegroom cometh; go ye out to meet him.

Then all those virgins arose, and trimmed their lamps.

And the foolish said unto the wise, Give us of your oil; for our lamps are gone out.

But the wise answered, saying, Not so; lest there be not enough for us and you: but go ye rather to them that sell, and buy for yourselves.

And while they went to buy, the bridegroom came; and they that were ready went in with him to the marriage: and the door was shut.

Afterward came also the other virgins, saying, Lord, Lord, open to us.

But he answered and said, Verily I say unto you, I know you not.

Watch therefore, for ye know neither the day nor the hour wherein the Son of man cometh.

Let your loins be girded about, and your lights burning;

And ye yourselves like unto men that wait for their lord, when he will return from the wedding; that when he cometh and knocketh, they may open unto him immediately.

Parable: Talents

Matt. 25:14–30

For the kingdom of heaven is as a man travelling into a far country, who called his own servants, and delivered unto them his goods.

And unto one he gave five talents, to another two, and to another one; to every man according to his several ability; and straightway took his journey.

Then he that had received the five talents went and traded with the same, and made them other five talents.

And likewise he that had received two, he also gained other two.

But he that had received one went and digged in the earth, and hid his lord's money.

After a long time the lord of those servants cometh, and reckoneth with them.

And so he that had received five talents came and brought other five talents, saying, Lord, thou deliveredst unto me five talents: behold, I have gained beside them five talents more.

His lord said unto him, Well done, thou good and faithful servant: thou hast been faithful over a few things, I will make thee ruler over many things: enter thou into the joy of thy lord.

He also that had received two talents came and said, Lord, thou deliveredst unto me two talents: behold, I have gained two other talents beside them.

His lord said unto him, Well done, good and faithful servant; thou hast been faithful over a few things, I will make thee ruler over many things: enter thou into the joy of thy lord.

Then he which had received the one talent came and said, Lord, I knew thee that thou art an hard man, reaping where thou hast not sown, and gathering where thou hast not strawed:

And I was afraid, and went and hid thy talent in the earth: lo, there thou hast that is thine.

His lord answered and said unto him, Thou wicked and slothful servant, thou knewest that I reap where I sowed not, and gather where I have not strawed:

Thou oughtest therefore to have put my money to the exchangers, and then at my coming I should have received mine own with usury.

Take therefore the talent from him, and give it unto him which hath ten talents.

For unto every one that hath shall be given, and he shall have abundance: but from him that hath not shall be taken away even that which he hath.

And cast ye the unprofitable servant into outer darkness: there shall be weeping and gnashing of teeth.

Parable: Sheep, Goats
Matt. 25:31–46

When the Son of man shall come in his glory, and all the holy angels with him, then shall he sit upon the throne of his glory:

And before him shall be gathered all nations: and he shall separate them one from another, as a shepherd divideth his sheep from the goats:

And he shall set the sheep on his right hand, but the goats on the left.

Then shall the King say unto them on his right hand, Come, ye blessed of my Father, inherit the kingdom prepared for you from the foundation of the world:

For I was an hungred, and ye gave me meat: I was thirsty, and ye gave me drink: I was a stranger, and ye took me in:

Naked, and ye clothed me: I was sick, and ye visited me: I was in prison, and ye came unto me.

Then shall the righteous answer him, saying, Lord, when saw we thee an hungred, and fed thee? or thirsty, and gave thee drink?

When saw we thee a stranger, and took thee in? or naked, and clothed thee?

Or when saw we thee sick, or in prison, and came unto thee?

And the King shall answer and say unto them, Verily I say unto you, Inasmuch as ye have done it unto one of the least of these my brethren, ye have done it unto me.

Then shall he say also unto them on the left hand, Depart from me, ye cursed, into everlasting fire, prepared for the devil and his angels:

For I was an hungred, and ye gave me no meat: I was thirsty, and ye gave me no drink:

I was a stranger, and ye took me not in: naked, and ye clothed me not: sick, and in prison, and ye visited me not.

Then shall they also answer him, saying, Lord, when saw we thee an hungred, or athirst, or a stranger, or naked, or sick, or in prison, and did not minister unto thee?

Then shall he answer them, saying, Verily I say unto you, Inasmuch as ye did it not to one of the least of these, ye did it not to me.

And these shall go away into everlasting punishment: but the righteous into life eternal.

The Second Day Before Passover
Matt. 26:2, Mark 14:1

Ye know that after two days is the feast of the passover, and of unleavened bread: and the chief priests and the scribes sought how they might take the Son of man by craft, and put him to death to be crucified.

Conspiracy at Caiaphas's Palace
Matt 26:3–5, Mark 14:2

Then assembled together the chief priests, and the scribes, and the elders of the people, unto the palace of the high priest, who was called Caiaphas,

And consulted that they might take Jesus by subtilty, [or] by craft, and kill him.

But they said, Not on the feast day, lest there be an uproar among the people.

Feast with Simon the Pharisee
Matt. 26:6, Mark 14:3, Luke 7:36

Now when Jesus was in Bethany one of the Pharisees desired him that he would eat with him. And he went into the house of Simon the leper, the Pharisee, as he sat down to meat, there came a woman having an alabaster box of ointment of spikenard very precious; and she brake the box, and poured it on his head.

Jesus Anointed by Woman

Matt. 26:7–13, Mark 14:3–9, Luke 7:37–50, JST Mark 14:8

And being in Bethany in the house of Simon the leper, as he sat at meat, behold, a woman in the city, which was a sinner, when she knew that Jesus sat at meat in the Pharisee's house, came unto him having an alabaster box of very precious ointment of spikenard.

And she stood at his feet behind him weeping, and began to wash his feet with tears, and did wipe them with the hairs of her head, and kissed his feet, [and] she brake the box, and anointed them with the ointment, and poured it on his head, as he sat at meat.

Now when the Pharisee which had bidden him saw it, he spake within himself, saying, This man, if he were a prophet, would have known who and what manner of woman this is that toucheth him: for she is a sinner.

And Jesus answering said unto him, Simon, I have somewhat to say unto thee. And he saith, Master, say on.

There was a certain creditor which had two debtors: the one owed five hundred pence, and the other fifty.

And when they had nothing to pay, he frankly forgave them both. Tell me therefore, which of them will love him most?

Simon answered and said, I suppose that he, to whom he forgave most. And he said unto him, Thou hast rightly judged.

And he turned to the woman, and said unto Simon, Seest thou this woman? I entered into thine house, thou gavest me no water for my feet: but she hath washed my feet with tears, and wiped them with the hairs of her head.

Thou gavest me no kiss: but this woman since the time I came in hath not ceased to kiss my feet.

My head with oil thou didst not anoint: but this woman hath anointed my feet with ointment.

Wherefore I say unto thee, Her sins, which are many, are forgiven; for she loved much: but to whom little is forgiven, the same loveth little.

And he said unto her, Thy sins are forgiven.

And they that sat at meat with him began to say within themselves, Who is this that forgiveth sins also?

And he said to the woman, Thy faith hath saved thee; go in peace. But when his disciples saw it, there were some that had indignation within themselves, and said, To what purpose was this waste of the ointment made?

For this ointment might have been sold for more than three hundred pence, and have been given to the poor. And they murmured against her.

When Jesus understood it, he said unto them, Let her alone; Why trouble ye the woman? for she hath wrought a good work upon me.

For ye have the poor always with you, and whensoever ye will ye may do them good: but me ye have not always. She hath done what she could:

For in that she hath poured this ointment on my body, she is come aforehand and this which she has done unto me, shall be had in remembrance in generations to come, wheresoever my gospel shall be preached; for verily she has come beforehand to anoint my body for my burial.

Verily I say unto you, Wheresoever this gospel shall be preached throughout the whole world, there shall also this, that this woman hath done, be told, and spoken of for a memorial of her.

Judas's Conspiracy to Betray Jesus
Matt. 26:14–16, Mark 14:10–11, Luke 22:1–6

Now the feast of unleavened bread drew nigh, which is called the Passover.

And the chief priests and scribes sought how they might kill him; for they feared the people.

Then entered Satan into Judas surnamed Iscariot, being of the number of the twelve.

And he went his way, and communed with the chief priests and captains, how he might betray him unto them.

And said unto them, What will ye give me, and I will deliver him unto you? And when they heard it, they were glad, and promised, and covenanted with him for thirty pieces of silver.

And he promised, and from that time he sought opportunity to conveniently betray him unto them in the absence of the multitude.

The First Day of Unleavened Bread
Matt. 26:17–19, Mark 14:12–16, Luke 22:7–13

Now the first day of the feast of unleavened bread, when the passover must be killed, the disciples came to Jesus.

And he sent Peter and John, saying, Go and prepare us the passover, that we may eat.

And they said unto him, Where wilt thou that we go and prepare for thee that thou mayest eat the passover?

And he said unto them, Behold, Go ye into the city, and when ye are entered into the city there shall meet you a man bearing a pitcher of water: follow him into the house where he entereth in.

And wheresoever he shall go in, say ye unto the goodman of the house, The Master saith unto thee, My time is at hand; Where is the guestchamber, where I shall eat the passover with my disciples?

And he will shew you a large upper room furnished and prepared: there make ready for us.

And the disciples did as Jesus had appointed them;

And they went forth, and came into the city, and found as he had said unto them: and they made ready the passover.

Eve of the Passover
Matt. 26:20, Mark 14:17, Luke 22:14, John 13:1–2

Now before the feast of the passover, when Jesus knew that his hour was come that he should depart out of this world unto the Father, having loved his own which were in the world, he loved them unto the end.

Now when the evening hour was come, he cometh and sat down with the twelve apostles.

And supper being ended, the devil having now put into the heart of Judas Iscariot, Simon's son, to betray him.

"One of You Shall Betray Me"
Matt. 26:2–24, Mark 14:18–21, Luke 22:21–23, John 13:18–22

And as they sat and did eat, Jesus said, I speak not of you all: I know whom I have chosen: but that the scripture may be fulfilled, He that eateth bread with me hath lifted up his heel against me.

Now I tell you before it come, that, when it is come to pass, ye may believe that I am he.

Verily, verily, I say unto you, He that receiveth whomsoever I send receiveth me; and he that receiveth me receiveth him that sent me.

When Jesus had thus said, he was troubled in spirit, and testified, and said,

Verily, verily, I say unto you, that the hand of him that betrayeth me is with me and eateth with me on the table.

And truly the Son of man goeth, as it was determined: but woe unto that man by whom he is betrayed!

And they were exceeding sorrowful, and the disciples looked one on another, and began to enquire among themselves, which of them it was that should do this thing, doubting of whom he spake.

And one by one began every one of them to say unto him, Lord, is it I? and another said, Is it I?

And he answered and said unto them, It is one of the twelve, He that dippeth his hand with me in the dish, the same shall betray me.

The Son of man indeed goeth, as it is written of him: but woe unto that man by whom the Son of man is betrayed! it had been good for that man if he had not been born.

Betrayer Identified

Matt. 26:25, John 13:23–30

Now there was leaning on Jesus' bosom one of his disciples, whom Jesus loved.

Simon Peter therefore beckoned to him, that he should ask who it should be of whom he spake.

He then lying on Jesus' breast saith unto him, Lord, who is it? Jesus answered, He it is, to whom I shall give a sop, when I have dipped it. And when he had dipped the sop, he gave it to Judas Iscariot, the son of Simon.

Then Judas, which betrayed him, answered and said, Master, is it I? He said unto him, Thou hast said.

And after the sop Satan entered into him. Then said Jesus unto him, That thou doest, do quickly.

Now no man at the table knew for what intent he spake this unto him.

For some of them thought, because Judas had the bag, that Jesus had said unto him, Buy those things that we have need of against the feast; or, that he should give something to the poor.

He then having received the sop went immediately out: and it was night.

Sacrament Instituted

Matt. 26:26–29, Mark 14:22–25, Luke 22:15–20,
JST Matt. 26:22, 24–25, JST Mark 14:20–25, JST Luke 22:16

And he said unto them, With desire I have desired to eat this passover with you before I suffer:

And as they were eating, Jesus took bread, and gave thanks, and brake it, and blessed it[102] and gave it to his disciples, and said, Take it, eat;

Behold this is for you to do in remembrance of my body, which is given a ransom for you: this do in remembrance of me; for as oft as ye do this ye will remember this hour that I was with you.

For I say unto you, I will not any more eat thereof, until it be fulfilled which is written in the prophets concerning me. Then I will partake with you in the kingdom of God.

---

102 Matthew reads, "blessed it, and brake it,"

". . . for you to do in remembrance of my body. . . ."

Likewise also, he took the cup, after supper, and when he had given thanks, and gave it to them, and said, Take this, and divide it among yourselves: saying, Drink ye all of it; and they all drank of it.

And he said unto them, For this cup is in remembrance of my blood of the new testament which I give unto you, which is shed for as many as shall believe on my name for the remission of sins, for of me ye shall bear record unto all the world.

And I give unto you a commandment, that ye shall observe to do the things which ye have seen me do, and bear record of me even unto the end.

And as oft as ye do this ordinance, ye will remember me in this hour that I was with you and drank with you of this cup, even the last time in my ministry.

But verily, I say unto you, Of this ye shall bear record; for I will not drink henceforth of this fruit of the vine, until that day when I drink it new with you, [when] my Father's kingdom, the kingdom of God, shall come.

Jesus Washes Disciples' Feet
John 13:2–5

And supper being ended, the devil having now put into the heart of Judas Iscariot, Simon's son, to betray him;

Jesus knowing that the Father had given all things into his hands, and that he was come from God, and went to God;

He riseth from supper, and laid aside his garments; and took a towel, and girded himself.

After that he poureth water into a bason, and began to wash the disciples' feet, and to wipe them with the towel wherewith he was girded.

"After that he poureth water into a bason, and began to wash the disciples' feet. . . ."

Peter's Protest

John 13:6–12, JST John 13:8–10

Then cometh he to Simon Peter: and Peter saith unto him, <u>Thou needest not to wash my feet.</u>[103] Jesus answered and said unto him, If I wash thee not, thou hast no part with me.

Simon Peter saith unto him, Lord, not my feet only, but also my hands and my head.

Jesus saith to him, He that is washed needeth not save to wash his feet, but is clean every whit: and ye are clean, but not all.

For he knew who should betray him; therefore said he, Ye are not all clean.

So after he had washed their feet, and had taken his garments, and was set down again, he said unto them, Know ye what I have done to you?

Jesus' Example

John 13:13–17

Ye call me Master and Lord: and ye say well; for so I am.

If I then, your Lord and Master, have washed your feet; ye also ought to wash one another's feet.

For I have given you an example, that ye should do as I have done to you.

Verily, verily, I say unto you, The servant is not greater than his lord; neither he that is sent greater than he that sent him.

If ye know these things, happy are ye if ye do them.

A New Commandment

John 13:31–35

Therefore, when he was gone out, Jesus said, Now is the Son of man glorified, and God is glorified in him.

If God be glorified in him, God shall also glorify him in himself, and shall straightway glorify him.

Little children, yet a little while I am with you. Ye shall seek me: and as I said unto the Jews, Whither I go, ye cannot come; so now I say to you.

A new commandment I give unto you, That ye love one another; as I have loved you, that ye also love one another. By this shall all men know that ye are my disciples, if ye have love one to another.

---

103 John reads, "Thou shalt never wash my feet"

Jesus Comforts the Disciples
John 14:1–15

LET not your heart be troubled: ye believe in God, believe also in me.

In my Father's house are many mansions: if it were not so, I would have told you. I go to prepare a place for you.

And if I go and prepare a place for you, I will come again, and receive you unto myself; that where I am, there ye may be also.

And whither I go ye know, and the way ye know.

Thomas saith unto him, Lord, we know not whither thou goest; and how can we know the way?

Jesus saith unto him, I am the way, the truth, and the life: no man cometh unto the Father, but by me.

If ye had known me, ye should have known my Father also: and from henceforth ye know him, and have seen him.

Philip saith unto him, Lord, shew us the Father, and it sufficeth us.

Jesus saith unto him, Have I been so long time with you, and yet hast thou not known me, Philip? he that hath seen me hath seen the Father; and how sayest thou then, Shew us the Father?

Believest thou not that I am in the Father, and the Father in me? the words that I speak unto you I speak not of myself: but the Father that dwelleth in me, he doeth the works.

Believe me that I am in the Father, and the Father in me: or else believe me for the very works' sake.

Verily, verily, I say unto you, He that believeth on me, the works that I do shall he do also; and greater works than these shall he do; because I go unto my Father.

And whatsoever ye shall ask in my name, that will I do, that the Father may be glorified in the Son.

If ye shall ask any thing in my name, I will do it.

If ye love me, keep my commandments.

Another Comforter
John 14:16–31, JST John 14:30

And I will pray the Father, and he shall give you another Comforter, that he may abide with you for ever;

Even the Spirit of truth; whom the world cannot receive, because it seeth him not, neither knoweth him: but ye know him; for he dwelleth with you, and shall be in you.

I will not leave you comfortless: I will come to you.

Yet a little while, and the world seeth me no more; but ye see me: because I live, ye shall live also.

At that day ye shall know that I am in my Father, and ye in me, and I in you.

He that hath my commandments, and keepeth them, he it is that loveth me: and he that loveth me shall be loved of my Father, and I will love him, and will manifest myself to him.

Judas saith unto him, not Iscariot, Lord, how is it that thou wilt manifest thyself unto us, and not unto the world?

Jesus answered and said unto him, If a man love me, he will keep my words: and my Father will love him, and we will come unto him, and make our abode with him.

He that loveth me not keepeth not my sayings: and the word which ye hear is not mine, but the Father's which sent me.

These things have I spoken unto you, being yet present with you.

But the Comforter, which is the Holy Ghost, whom the Father will send in my name, he shall teach you all things, and bring all things to your remembrance, whatsoever I have said unto you.

Peace I leave with you, my peace I give unto you: not as the world giveth, give I unto you. Let not your heart be troubled, neither let it be afraid.

Ye have heard how I said unto you, I go away, and come again unto you. If ye loved me, ye would rejoice, because I said, I go unto the Father: for my Father is greater than I.

And now I have told you before it come to pass, that, when it is come to pass, ye might believe.

Hereafter I will not talk much with you: for the prince of <u>darkness, who is of</u> this world cometh, <u>but</u> hath <u>no power over me</u>[104]<u>, but he hath power over you</u>.

But that the world may know that I love the Father; and as the Father gave me commandment, even so I do. Arise, let us go hence.

The True Vine

John 15:1–8

I AM the true vine, and my Father is the husbandman.

Every branch in me that beareth not fruit he taketh away: and every branch that beareth fruit, he purgeth it, that it may bring forth more fruit.

Now ye are clean through the word which I have spoken unto you.

Abide in me, and I in you. As the branch cannot bear fruit of itself, except it abide in the vine; no more can ye, except ye abide in me.

---

104 John reads, "nothing in me"

I am the vine, ye are the branches: He that abideth in me, and I in him, the same bringeth forth much fruit: for without me ye can do nothing.

If a man abide not in me, he is cast forth as a branch, and is withered; and men gather them, and cast them into the fire, and they are burned.

If ye abide in me, and my words abide in you, ye shall ask what ye will, and it shall be done unto you.

Herein is my Father glorified, that ye bear much fruit; so shall ye be my disciples.

Love One Another
John 15:9–17

As the Father hath loved me, so have I loved you: continue ye in my love.

If ye keep my commandments, ye shall abide in my love; even as I have kept my Father's commandments, and abide in his love.

These things have I spoken unto you, that my joy might remain in you, and that your joy might be full.

This is my commandment, That ye love one another, as I have loved you.

Greater love hath no man than this, that a man lay down his life for his friends. Ye are my friends, if ye do whatsoever I command you.

Henceforth I call you not servants; for the servant knoweth not what his lord doeth: but I have called you friends; for all things that I have heard of my Father I have made known unto you.

Ye have not chosen me, but I have chosen you, and ordained you, that ye should go and bring forth fruit, and that your fruit should remain: that whatsoever ye shall ask of the Father in my name, he may give it you.

These things I command you, that ye love one another.

Hatred of the World
John 15:18–25

If the world hate you, ye know that it hated me before it hated you.

If ye were of the world, the world would love his own: but because ye are not of the world, but I have chosen you out of the world, therefore the world hateth you.

Remember the word that I said unto you, The servant is not greater than his lord. If they have persecuted me, they will also persecute you; if they have kept my saying, they will keep yours also.

But all these things will they do unto you for my name's sake, because they know not him that sent me.

If I had not come and spoken unto them, they had not had sin: but now they have no cloke for their sin.

He that hateth me hateth my Father also.

If I had not done among them the works which none other man did, they had not had sin: but now have they both seen and hated both me and my Father.

But this cometh to pass, that the word might be fulfilled that is written in their law, They hated me without a cause.

The Spirit of Truth Testifies
John 15:26–27

But when the Comforter is come, whom I will send unto you from the Father, even the Spirit of truth, which proceedeth from the Father, he shall testify of me:

And ye also shall bear witness, because ye have been with me from the beginning.

Warnings to the Apostles
John 16:1–6

THESE things have I spoken unto you, that ye should not be offended.

They shall put you out of the synagogues: yea, the time cometh, that whosoever killeth you will think that he doeth God service.

And these things will they do unto you, because they have not known the Father, nor me.

But these things have I told you, that when the time shall come, ye may remember that I told you of them. And these things I said not unto you at the beginning, because I was with you.

But now I go my way to him that sent me; and none of you asketh me, Whither goest thou?

But because I have said these things unto you, sorrow hath filled your heart.

The Comforter
John 16:7–16

Nevertheless I tell you the truth; It is expedient for you that I go away: for if I go not away, the Comforter will not come unto you; but if I depart, I will send him unto you.

And when he is come, he will reprove the world of sin, and of righteousness, and of judgment:

Of sin, because they believe not on me;

Of righteousness, because I go to my Father, and ye see me no more;

Of judgment, because the prince of this world is judged.

I have yet many things to say unto you, but ye cannot bear them now.

Howbeit when he, the Spirit of truth, is come, he will guide you into all truth: for he shall not speak of himself; but whatsoever he shall hear, that shall he speak: and he will shew you things to come.

He shall glorify me: for he shall receive of mine, and shall shew it unto you.

All things that the Father hath are mine: therefore said I, that he shall take of mine, and shall shew it unto you.

A little while, and ye shall not see me: and again, a little while, and ye shall see me, because I go to the Father.

Opposition: Joy and Sorrow
John 16:17–31, JST John 16:23

Then said some of his disciples among themselves, What is this that he saith unto us, A little while, and ye shall not see me: and again, a little while, and ye shall see me: and, Because I go to the Father?

They said therefore, What is this that he saith, A little while? we cannot tell what he saith.

Now Jesus knew that they were desirous to ask him, and said unto them, Do ye enquire among yourselves of that I said, A little while, and ye shall not see me: and again, a little while, and ye shall see me?

Verily, verily, I say unto you, That ye shall weep and lament, but the world shall rejoice: and ye shall be sorrowful, but your sorrow shall be turned into joy.

A woman when she is in travail hath sorrow, because her hour is come: but as soon as she is delivered of the child, she remembereth no more the anguish, for joy that a man is born into the world.

And ye now therefore have sorrow: but I will see you again, and your heart shall rejoice, and your joy no man taketh from you.

And in that day ye shall ask me nothing <u>but it shall be done unto you</u>. Verily, verily, I say unto you, Whatsoever ye shall ask the Father in my name, he will give it you.

Hitherto have ye asked nothing in my name: ask, and ye shall receive, that your joy may be full.

These things have I spoken unto you in proverbs: but the time cometh, when I shall no more speak unto you in proverbs, but I shall shew you plainly of the Father.

At that day ye shall ask in my name: and I say not unto you, that I will pray the Father for you:

For the Father himself loveth you, because ye have loved me, and have believed that I came out from God.

I came forth from the Father, and am come into the world: again, I leave the world, and go to the Father.

His disciples said unto him, Lo, now speakest thou plainly, and speakest no proverb. Now are we sure that thou knowest all things, and needest not that any man should ask thee: by this we believe that thou camest forth from God.

Jesus answered them, Do ye now believe?

Prophecy: Flock to Be Scattered
Matt. 26:31–32, John 16:32–33

Then saith Jesus unto them, All ye shall be offended because of me this night: for it is written, I will smite the shepherd, and the sheep of the flock shall be scattered abroad.

But after I am risen again, I will go before you into Galilee. Behold, the hour cometh, yea, is now come, that ye shall be scattered, every man to his own, and shall leave me alone: and yet I am not alone, because the Father is with me.

These things I have spoken unto you, that in me ye might have peace. In the world ye shall have tribulation: but be of good cheer; I have overcome the world.

Jesus' Great Intercessory Prayer
John 17:1–26

THESE words spake Jesus, and lifted up his eyes to heaven, and said, Father, the hour is come; glorify thy Son, that thy Son also may glorify thee:

As thou hast given him power over all flesh, that he should give eternal life to as many as thou hast given him.

And this is life eternal, that they might know thee the only true God, and Jesus Christ, whom thou hast sent.

I have glorified thee on the earth: I have finished the work which thou gavest me to do.

And now, O Father, glorify thou me with thine own self with the glory which I had with thee before the world was.

I have manifested thy name unto the men which thou gavest me out of the world: thine they were, and thou gavest them me; and they have kept thy word.

Now they have known that all things whatsoever thou hast given me are of thee.

For I have given unto them the words which thou gavest me; and they have received them, and have known surely that I came out from thee, and they have believed that thou didst send me.

I pray for them: I pray not for the world, but for them which thou hast given me; for they are thine.

And all mine are thine, and thine are mine; and I am glorified in them.

And now I am no more in the world, but these are in the world, and I come to thee. Holy Father, keep through thine own name those whom thou hast given me, that they may be one, as we are.

While I was with them in the world, I kept them in thy name: those that thou gavest me I have kept, and none of them is lost, but the son of perdition; that the scripture might be fulfilled.

And now come I to thee; and these things I speak in the world, that they might have my joy fulfilled in themselves.

I have given them thy word; and the world hath hated them, because they are not of the world, even as I am not of the world.

I pray not that thou shouldest take them out of the world, but that thou shouldest keep them from the evil.

They are not of the world, even as I am not of the world. Sanctify them through thy truth: thy word is truth.

As thou hast sent me into the world, even so have I also sent them into the world.

And for their sakes I sanctify myself, that they also might be sanctified through the truth.

Neither pray I for these alone, but for them also which shall believe on me through their word;

That they all may be one; as thou, Father, art in me, and I in thee, that they also may be one in us: that the world may believe that thou hast sent me.

And the glory which thou gavest me I have given them; that they may be one, even as we are one:

I in them, and thou in me, that they may be made perfect in one; and that the world may know that thou hast sent me, and hast loved them, as thou hast loved me.

Father, I will that they also, whom thou hast given me, be with me where I am; that they may behold my glory, which thou hast given me: for thou lovedst me before the foundation of the world.

O righteous Father, the world hath not known thee: but I have known thee, and these have known that thou hast sent me.

And I have declared unto them thy name, and will declare it: that the love wherewith thou hast loved me may be in them, and I in them.

Retirement to Gethsemane

Matt. 26:30, Mark 14:26, Luke 22:39, John 18:1

Luke adds no additional information

WHEN Jesus had spoken these words, and when they had sung an hymn, he came out, and went, as he was wont, [and] he went forth with his disciples over the brook Cedron, and they went out into the mount of Olives, where was a garden, into the which he entered, and his disciples also followed him.

Peter: "When Thou Art Converted"

Luke 22:31–32, JST Luke 22:31

And the Lord said, Simon, Simon, behold, Satan hath desired to have you, that he may sift the children of the kingdom[105] as wheat:

But I have prayed for thee, that thy faith fail not: and when thou art converted, strengthen thy brethren.

Prophecy: "Before the Cock Crow"

Matt. 26:33–35, Mark 14:29–31, Luke 22:33–34, John 13:36–38

Simon Peter said unto him, Lord, whither goest thou? Jesus answered him, Whither I go, thou canst not follow me now; but thou shalt follow me afterwards. Peter answered and said unto him, Lord, why cannot I follow thee now? I will lay down my life for thy sake. I am ready to go with thee, both into prison, and to death.

Although all men shall be offended because of thee, yet will I never be offended.

Jesus answered him, and said unto him, Wilt thou lay down thy life for my sake? Verily, verily, I say unto thee, That this day, even in this night, before the cock crow twice, thou shalt deny that thou knowest me thrice.

But Peter spake the more vehemently, unto him, Though I should die with thee, yet will I not deny thee in any wise. Likewise also said all the disciples.

---

105 Luke reads, "you"

"Reckoned Among the Transgressors"
Luke 22:35–38

And he said unto them, When I sent you without purse, and scrip, and shoes, lacked ye any thing? And they said, Nothing.

Then said he unto them, But now, he that hath a purse, let him take it, and likewise his scrip: and he that hath no sword, let him sell his garment, and buy one.

For I say unto you, that this that is written must yet be accomplished in me, And he was reckoned among the transgressors: for the things concerning me have an end.

And they said, Lord, behold, here are two swords. And he said unto them, It is enough.

Jesus' Suffering and Prayers
Matt. 26:36–46, Mark 14:32–42, Luke 22:40–46, JST Mark 14:36–38, JST Luke 22:44

Then cometh Jesus with them unto a place called Gethsemane which was a garden, and the disciples began to be sore amazed, and to be very heavy, and to complain in their hearts, wondering if this be the Messiah. And Jesus knowing their hearts saith unto the disciples, Sit ye here, while I shall go and pray yonder.

And he took with him Peter and the two sons of Zebedee, James and John, and rebuked them, and said unto them, My soul is exceeding sorrowful, and sore amazed, and very heavy.

And when he was at the place, Then saith he unto them, My soul is exceeding sorrowful, even unto death: tarry ye here, and watch with me. Pray that ye enter not into temptation.

And he went forward a little further, And he was withdrawn from them about a stone's cast, and fell on the ground, on his face, and kneeled down and prayed, saying, Abba, O my Father, if it be possible, or if thou be willing, let the hour [of] this cup pass from me: nevertheless not as I will, but as thou wilt.

And he cometh unto the disciples, and findeth them asleep for sorrow, and saith unto Simon Peter, Why sleepest thou? What, could ye not watch with me one hour?

Rise, Watch and pray, that ye enter not into temptation: the spirit indeed is truly willing, and ready, but the flesh is weak.

He went away again the second time, and prayed, and spake the same words, saying, O my Father, if this cup may not pass away from me, except I drink it, thy will be done.

And he returned [and] came and found

them asleep again: for their eyes were heavy, neither wist they what to answer him.

And he left them, and went away again, and prayed the third time, saying the same words.

And there appeared an angel unto him from heaven, strengthening him.

And being in an agony he prayed more earnestly: and he sweat as it were[106], great drops of blood falling down to the ground.

And when he rose up from prayer, cometh he to his disciples, the third time, and saith unto them, Sleep on now, and take your rest: it is enough, behold, the hour is at hand, and the Son of man is betrayed into the hands of sinners.

Rise up, let us be going: behold, he is at hand that doth betray me.

Judas's Betrayal
Matt. 26:47–50, Mark 14:43–46, Luke 22:47–48, John 18:2–3

And Judas also, which betrayed him, knew the place: for Jesus ofttimes resorted thither with his disciples.

Judas then, having received a band of men and officers from the chief priests and Pharisees, cometh thither with lanterns and torches and weapons.

And immediately, while he yet spake, lo, Judas, one of the twelve, came, and drew near unto Jesus to kiss him, and with him a great multitude with swords and staves, from the chief priests and the scribes and elders of the people.

Now he that betrayed had given them a token, [or] a sign, saying, Whomsoever I shall kiss, that same is he: hold him fast, take him, and lead him away safely.

And forthwith he came to Jesus, [and] he goeth straightway to him, and said, Hail, Master; master; and kissed him.

And Jesus said unto him, Friend, wherefore art thou come? Judas, betrayest thou the Son of man with a kiss? Then came they, and they laid their hands on Jesus, and took him.

Arresting Officers Fall
John 18:4–9

Jesus therefore, knowing all things that should come upon him, went forth, and said unto them, Whom seek ye?

They answered him, Jesus of Nazareth. Jesus saith unto them, I am he. And Judas also, which betrayed him, stood with them.

As soon then as he had said unto them, I am he, they went backward, and fell to the ground.

Then asked he them again, Whom seek ye? And they said, Jesus of Nazareth.

Jesus answered, I have told you that I am he: if therefore ye seek me, let these go their way.

---

106 Luke reads, "his sweat was as it were"

Peter Defends Jesus with a Sword
Matt. 26:51–55, Mark 14:47, Luke 22:49–53, John 18:10–11

When they which were about him saw what would follow, they said unto him, Lord, shall we smite with the sword?

And, behold, one of them that stood which were with Jesus stretched out his hand, and drew his sword, and struck a servant of the high priest's, and smote off his right ear. The servant's name was Malchus.

Then Jesus answered and said unto Peter, Suffer ye thus far. Put up again thy sword into the sheath: the cup which my Father hath given me, shall I not drink it? for all they that take the sword shall perish with the sword.

Thinkest thou that I cannot now pray to my Father, and he shall presently give me more than twelve legions of angels?

But how then shall the scriptures be fulfilled, that thus it must be? And he touched his ear, and healed him.

Then Jesus said unto the chief priests, and captains of the temple, and the elders, which were come to him, Be ye come out, as against a thief, with swords and staves for to take me?

When I was daily with you teaching in the temple, ye stretched forth no hands against me, and ye laid no hold on me. [B]ut this is your hour, and the power of darkness.

Disciples Flee
Matt. 26:56, Mark 14:50

Mark adds no additional information

But all this was done, that the scriptures of the prophets might be fulfilled. Then all the disciples forsook him, and fled.

Jesus Arrested
Matt. 26:57, Mark 14:51–52, Luke 22:54, John 18:12, JST Mark 14:51

Then the band and the captain and officers of the Jews took Jesus, and bound him,

And they that had laid hold on Jesus led him away and took him to Caiaphas the high priest, where the scribes and the elders were assembled.

And there followed him a disciple[107], having a linen cloth cast about his naked body; and the young men laid hold on him:

And he left the linen cloth, and fled from them naked.

---

107 Marks reads, "certain young man"

Hearing Before the Chief Priests

Matt. 26:57–68, Mark 14:53–65,
Luke 22:54, John 18:13, 19–24

And led him away to Annas first; for he was father in law to Caiaphas, which was the high priest that same year.

The high priest then asked Jesus of his disciples, and of his doctrine.

Jesus answered him, I spake openly to the world; I ever taught in the synagogue, and in the temple, whither the Jews always resort; and in secret have I said nothing.

Why askest thou me? ask them which heard me, what I have said unto them: behold, they know what I said.

And when he had thus spoken, one of the officers which stood by struck Jesus with the palm of his hand, saying, Answerest thou the high priest so?

Jesus answered him, If I have spoken evil, bear witness of the evil: but if well, why smitest thou me?

Now Annas had sent him bound unto Caiaphas the high priest.

And they that had laid hold on Jesus led him away and took him to Caiaphas the high priest, where all the chief priests, the scribes and the elders were assembled.

But Peter followed him afar off even unto the high priest's palace, and went in, and sat with the servants, and warmed himself at the fire to see the end.

Now the chief priests, and elders, and all the council, sought false witness against Jesus, to put him to death;

But found none: yea, though many false witnesses came, but their witness agreed not together. At the last came two certain false witnesses,

And said, We heard this fellow say, I am able to destroy the temple of God that is made with hands, and to build another in three days without hands.

But neither so did their witness agree together.

And the high priest arose in the midst, and said unto him, Answerest thou nothing? what is it which these witness against thee?

But Jesus held his peace and answered nothing. And the high priest answered and said unto him, I adjure thee by the living God, that thou tell us whether thou be the Christ, the Son of the Blessed God?

Jesus saith unto him, Thou hast said: nevertheless I say unto you, I am. Hereafter shall ye see the Son of man sitting on the right hand of power, and coming in the clouds of heaven.

Then the high priest rent his clothes, saying, He hath spoken blasphemy; what further need have we of witnesses? behold, now ye have heard his blasphemy.

What think ye? They answered and said, He is guilty of death.

Then did they spit on him and to cover his face, and buffeted him; and others smote him with the palms of their hands,

Saying, Prophesy unto us, thou Christ, Who is he that smote thee?

Peter's Denial
Matt. 26:69–75, Mark 14:66–72, Luke 22:55–62, John 18:15–18, 25–27

And Simon Peter followed Jesus, and so did another disciple: that disciple was known unto the high priest, and went in with Jesus into the palace of the high priest.

But Peter stood at the door without. Then went out that other disciple, which was known unto the high priest,

And as Peter was beneath in the palace, there cometh one of the maids of the high priest: and [he] spake unto her that kept the door, and brought in Peter.

And the servants and officers stood there, and they kindled a fire in the midst of the hall made of coals; for it was cold: and they warmed themselves: and were set down together, and Peter stood with them, and warmed himself.

Now Peter sat without in the palace: and there cometh a damsel, one of the maids of the high priest that kept the door unto Peter:

And when she saw Peter warming himself, came unto him, and earnestly looked upon him, saying, Thou also wast with Jesus of Galilee.

Jesus of Nazareth. Art not thou also one of this man's disciples? But he denied him, before them all, saying, I am not, I know him not, neither understand I what thou sayest.

And he went out into the porch; and the cock crew. And when he was gone out into the porch,

And after a little while another maid saw him again, and began to say unto them that were there, This is one of them, Thou art also of them. This fellow was also with Jesus of Nazareth. They said therefore unto him, Art not thou also one of his disciples? And again he denied with an oath, I am not. I do not know the man. And after a little while about the space of one hour after another confidently affirmed, saying, Of a truth this fellow also was with him: for he is a Galilæan.

One of the servants of the high priest, being his kinsman whose ear Peter cut off, came unto him they that stood by, and said again to Peter, Did not I see thee in the garden with him? Surely thou also art one of them; for thou art a Galilæan, for thy speech bewrayeth thee.

Then began he to curse and to swear, saying, Man, I know not what thou sayest. I know not the man of whom ye speak. And immediately while he yet spake, the cock crew the second time.

And the Lord turned, and looked upon Peter. And Peter called to mind, and remembered the word of the Lord, Jesus, which said unto him, Before the cock crow twice, thou shalt deny me thrice. And when he thought thereon, he went out, and wept bitterly.

". . . And the Lord turned, and looked upon Peter."

Soldiers Mock Jesus
Luke 22:63–65

And the men that held Jesus mocked him, and smote him.

And when they had blindfolded him, they struck him on the face, and asked him, saying, Prophesy, who is it that smote thee?

And many other things blasphemously spake they against him.

The Next Morning
Matt. 27:1, Mark 15:1, Luke 22:66, John 18:28

And straightway as soon as it was day, when the morning was come, all the chief priests and elders of the people and the scribes and the whole council came together, took counsel against Jesus to put him to death: and bound Jesus,

Then led they Jesus from Caiaphas unto the hall of judgment, and delivered him to Pilate, and it was early; and they themselves went not into the judgment hall, lest they should be defiled; but that they might eat the passover.

Hearing before Caiaphas
Matt. 27:1, Mark 15:1, Luke 22:66–71, John 18:24, 28

Now Annas had sent him bound unto Caiaphas the high priest.

And straightway as soon as it was day, when the morning was come, the elders of the people and the chief priests and the scribes, and the whole council came together, and led him into their council, saying,

Art thou the Christ? tell us. And he said unto them, If I tell you, ye will not believe:

And if I also ask you, ye will not answer me, nor let me go.

Hereafter shall the Son of man sit on the right hand of the power of God.

Then said they all, Art thou then the Son of God? And he said unto them, Ye say that I am.

And they said, What need we any further witness? for we ourselves have heard of his own mouth.

Then led they Jesus from Caiaphas unto the hall of judgment: and it was early; and they themselves went not into the judgment hall, lest they should be defiled; but that they might eat the passover.

Hearing Before Pilate
Matt. 27:2, 11–14, Mark 15:1–5, Luke 23:1–6, John 18:29–38, JST Mark 15:4

And straightway in the morning the chief priests held a consultation with the elders and scribes and the whole council,

And when they had bound him, And the whole multitude of them arose, they led him away, and delivered him to Pontius Pilate the governor.

And Jesus stood before the governor:

Pilate then went out unto them, and said, What accusation bring ye against this man? They answered and said unto him,

And they began to accuse him, saying, We found this fellow perverting the nation, and forbidding to give tribute to Cæsar, saying that he himself is Christ a King.

If he were not a malefactor, we would not have delivered him up unto thee.

Then said Pilate unto them, Take ye him, and judge him according to your law. The Jews therefore said unto him, It is not lawful for us to put any man to death:

That the saying of Jesus might be fulfilled, which he spake, signifying what death he should die.

Then Pilate entered into the judgment hall again, and Pilate the governor called Jesus, and asked him, saying, Art thou the King of the Jews?

Jesus answered him, Sayest thou this thing of thyself, or did others tell it thee of me?

Pilate answered, Am I a Jew? Thine own nation and the chief priests have delivered thee unto me: what hast thou done?

Jesus answered, My kingdom is not of this world: if my kingdom were of this world, then would my servants fight, that I should not be delivered to the Jews: but now is my kingdom not from hence.

Pilate therefore said unto him, Art thou a king then? And Jesus answering said unto him, Thou sayest that I am a king. I am even as thou sayest. To this end was I born, and for this cause came I into the world, that I should bear witness unto the truth. Every one that is of the truth heareth my voice.

Pilate saith unto him, What is truth?

And when he was accused of the chief priests and elders of many things, he answered nothing.

Then said Pilate unto him, again, saying, Answerest thou nothing? behold Hearest thou not how many things they witness against thee? And Jesus yet answered him nothing; insomuch that Pilate the governor marvelled greatly, and he went out again unto the Jews,

Then said Pilate to the chief priests and to the people, I find no fault in this man.

And they were the more fierce, saying, He stirreth up the people, teaching throughout all Jewry, beginning from Galilee to this place.

When Pilate heard of Galilee, he asked whether the man were a Galilæan.

Judas's Remorse and Death
Matt. 27:3–10, JST Matt. 27:5–6

Then Judas, which had betrayed him, when he saw that he was condemned, repented himself, and brought again the thirty pieces of silver to the chief priests and elders,

Saying, I have sinned in that I have betrayed the innocent blood. And they said, What is that to us? see thou to it; thy sins be upon thee[108].

And he cast down the pieces of silver in the temple, and departed, and went and hanged himself on a tree. And straightway he fell down, and his bowels gushed out, and he died.

And the chief priests took the silver pieces, and said, It is not lawful for to put them into the treasury, because it is the price of blood.

And they took counsel, and bought with them the potter's field, to bury strangers in.

Wherefore that field was called, The field of blood, unto this day.

Then was fulfilled that which was spoken by Jeremy the prophet, saying, And they took the thirty pieces of silver, the price of him that was valued, whom they of the children of Israel did value;

And gave them for the potter's field, as the Lord appointed me.

Hearing Before Herod
Luke 23:7–10

And as soon as he knew that he belonged unto Herod's jurisdiction, he sent him to Herod, who himself also was at Jerusalem at that time.

And when Herod saw Jesus, he was exceeding glad: for he was desirous to see him of a long season, because he had heard many things of him; and he hoped to have seen some miracle done by him.

Then he questioned with him in many words; but he answered him nothing.

And the chief priests and scribes stood and vehemently accused him.

Herod and Soldiers Mock Jesus
Luke 23:11–12

And Herod with his men of war set him at nought, and mocked him, and arrayed him in a gorgeous robe, and sent him again to Pilate.

And the same day Pilate and Herod were made friends together: for before they were at enmity between themselves.

---

108   Matthew reads, "see thou to that"

Second Hearing Before Pilate

Matt. 27:15–31, Mark 15:6–15, Luke 23:13–17

Now at that feast the governor was wont to release unto the people one prisoner, whomsoever they would desire.

And they had then a notable prisoner, called Barabbas, which lay bound with them that had made insurrection with him, who had committed murder in the insurrection.

Therefore when they were gathered together, the multitude crying aloud began to desire him to do as he had ever done unto them.

And Pilate, Said unto them, Ye have brought this man unto me, as one that perverteth the people: and, behold, I, having examined him before you, have found no fault in this man touching those things whereof ye accuse him:

No, nor yet Herod: for I sent you to him; and, lo, nothing worthy of death is done unto him.

I will therefore chastise him, and release him. (For of necessity he must release one unto them at the feast.)

Pilate said unto them, Whom will ye that I release unto you? Barabbas, or Will ye that I release unto you the King of the Jews, Jesus, which is called Christ?

For he knew that the chief priests for envy had delivered him.

When he was set down on the judgment seat, his wife sent unto him, saying, Have thou nothing to do with that just man: for I have suffered many things this day in a dream because of him.

But the chief priests and elders persuaded the multitude that they should rather ask release

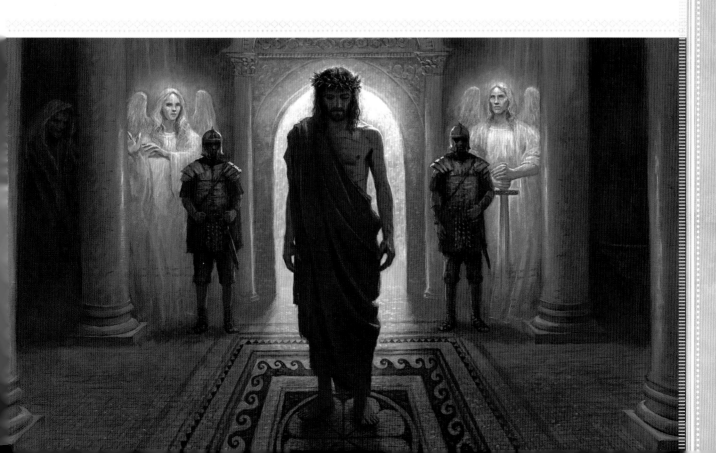

[of] Barabbas unto them, and destroy Jesus.

The governor answered and said unto them, Whether of the twain will ye that I release unto you? They said, Barabbas.

Pilate saith unto them, What will ye then that I shall do unto him whom ye call the King of the Jews, Jesus which is called Christ? They all say unto him, Let him be crucified.

And they cried out again, Crucify him.

And then Pilate the governor said, Why, what evil hath he done? But they cried out the more exceedingly, saying, Let him be crucified.

When Pilate saw that he could prevail nothing, but that rather a tumult was made, he took water, and washed his hands before the multitude, saying, I am innocent of the blood of this just person: see ye to it.

Then answered all the people, and said, His blood be on us, and on our children.

And so Pilate, willing to content the people, released Barabbas unto them: and when he had scourged Jesus, he delivered him to be crucified.

Then the soldiers of the governor took Jesus into the common hall, and gathered unto him the whole band of soldiers. And they stripped him, and put on him a <u>purple</u>[109] robe.

And when they had platted a crown of thorns, they put it upon his head, and a reed in his right hand: and they bowed the knee before him, and mocked him, saying, Hail, King of the Jews!

And they spit upon him, and took the reed, and smote him on the head.

And after that they had mocked him, they took the robe off from him, and put his own raiment on him, and led him away to crucify him.

---

109   Matthew reads, "scarlet"

A Murderer Released

Matt. 27:15–21, 26, Mark 15:6–15, Luke 23:18–25, John 18:39–40

Now at that feast the governor was wont to release unto the people one prisoner, whomsoever they would desire.

And they had then a notable prisoner, called Barabbas, which lay bound with them that had made insurrection with him, who had committed murder in the insurrection.

Therefore when they were gathered together, the multitude crying aloud began to desire him to do as he had ever done unto them.

But Pilate said unto them, ye have a custom, that I should release unto you one at the passover,

Whom will ye that I release unto you? Barabbas, or the King of the Jews, Jesus which is called Christ?

For he knew that for envy they, the chief priests, had delivered him.

When he was set down on the judgment seat, his wife sent unto him, saying, Have thou nothing to do with that just man: for I have suffered many things this day in a dream because of him.

But the chief priests and elders moved [and] persuaded the multitude [of] people that they that he should rather release Barabbas unto them, and destroy Jesus.

The governor answered and said again unto them, Whether of the twain will ye that I release unto you? And they all cried out all at once, saying, Not this man, away with this man, and release unto us Barabbas:

(Who for a certain sedition made in the city, and for murder, was cast into prison, [and] was a robber.)

And Pilate, willing to release Jesus, answered and said again unto them, What will ye then that I shall do unto him whom ye call the King of the Jews?

And they cried out again, Crucify him.

Then Pilate said unto them, Why, what evil hath he done? And they cried out the more exceedingly, Crucify him, crucify him.

And he said unto them the third time, Why, what evil hath he done? I have found no cause of death in him: I will therefore chastise him, and let him go.

And they were instant with loud voices, requiring that he might be crucified. And the voices of them and of the chief priests prevailed.

And so Pilate, willing to content the people, gave sentence that it should be as they required.

And he released Barabbas unto them, that for sedition and murder was cast into prison, whom they had desired; and when he had scourged Jesus, he delivered Jesus to their will to be crucified.

Pilate Proclaims His Innocence
Matt. 27:24–25, Luke 23:4, 14, 22, John 19:4

Then said Pilate to the chief priests and to the people, I find no fault in this man.

Pilate therefore went forth again, and saith unto them, Ye have brought this man unto me, as one that perverteth the people: and, behold, I bring him forth to you, having examined him before you, that ye may know that I have found no fault in this man touching those things whereof ye accuse him.

And he said unto them the third time, Why, what evil hath he done? I have found no cause of death in him: I will therefore chastise him, and let him go.

When Pilate saw that he could prevail nothing, but that rather a tumult was made, he took water, and washed his hands before the multitude, saying, I am innocent of the blood of this just person: see ye to it.

Then answered all the people, and said, His blood be on us, and on our children.

Jesus Scourged and Mocked
Matt. 27:27–31, Mark 15:15–20, John 19:1–12

And so Pilate, willing to content the people, released Barabbas unto them, and delivered Jesus, when he had scourged him, to be crucified.

Then the soldiers of the governor took Jesus into the common hall, Prætorium; and they call together, and gathered unto him the whole band of soldiers.

And they stripped him, And they clothed him with purple and put on him a scarlet robe.

And when they had platted a crown of thorns, they put it upon his head, and a reed in his right hand: and they bowed the knee before him And began to salute him, and mocked him,

saying, Hail, King of the Jews! and they smote him with their hands.

And they spit upon him, and took the reed, and smote him on the head.

Pilate therefore went forth again, and saith unto them, Behold, I bring him forth to you, that ye may know that I find no fault in him.

Then came Jesus forth, wearing the crown of thorns, and the purple robe. And Pilate saith unto them, Behold the man!

When the chief priests therefore and officers saw him, they cried out, saying, Crucify him, crucify him. Pilate saith unto them, Take ye him, and crucify him: for I find no fault in him.

The Jews answered him, We have a law,

and by our law he ought to die, because he made himself the Son of God.

When Pilate therefore heard that saying, he was the more afraid;

And went again into the judgment hall, and saith unto Jesus, Whence art thou? But Jesus gave him no answer.

Then saith Pilate unto him, Speakest thou not unto me? knowest thou not that I have power to crucify thee, and have power to release thee?

Jesus answered, Thou couldest have no power at all against me, except it were given thee from above: therefore he that delivered me unto thee hath the greater sin.

And from thenceforth Pilate sought to release him: but the Jews cried out, saying, If thou let this man go, thou art not Cæsar's friend: whosoever maketh himself a king speaketh against Cæsar.

And after that they had mocked him, they took the robe off from him, and put his own raiment on him, and led him away to crucify him.

Jesus Taken to Golgotha
Matt. 27:32–34, Mark 15:21–23, Luke 23:26–31, John 19:13–17,
JST Matt. 27:35, JST Luke 23:32, JST John 19:17

When Pilate therefore heard that saying, he brought Jesus forth, and sat down in the judgment seat in a place that is called the Pavement, but in the Hebrew, Gabbatha.

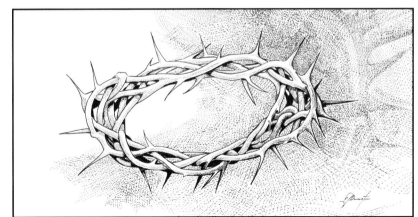

And it was the preparation of the passover, and about the sixth hour: and he saith unto the Jews, Behold your King!

But they cried out, Away with him, away with him, crucify him. Pilate saith unto them, Shall I crucify your King? The chief priests answered, We have no king but Cæsar.

Then delivered he him therefore unto them to be crucified. And they took Jesus, and led him away.

And as they came out, they found a man of Cyrene, Simon by name: who passed by, coming out of the country, the father of Alexander and Rufus, him they compelled to bear his cross, and on him they laid the cross, that he might bear it after Jesus.

And there followed him a great company of people, and of women, which also bewailed and lamented him.

But Jesus turning unto them said, Daughters of Jerusalem, weep not for me, but weep for yourselves, and for your children.

For, behold, the days are coming, in the which they shall say, Blessed are the barren, and the wombs that never bare, and the paps which never gave suck.

Then shall they begin to say to the mountains, Fall on us; and to the hills, Cover us.

For if they do these things in a green tree, what shall be done in the dry? This he spake, signifying the scattering of Israel, and the desolation of the heathen, or in other words, the Gentiles. And when they were come unto a place which is called in the Hebrew Golgotha: which is, being interpreted, The place of burial[110], They gave him vinegar to drink mingled with gall, wine mingled with myrrh: and when he had tasted thereof, he would not drink.

The Crucifixion
Matt. 27:35–44, Mark 15:24–33, Luke 23:32–43,
John 19:18–22, JST Luke 23:35

And they crucified him, and parted his garments, casting lots upon them, what every man should take: that it might be fulfilled which was spoken by the prophet, They parted my garments among them, and upon my vesture did they cast lots.

And sitting down they watched him there; And Pilate wrote a title, and put it on the cross.

And set up over his head his superscription of his accusation was written, THIS IS JESUS OF NAZARETH THE KING OF THE JEWS.

This title then read many of the Jews: for the place where Jesus was crucified was nigh to the city: and it was written in Hebrew, and Greek, and Latin.

Then said the chief priests of the Jews to Pilate, Write not, The King of the Jews; but that he said, I am King of the Jews.

Pilate answered, What I have written I have written.

And there were also two other, malefactors, thieves, led with him to be crucified with him.

And when they were come to the place, which is called Calvary, there they crucified him, and the malefactors, one on his right hand, and another on his left, and Jesus in the midst. Then said Jesus, Father, forgive them; for they know not what they do (Meaning the soldiers who crucified him). And they parted his raiment, and cast lots.

And the scripture was fulfilled, which saith, And he was numbered with the transgressors. And the people stood beholding.

And they that passed by reviled him, railed on him, wagging their heads,

And saying, Ah, thou that destroyest the temple, and buildest it in three days, save thyself. If thou be the Son of God, come down from the cross.

Likewise also the chief priests mocking him, among themselves with the scribes and elders, said,

He saved others; himself he cannot save. If he be Christ, the chosen of God, If he be the King of Israel, let him now come down from the cross, that we may see and we will believe him.

---

110   Matthew and John read, "a skull"

"Father, forgive them; for they know
not what they do."

He trusted in God; let him deliver him now, if he will have him: for he said, I am the Son of God.

And the soldiers also mocked him, coming to him, and offering him vinegar,

And saying, If thou be the king of the Jews, save thyself.

The thieves also, which were crucified with him, cast the same in his teeth.

And one of the malefactors which were hanged railed on him, saying, If thou be Christ, save thyself and us.

But the other answering rebuked him, saying, Dost not thou fear God, seeing thou art in the same condemnation?

And we indeed justly; for we receive the due reward of our deeds: but this man hath done nothing amiss.

And he said unto Jesus, Lord, remember me when thou comest into thy kingdom.

And Jesus said unto him, Verily I say unto thee, To day shalt thou be with me in paradise.

And it was the third hour, and they crucified him.

And when the sixth hour was come, there was darkness over the whole land until the ninth hour.

Soldiers Cast Lots for Jesus' Robe
Matt. 27:35, Mark 15:24, Luke 23:34, John 19:23–24

Then said Jesus, Father, forgive them; for they know not what they do.

Then the soldiers, when they had crucified Jesus, they took his garments, and made four parts, to every soldier a part; and also his coat: now the coat was without seam, woven from the top throughout.

They said therefore among themselves, Let us not rend it, but cast lots for it, whose it shall be: that the scripture might be fulfilled which was spoken by the prophet, They parted my raiment, garments, among them, and upon my vesture did they cast lots. These things therefore the soldiers did.

The Sign: King of the Jews
Matt.27:37, Mark 15:26, Luke 23:38, John 19:19–22

And Pilate wrote a title, and put it on the cross.

This title then read many of the Jews: for the place where Jesus was crucified was nigh to the city. And set up over his head the superscription of his accusation was written in letters of Greek, and Latin, and Hebrew, THIS IS JESUS OF NAZARETH THE KING OF THE JEWS. Then said the chief priests of the Jews to Pilate, Write not, The King of the Jews; but that he said, I am King of the Jews.

Pilate answered, What I have written I have written.

Darkness: Sixth to Ninth Hour
Matt. 27:45, Mark 15:33–36, Luke 23:44–45

Now from the sixth hour there was darkness over all the land unto the ninth hour.

And at the ninth hour Jesus cried with a loud voice, saying, Eloi, Eloi, lama sabachthani? which is, being interpreted, My God, my God, why hast thou forsaken me?

And some of them that stood by, when they heard it, said, Behold, he calleth Elias. And one ran and filled a spunge full of vinegar, and put it on a reed, and gave him to drink, saying, Let alone; let us see whether Elias will come to take him down.

And the sun was darkened, and the veil of the temple was rent in the midst.

Jesus' Mother Put in John's Care
John 19:25–27

Now there stood by the cross of Jesus his mother, and his mother's sister, Mary the wife of Cleophas, and Mary Magdalene.

When Jesus therefore saw his mother, and the disciple standing by, whom he loved, he saith unto his mother, Woman, behold thy son!

Then saith he to the disciple, Behold thy mother! And from that hour that disciple took her unto his own home.

Death of Jesus
Matt. 27:46–50, Mark 15:37, Luke 23:46, John 19:28–30, JST Matt. 27:54

And about the ninth hour Jesus cried with a loud voice, saying, Eli, Eli, lama sabachthani? that is to say, My God, my God, why hast thou forsaken me?

Some of them that stood there, when they heard that, said, This man calleth for Elias.

And straightway one of them ran, and took a spunge, and filled it with vinegar, and put it on a reed, and gave him to drink.

The rest said, Let be, let us see whether Elias will come to save him.

After this, Jesus knowing that all things were now accomplished, that the scripture might be fulfilled, saith, I thirst.

Now there was set a vessel full of vinegar: and they filled a spunge with vinegar, and put it upon hyssop, and put it to his mouth.

When Jesus therefore had received the vinegar he cried again with a loud voice and he said, Father, It is finished: thy will is done, into thy hands I commend my spirit: and having said thus, he bowed his head and yielded [and] gave up the ghost.

Earthquake: Veil of Temple Rent
Matt. 27:51–53, Mark 15:38, Luke 23:45

Mark adds no additional information

And the sun was darkened, And, behold, the veil of the temple was rent in twain in the midst from the top to the bottom; and the earth did quake, and the rocks rent;

And the graves were opened; and many bodies of the saints which slept arose,

And came out of the graves after his resurrection, and went into the holy city, and appeared unto many.

Pierced by a Spear
John 19:31–34

The Jews therefore, because it was the preparation, that the bodies should not remain upon the cross on the sabbath day, (for that sabbath day was an high day,) besought Pilate that their legs might be broken, and that they might be taken away.

Then came the soldiers, and brake the legs of the first, and of the other which was crucified with him.

But when they came to Jesus, and saw that he was dead already, they brake not his legs:

But one of the soldiers with a spear pierced his side, and forthwith came there out blood and water.

Passover Scripture Fulfilled
John 19:35–37

And he that saw it bare record, and his record is true: and he knoweth that he saith true, that ye might believe.

For these things were done, that the scripture should be fulfilled, A bone of him shall not be broken.

And again another scripture saith, They shall look on him whom they pierced.

Watchers Near the Cross

Matt. 27:54–56, Mark 15:39–41, Luke 23:47–49

Now when the centurion, which stood over against him, saw what was done, he glorified God, saying, Certainly this was a righteous man. and they that were with him, watching Jesus, saw that he so cried out, and gave up the ghost, [and] saw the earthquake, and those things that were done, they feared greatly, saying, Truly this man was the Son of God.

And all the people that came together to that sight, beholding the things which were done, smote their breasts, and returned.

There were also all his acquaintance, and many women that followed him from Galilee there beholding these things afar off, which followed Jesus from Galilee, ministering unto him:

Among which was Mary Magdalene, and Mary the mother of James the less and of Joses, and the mother of Zebedee's children, and Salome;

(Who also, when he was in Galilee, followed him, and ministered unto him;) and many other women which came up with him unto Jerusalem.

Jesus' Burial

Matt. 27:57–61, Mark 15:42–47, Luke 23:50–56, John 19:38–42

And now when the even was come, because it was the preparation, that is, the day before the sabbath, there came a rich man of Arimathæa, a city of the Jews: named Joseph, an honourable counselor and he was a good man, and a just:

(The same had not consented to the counsel and deed of them;) which also waited for the kingdom of God, who also himself was Jesus' disciple, but secretly for fear of the Jews,

He went in boldly unto to Pilate, and craved and begged the body of Jesus.

And Pilate marvelled if he were already dead: and calling unto him the centurion, he asked him whether he had been any while dead.

And when he knew it of the centurion, Then Pilate commanded the body to be delivered to Joseph.

And when Joseph had taken the body, he bought fine linen, and took him down.

And there came also Nicodemus, which at the first came to Jesus by night, and brought a mixture of myrrh and aloes, about an hundred pound weight.

Then took they the body of Jesus, and wrapped it in a clean linen cloth with the spices, as the manner of the Jews is to bury.

Now in the place where he was crucified there was a garden; and in the garden a new sepulchre,

There laid they Jesus in his [Joseph's] own new tomb, which he had hewn out in the rock, wherein never man before was laid:

There laid they Jesus therefore because of the Jews' preparation day; for the sepulchre was nigh at hand. And he rolled a great stone to the door of the sepulchre, and departed.

And the women also, which came with him from Galilee, followed after And there was Mary Magdalene, and the other Mary the mother of Joses sitting over against the sepulchre, and beheld the sepulchre where he was laid, and how his body was laid.

And they returned, and prepared spices and ointments; and rested the sabbath day according to the commandment.

Chief Priests and Pharisees Seal the Tomb
Matt. 27:62–66

Now the next day, that followed the day of the preparation, the chief priests and Pharisees came together unto Pilate,

Saying, Sir, we remember that that deceiver said, while he was yet alive, After three days I will rise again.

Command therefore that the sepulchre be made sure until the third day, lest his disciples come by night, and steal him away, and say unto the people, He is risen from the dead: so the last error shall be worse than the first.

Pilate said unto them, Ye have a watch: go your way, make it as sure as ye can.

So they went, and made the sepulchre sure, sealing the stone, and setting a watch.

First Day: Earthquake, Angels Open Tomb
Matt. 28:1–2, Luke 24:1–2, JST Luke 24:2–4

In the end of the sabbath, very early in the morning, as it began to dawn toward the first day of the week, came Mary Magdalene and the other Mary to see the sepulcher, bringing the spices which they had prepared, and certain others with them.

And, behold, there was a great earthquake: for the angel of the Lord descended from heaven, and came and rolled back the stone from the door, and sat upon it.

And they found the stone rolled away from the sepulchre, and two angels standing by it in shining garments.

And they entered into the sepulcher, and not finding the body of the Lord Jesus, they were much perplexed thereabout;

And were affrighted, and bowed down their faces to the earth. But behold the angels said unto them, Why seek ye the living among the dead?

Mary Magdalene Comes to the Open Tomb
John 20:1–2, JST John 20:1

The first day of the week cometh Mary Magdalene early, when it was yet dark, unto the sepulchre, and seeth the stone taken away from the sepulchre, <u>and two angels sitting thereon.</u>

Then she runneth, and cometh to Simon Peter, and to the other disciple, whom Jesus loved, and saith unto them, They have taken away the Lord out of the sepulchre, and we know not where they have laid him.

Peter and John Run to the Tomb
Luke 24:12, 24, John 20:3–10

Then arose Peter went forth, and that other disciple ran unto the sepulchre;

So they ran both together: and the other disciple did outrun Peter, and came first to the sepulchre.

And he and stooping down and looking in, he beheld the linen clothes laid by themselves, yet went he not in.

Then cometh Simon Peter following him, and went into the sepulchre, and seeth the linen clothes lie,

And the napkin, that was about his head, not lying with the linen clothes, but wrapped together in a place by itself.

Then went in also that other disciple, which came first to the sepulchre, and he saw, and believed.

For as yet they knew not the scripture, that he must rise again from the dead.

Then the disciples went away again and departed, unto their own home, wondering in himself at that which was come to pass.

And certain of them which were with us went to the sepulchre, and found it even so as the women had said: but him they saw not.

"Woman, Why Weepest Thou?"
John 20:11–13

But Mary stood without at the sepulchre weeping: and as she wept, she stooped down, and looked into the sepulchre,

And seeth two angels in white sitting, the one at the head, and the other at the feet, where the body of Jesus had lain.

And they say unto her, Woman, why weepest thou? She saith unto them, Because they have taken away my Lord, and I know not where they have laid him.

"Touch Me Not"
John 20:14–17, JST John 20:17

And when she had thus said, she turned herself back, and saw Jesus standing, and knew not that it was Jesus.

Jesus saith unto her, Woman, why weepest thou? whom seekest thou? She, supposing him to be the gardener, saith unto him, Sir, if thou have borne him hence, tell me where thou hast laid him, and I will take him away.

Jesus saith unto her, Mary. She turned herself, and saith unto him, Rabboni; which is to say, Master. Jesus saith unto her,

Hold me not[111]; for I am not yet ascended to my Father: but go to my brethren, and say unto them, I ascend unto my Father, and your Father; and to my God, and your God.

---

111 John reads, "Touch me not"

Disciples Told, But Disbelieve
Mark 16:10–11, Luke 24:9–11, John 20:18

And **Mary Magdalene** went and returned from the sepulchre, and told all these things unto the eleven, and to all the rest [of] them that had been with him, as they mourned and wept **that she had seen the Lord, and that he had spoken these things unto her.**

It was Mary Magdalene, and Joanna, and Mary the mother of James, and other women that were with them, which told these things unto the apostles.

And they, when they had heard that he was alive, and had been seen of her, **and their words seemed to them as idle tales, and they** believed **them** not.

Two Marys Come to the Tomb
Matt. 28:1, Mark 16:1–4, Luke 24:3, JST Mark 16:3-6

And when the sabbath was past, Mary Magdalene, and Mary the mother of James, and Salome, had bought sweet spices, that they might come and anoint him.

In the end of the sabbath, very early in the morning, **as it began to dawn toward the first day of the week,** they came unto the sepulchre.

And they said among themselves, Who shall roll us away the stone from the door of the sepulchre?

<u>But</u> when they looked, they saw that the stone was rolled away: for it was very great, <u>and two angels sitting thereon, clothed in long white garments; and they were affrighted. But the angels said unto them, Be not affrighted; ye seek Jesus of Nazareth, who was crucified; he is risen; he is not here; behold the place where they laid him;</u>

<u>And go your way, tell his disciples and Peter, that he goeth before you into Galilee; there shall ye see him as he said unto you.</u>

And they entered <u>into the sepulcher,</u> and <u>saw the place where they laid Jesus</u> [and] found not the body of the Lord Jesus.

Angels: "He Is Risen"
Matt. 28:2–8, Mark 16:5–8, Luke 24:4–8, JST Matt. 28:4

And, behold, there was a great earthquake: for the angel of the Lord descended from heaven, and came and rolled back the stone from the door, and sat upon it.

His countenance was like lightning, and his raiment white as snow:

And for fear of him the keepers did shake, and became as dead men.

And entering into the sepulchre, they saw a young man sitting on the right side, clothed in a long white garment; and they were affrighted.

And it came to pass, as they were much perplexed thereabout, behold, two men stood by them in shining garments: And as they were afraid, and bowed down their faces to the earth, the angel<u>s</u> answered and said unto the women, Why seek ye the living among the dead? Fear not ye: for <u>we</u>[112] know that ye seek Jesus of Nazareth, which was crucified.

He is not here: for he is risen, as he said. Come, see the place where the Lord lay.

And go your way quickly, and tell his disciples and Peter that he is risen from the dead; remember how he spake unto you when he was yet in Galilee,

Saying, The Son of man must be delivered into the hands of sinful men, and be crucified, and the third day rise again, and, behold, he goeth before you into Galilee; there shall ye see him as he said unto you: lo, I have told you.

And they remembered his words.

And they departed quickly and fled from the sepulchre with fear and great joy; and did run to bring his disciples word, for they trembled and were amazed: neither said they any thing to any man; for they were afraid.

Women Meet Jesus
Matt. 28:9–10, Luke 16:9

Now when Jesus was risen early the first day of the week, he appeared first to Mary Magdalene, out of whom he had cast seven devils.

And as they went to tell his disciples, behold, Jesus met them, saying, All hail. And they came and held him by the feet, and worshipped him.

Then said Jesus unto them, Be not afraid: go tell my brethren that they go into Galilee, and there shall they see me.

Officials Bribe Soldiers
Matt. 28:11–15

Now when they were going, behold, some of the watch came into the city, and shewed unto the chief priests all the things that were done.

And when they were assembled with the elders, and had taken counsel, they gave large money unto the soldiers,

Saying, Say ye, His disciples came by night, and stole him away while we slept.

And if this come to the governor's ears, we will persuade him, and secure you.

So they took the money, and did as they were taught: and this saying is commonly reported among the Jews until this day.

---

112   Matthew reads, "I"

Jesus Appears to Two Disciples
Mark 16:12, Luke 24:13–32

After that he appeared in another form unto two of them, as they walked, and went into the country.

And, behold, two of them went that same day to a village called Emmaus, which was from Jerusalem about threescore furlongs.

And they talked together of all these things which had happened.

And it came to pass, that, while they communed together and reasoned, Jesus himself drew near, and went with them.

But their eyes were holden that they should not know him.

And he said unto them, What manner of communications are these that ye have one to another, as ye walk, and are sad?

And the one of them, whose name was Cleopas, answering said unto him, Art thou only a stranger in Jerusalem, and hast not known the things which are come to pass there in these days?

And he said unto them, What things? And they said unto him, Concerning Jesus of Nazareth, which was a prophet mighty in deed and word before God and all the people:

And how the chief priests and our rulers delivered him to be condemned to death, and have crucified him.

But we trusted that it had been he which should have redeemed Israel: and beside all this, to day is the third day since these things were done.

Yea, and certain women also of our company made us astonished, which were early at the sepulchre;

And when they found not his body, they came, saying, that they had also seen a vision of angels, which said that he was alive.

And certain of them which were with us went to the sepulchre, and found it even so as the women had said: but him they saw not.

Then he said unto them, O fools, and slow of heart to believe all that the prophets have spoken:

Ought not Christ to have suffered these things, and to enter into his glory?

And beginning at Moses and all the prophets, he expounded unto them in all the scriptures the things concerning himself.

And they drew nigh unto the village, whither they went: and he made as though he would have gone further.

But they constrained him, saying, Abide with us: for it is toward evening, and the day is far spent. And he went in to tarry with them.

And it came to pass, as he sat at meat with them, he took bread, and blessed it, and brake, and gave to them.

And their eyes were opened, and they knew him; and he vanished out of their sight.

And they said one to another, Did not our heart burn within us, while he talked with us by the way, and while he opened to us the scriptures?

Two Tell Others Who Disbelieve
Mark 16:13, Luke 24:33–35

And they rose up the same hour, and returned to Jerusalem, and found the eleven gathered together, and them that were with them,

And they went and told it unto the residue: Saying, The Lord is risen indeed, and hath appeared to Simon.

And they told what things were done in the way, and how he was known of them in breaking of bread, neither believed they them.

Evening: Jesus Appears to Disciples
Mark 16:14, Luke 24:36–49, John 20:19–23

Then the same day at evening, being the first day of the week, when the doors were shut where the disciples were assembled for fear of the Jews,

And as they thus spake, came Jesus himself appeared and stood in the midst of them, unto the eleven as they sat at meat. And [he] saith unto them, Peace be unto you.

But they were terrified and affrighted, and supposed that they had seen a spirit.

And upbraided them with their unbelief and hardness of heart, because they believed not them which had seen him after he was risen.

And he said unto them, Why are ye troubled? and why do thoughts arise in your hearts?

Behold my hands and my feet, that it is I myself: handle me, and see; for a spirit hath not flesh and bones, as ye see me have.

And when he had thus spoken, he shewed unto them his hands and his feet and his side.

Then were the disciples glad, when they saw the Lord.

And while they yet believed not for joy, and wondered, he said unto them, Have ye here any meat? And they gave him a piece of a broiled fish, and of an honeycomb.

And he took it, and did eat before them.

And he said unto them, These are the words which I spake unto you, while I was yet with you, that all things must be fulfilled, which were written in the law of Moses, and in the prophets, and in the psalms, concerning me.

Then opened he their understanding, that they might understand the scriptures,

And said unto them, Thus it is written, and thus it behoved Christ to suffer, and to rise from the dead the third day:

And that repentance and remission of sins should be preached in his name among all nations, beginning at Jerusalem.

And ye are witnesses of these things.

And, behold, I send the promise of my Father upon you: but tarry ye in the city of Jerusalem, until ye be endued with power from on high.

Then said Jesus to them again, Peace be unto you: as my Father hath sent me, even so send I you.

And when he had said this, he breathed on them, and saith unto them, Receive ye the Holy Ghost:

Whose soever sins ye remit, they are remitted unto them; and whose soever sins ye retain, they are retained.

Thomas, Absent, Does Not Believe
John 20:24–25

But Thomas, one of the twelve, called Didymus, was not with them when Jesus came.

The other disciples therefore said unto him, We have seen the Lord. But he said unto them, Except I shall see in his hands the print of the nails, and put my finger into the print of the nails, and thrust my hand into his side, I will not believe.

Eight Days Later: With Thomas
John 20:26–29

And after eight days again his disciples were within, and Thomas with them: then came Jesus, the doors being shut, and stood in the midst, and said, Peace be unto you.

Then saith he to Thomas, Reach hither thy finger, and behold my hands; and reach hither thy hand, and thrust it into my side: and be not faithless, but believing.

And Thomas answered and said unto him, My Lord and my God.

Jesus saith unto him, Thomas, because thou hast seen me, thou hast believed: blessed are they that have not seen, and yet have believed.

Purpose of John's Gospel
John 20:30–31

And many other signs truly did Jesus in the presence of his disciples, which are not written in this book:

But these are written, that ye might believe that Jesus is the Christ, the Son of God; and that believing ye might have life through his name.

Peter: "I Go Fishing"

John 21:1–19

AFTER these things Jesus shewed himself again to the disciples at the sea of Tiberias; and on this wise shewed he himself. There were together Simon Peter, and Thomas called Didymus, and Nathanael of Cana in Galilee, and the sons of Zebedee, and two other of his disciples.

Simon Peter saith unto them, I go a fishing. They say unto him, We also go with thee. They went forth, and entered into a ship immediately; and that night they caught nothing.

But when the morning was now come, Jesus stood on the shore: but the disciples knew not that it was Jesus.

Then Jesus saith unto them, Children, have ye any meat? They answered him, No.

And he said unto them, Cast the net on the right side of the ship, and ye shall find. They cast therefore, and now they were not able to draw it for the multitude of fishes.

Therefore that disciple whom Jesus loved saith unto Peter, It is the Lord. Now when Simon Peter heard that it was the Lord, he girt his fisher's coat unto him, (for he was naked,) and did cast himself into the sea.

And the other disciples came in a little ship; (for they were not far from land, but as it were two hundred cubits,) dragging the net with fishes.

As soon then as they were come to land, they saw a fire of coals there, and fish laid thereon, and bread.

Jesus saith unto them, Bring of the fish which ye have now caught.

Simon Peter went up, and drew the net to land full of great fishes, an hundred and fifty and three: and for all there were so many, yet was not the net broken.

Jesus saith unto them, Come and dine. And none of the disciples durst ask him, Who art thou? knowing that it was the Lord.

Jesus then cometh, and taketh bread, and giveth them, and fish likewise.

This is now the third time that Jesus shewed himself to his disciples, after that he was risen from the dead.

So when they had dined, Jesus saith to Simon Peter, Simon, son of Jonas, lovest thou me more than these? He saith unto him, Yea, Lord; thou knowest that I love thee. He saith unto him, Feed my lambs.

He saith to him again the second time, Simon, son of Jonas, lovest thou me? He saith unto him, Yea, Lord; thou knowest that I love thee. He saith unto him, Feed my sheep.

He saith unto him the third time, Simon, son of Jonas, lovest thou me? Peter was grieved because he said unto him the third time, Lovest thou me? And he said unto him, Lord, thou knowest all things; thou knowest that I love thee. Jesus saith unto him, Feed my sheep.

Verily, verily, I say unto thee, When thou wast young, thou girdedst thyself, and walkedst whither thou wouldest: but when thou shalt be old, thou shalt stretch forth thy hands, and another shall gird thee, and carry thee whither thou wouldest not.

This spake he, signifying by what death he should glorify God. And when he had spoken this, he saith unto him, Follow me.

Peter Inquires about John

John 21:20–22

Then Peter, turning about, seeth the disciple whom Jesus loved following; which also leaned on his breast at supper, and said, Lord, which is he that betrayeth thee?

Peter seeing him saith to Jesus, Lord, and what shall this man do?

Jesus saith unto him, If I will that he tarry till I come, what is that to thee? follow thou me.

Testimony about John

John 21:23–25

Then went this saying abroad among the brethren, that that disciple should not die: yet Jesus said not unto him, He shall not die; but, If I will that he tarry till I come, what is that to thee?

This is the disciple which testifieth of these things, and wrote these things: and we know that his testimony is true.

And there are also many other things which Jesus did, the which, if they should be written every one, I suppose that even the world itself could not contain the books that should be written. Amen.

The Great Commission to the Twelve

Matt. 28:16–20, Mark 16:15–18

Then the eleven disciples went away into Galilee, into a mountain where Jesus had appointed them.

And when they saw him, they worshipped him: but some doubted.

And Jesus came and spake unto them, saying, All power is given unto me in heaven and in earth.

Go ye therefore into all the world, and teach all nations and preach the gospel to every creature, baptizing them in the name of the Father, and of the Son, and of the Holy Ghost:

He that believeth and is baptized shall be saved; but he that believeth not shall be damned.

And these signs shall follow them that believe; In my name shall they cast out devils; they shall speak with new tongues;

They shall take up serpents; and if they drink any deadly thing, it shall not hurt them: they shall lay hands on the sick, and they shall recover.

Teaching them to observe all things whatsoever I have commanded you: and, lo, I am with you alway, even unto the end of the world. Amen.

"Go ye therefore into all the world, and teach all nations and preach the gospel to every creature."

Ascension, Proclamation

Mark 16:19–20, Luke 24:50–53

So then after the Lord had spoken unto them, he led them out as far as to Bethany, and he lifted up his hands, and blessed them.

And it came to pass, while he blessed them, he was parted from them, and carried up into heaven, and sat on the right hand of God.

And they worshipped him, and returned to Jerusalem with great joy:

And they went forth, and preached every where, the Lord working with them, and confirming the word with signs following, and [they] were continually in the temple, praising and blessing God. Amen.

Art Credits

viii. *Christ Profile* © 2010 Christopher Young. For print information, go to www.christopheryoungart.com.

5. *The Annunciation* © 2010 James C. Christensen, © The Greenwich Workshop®, Inc. www.greenwichworkshop.com.

6. *The Annunciation to Joseph* © Joseph F. Brickey. For more information, go to www.josephbrickey.com.

7. *Mary's Visit to Elizabeth* by Carl Heinrich Bloch, courtesy of Det Nationalhistoriske Museum på Frederiksborg, Hillerød.

8. *A Savior Is Born* © Joseph F. Brickey. For more information, go to www.josephbrickey.com.

10. *The Nativity* © Cliff Dunston. For more information, call 801.766.9191.

12. *Depart to Egypt* © Cliff Dunston. For more information, call 801.766.9191.

13. *Herod's Plot* © Cliff Dunston. For more information, call 801.766.9191.

14. *Return to Jerusalem* © Cliff Dunston. For more information, call 801.766.9191.

16. *To Fulfill All Righteousness* © 2010 Simon Dewey. Courtesy of Altus Fine Art. For print information, go to www.altusfineart.com.

19. *To Fulfill All Righteousness* © 2010 Liz Lemon Swindle. Used with permission from Foundation Arts. For print information, go to www.foundationarts.com or call 1.800.366.2781.

20. *Stones of Temptation* © Cliff Dunston. For more information, call 801.766.9191.

23. *Wedding at Cana* by Carl Heinrich Bloch, courtesy of Det Nationalhistoriske Museum på Frederiksborg, Hillerød.

24. *Cleansing the Temple* by James Tissot.

26. *Nicodemus Came unto Him by Night* © Walter Rane. For more information, go to www.walterrane.com.

27. *John the Baptist* © Robert T. Barrett. For more information, go to www.roberttbarrett.com.

29. *Well of Life* © Robert T. Barrett. For more information, go to www.roberttbarrett.com.

31. *Light and Truth* © 2010 Simon Dewey. Courtesy of Altus Fine Art. For print information, go to www.altusfineart.com.

33. *Fishers of Men* © 2010 Simon Dewey. Courtesy of Altus Fine Art. For print information, go to www.altusfineart.com.

35. *The Grateful Leper* © Cliff Dunston. For more information, call 801.766.9191.

37. *Without Purse or Script* © 2010 Liz Lemon Swindle. Used with permission from Foundation Arts. For print information, go to www.foundationarts.com or call 1.800.366.2781.

39. *Cup for a Child* © Cliff Dunston. For more information, call 801.766.9191.

39. *The Sermon on the Mount* by Carl Heinrich Bloch, courtesy of Det Nationalhistoriske Museum på Frederiksborg, Hillerød.

41. *Let Your Light So Shine* © Cliff Dunston. For more information, call 801.766.9191.

44. *Coat and Cloak* © Cliff Dunston. For more information, call 801.766.9191.

45. *Hear Ye Him* © 2010 Simon Dewey. Courtesy of Altus Fine Art. For print information, go to www.altusfineart.com.

46. *Rust and Moth* © Cliff Dunston. For more information, call 801.766.9191.

47. *Two Masters, One Choice* © Cliff Dunston. For more information, call 801.766.9191.

48. *Beam and Mote* © Cliff Dunston. For more information, call 801.766.9191.

49. *Bread, Stone, and Fish* © Cliff Dunston. For more information, call 801.766.9191.

50. *Straight and Narrow Gate* © Cliff Dunston. For more information, call 801.766.9191.

51. *Good Fruit* © Cliff Dunston. For more information, call 801.766.9191.

52. *House Upon the Rock* © Cliff Dunston. For more information, call 801.766.9191.

54. *Lord I Believe* © 2010 Liz Lemon Swindle. Used with permission from Foundation Arts. For print information, go to www.foundationarts.com or call 1.800.366.2781.

55. *Birds Have Nests* © Cliff Dunston. For more information, call 801.766.9191.

56. *Peace, Be Still* © Arnold Friberg 2010. Used by permission from Friberg Fine Art. For print information, go to www.fribergfineart.com.

59. *The Paralytic* © J. Kirk Richards. For more information, go to www.jkirkrichards.com.

61. *Raising the Daughter of Jairus* © Jeffrey Hein. For more information, go to www.jeffreyhein.com.

63. *She Touched Him* © Cliff Dunston. For more information, call 801.766.9191.

63. *Two Blind Men Healed* © Cliff Dunston. For more information, call 801.766.9191.

64. *The Dumb Man Healed* © Cliff Dunston. For more information, call 801.766.9191.

67. Carl Heinrich Bloch (1834-1890), *Christ Healing the Sick at Bethesda,* 1883, oil on canvas, 101 x 126 inches. Brigham Young University Museum of Art, purchased with funds provided by Jack R. and Mary Lois Wheatley. All rights reserved. Uncropped image shown here:

68. *Man of Holiness* © Joseph F. Brickey. For more information, go to www.josephbrickey.com.

70. *The Corn* © Cliff Dunston. For more information, call 801.766.9191.

71. *Healing of the Withered Hand* © Cliff Dunston. For more information, call 801.766.9191.

74. *Mother* © 2010 Liz Lemon Swindle. Used with permission from Foundation Arts. For print information, go to www.foundationarts.com or call 1.800.366.2781.

75. *The Parable of the Seeds* © Cliff Dunston. For more information, call 801.766.9191.

77. *Parables* © 2010 James C. Christensen, © The Greenwich Workshop®, Inc., www.greenwichworkshop.com.

78. *The Wheat and Tares* © Cliff Dunston. For more information, call 801.766.9191.

79. *Mustard Seed Tree* © Cliff Dunston. For more information, call 801.766.9191.

81. *Parable of the Net* © Cliff Dunston. For more information, call 801.766.9191.

83. *Christ Went to the Desert to Lament John's Death* © Cliff Dunston. For more information, call 801.766.9191.

85. *Feeding of the Five Thousand* by Harry Anderson © Pacific Press Publishing Association, Nampa, Idaho.

86. *Christ Walking on the Waters* by Sergius Julius Von Kleaver. Courtesy of Sotheby's Picture Library, London. For information on art prints, go to www.foveditions.com.

89. *Bread of Life* by Roger Loveless © 2010 Roger Loveless.

91. *What Defiles a Man* © Cliff Dunston. For more information, call 801.766.9191.

92. *The Faithful Canaanite* © Cliff Dunston. For more information, call 801.766.9191.

93. *Christ Heals the Lame Man* © Cliff Dunston. For more information, call 801.766.9191.

96. *Approaching Storm* by Roger Loveless © 2010 Roger Loveless.

98. *Transfiguration of Christ* by Carl Heinrich Bloch, courtesy of Det Nationalhistoriske Museum på Frederiksborg, Hillerød.

101. *The Lost Sheep* © Cliff Dunston. For more information, call 801.766.9191.

102. *Lost Lamb* © Del Parson. For more information, go to www.delparson.com.

105. *The Prodigal Son* © 2010 Liz Lemon Swindle. Used with permission from Foundation Arts. For print information, go to www.foundationarts.com or call 1.800.366.2781.

106. *He That Is Without Sin* © Walter Rane. For more information, go to www.walterrane.com.

108. *From the Rooftops* © Al Rounds. For print information, call 801.287.6789 or visit www.alrounds.com.

110. *Come Unto Me* © Cliff Dunston. For more information, call 801.766.9191.

111. *The Good Samaritan* © Joseph F. Brickey. For more information, go to www.josephbrickey.com.

112. *Mary Heard His Word* © Walter Rane. For more information, go to www.walterrane.com.

114. *Woman With Crooked Back* © 2007 BiblicalPaintings.org. All Rights Reserved.

115. *Return to Jerusalem* © Cliff Dunston. For more information, call 801.766.9191.

117. *Where Are the Nine* © 2010 Liz Lemon Swindle. Used with permission from Foundation Arts. For print information, go to www.foundationarts.com or call 1.800.366.2781.

119. *Friends* © 2010 Liz Lemon Swindle. Used with permission from Foundation Arts. For print information, go to www.foundationarts.com or call 1.800.366.2781.

121. *He Who Is Without Sin* © 2010 Liz Lemon Swindle. Used with permission from Foundation Arts. For print information, go to www.foundationarts.com or call 1.800.366.2781.

122. *Light of the World* by Greg Olsen, © Greg Olsen Art. Used with permission. www.gregolsenart.com.

125. *Christ Healing the Blind Man* by Carl Heinrich Bloch, courtesy of Det Nationalhistoriske Museum på Frederiksborg, Hillerød.

126. *Whereas I Was Blind* © 2010 Tyson Snow. Used with permission from Foundation Arts. For print information, go to www.foundationarts.com or call 1.800.366.2781.

127. *The Lord Is My Shepherd* © 2010 Simon Dewey. Courtesy of Altus Fine Art. For print information, go to www.altusfineart.com.

129. *Let the Children Come* © 2010 Liz Lemon Swindle. Used with permission from Foundation Arts. For print information, go to www.foundationarts.com or call 1.800.366.2781.

130. *The Rich Young Man* © Cliff Dunston. For more information, call 801.766.9191.

131. *Workers in the Vineyard* © Cliff Dunston. For more information, call 801.766.9191.

132. *My Father's House* © Al Rounds. For print information, call 801.287.6789 or visit www.alrounds.com

135. *He Anointed the Eyes of the Blind Man* © Walter Rane. For more information, go to www.walterrane.com.

136. *Zaccheus* © J. Kirk Richards. For more information, go to www.jkirkrichards.com.

139. *I Am the Resurrection* © 2010 Liz Lemon Swindle. Used with permission from Foundation Arts. For print information, go to www.foundationarts.com or call 1.800.366.2781.

141. *For She Loved Much* © 2010 Simon Dewey. Courtesy of Altus Fine Art. For print information, go to www.altusfineart.com.

143. *Triumphal Entry* © Walter Rane. For more information, go to www.walterrane.com.

144. *Jesus Wept* © 2010 Liz Lemon Swindle. Used with permission from Foundation Arts. For print information, go to www.foundationarts.com or call 1.800.366.2781.

146. *Cleansing the Temple* by Carl Heinrich Bloch, courtesy of Det Nationalhistoriske Museum på Frederiksborg, Hillerød.

147. *The Fig Tree* © Cliff Dunston. For more information, call 801.766.9191.

149. *Wicked Husbandmen* © 2007 BiblicalPaintings.org. All Rights Reserved.

152. *Moses and the Burning Bush,* Arnold Friberg 2010. Used by permission from Friberg Fine Art. For print information, go to www.fribergfineart.com

155. *The Widow's Mite* © 2010 James C. Christensen, © The Greenwich Workshop®, Inc., www.greenwichworkshop.com.

157. *Jesus Christ* © 2010 Christopher Young. For print information, go to www.christopheryoungart.com.

159. *House of Desolate* © Cliff Dunston. For more information, call 801.766.9191.

161. *The Eagle Shall Gather* © Cliff Dunston. For more information, call 801.766.9191.

162. *In His Glory* © Del Parson. For more information, go to www.delparson.com.

163. *Noah's Ark* © Cliff Dunston. For more information, call 801.766.9191.

164. *Five of Them Were Wise Virgins* © Walter Rane. For more information, go to www.walterrane.com.

166. *The Talent* © Cliff Dunston. For more information, call 801.766.9191.

166. *Emblems of the Sacrament* © Cliff Dunston. For more information, call 801.766.9191.

168. *At Her Master's Feet* © Del Parson. For more information, go to www.delparson.com.

171. *Bread of Life* © 2010 Christopher Young. For print information, go to www.christopheryoungart.com.

172. *In Humility* © 2010 Simon Dewey. Courtesy of Altus Fine Art. For print information, go to www.altusfineart.com.

175. *Prince of Peace* © 2010 Simon Dewey. Courtesy of Altus Fine Art. For print information, go to www.altusfineart.com.

176. *Men of Galilee* © 2010 Simon Dewey. Courtesy of Altus Fine Art. For print information, go to www.altusfineart.com.

179. *Peace I Give Unto You* © Walter Rane. For more information, go to www.walterrane.com.

181. *The Cock's Crow* © Cliff Dunston. For more information, call 801.766.9191.

182. *Gethsemane* © 2010 Liz Lemon Swindle. Used with permission from Foundation Arts. For print information, go to www.foundationarts.com or call 1.800.366.2781.

185. *Judas Betrays Christ* by Ted Henninger © Intellectual Reserve.

187. *Peter's Denial* by Carl Heinrich Bloch, courtesy of Det Nationalhistoriske Museum på Frederiksborg, Hillerød.

188. *The Lord Accused Before Caiaphas* by Frank Adams.

191. *Awaiting the Command* by Jon McNaughton, © McNaughton Fine Art Co. For print information, go to www.mcnaughtonart.com.

192. *Behold the Man* © 2010 Simon Dewey. Courtesy of Altus Fine Art. For print information, go to www.altusfineart.com.

194. *Behold the Man* © 2010 Christopher Young. For print information, go to www.christopheryoungart.com.

195. *The Crown* © Cliff Dunston. For more information, call 801.766.9191.

197. *Man of Sorrows* © 2010 Christopher Young. For print information, go to www.christopheryoungart.com.

199. *It Is Finished* © 2010 Liz Lemon Swindle. Used with permission from Foundation Arts. For print information, go to www.foundationarts.com or call 1.800.366.2781.

201. *The Entombment* by Carl Heinrich Bloch, courtesy of Det Nationalhistoriske Museum på Frederiksborg, Hillerød.

203. *Hope* © 2010 Liz Lemon Swindle. Used with permission from Foundation Arts. For print information, go to www.foundationarts.com or call 1.800.366.2781.

204. *The Risen Hope* © Joseph F. Brickey. For more information, go to www.josephbrickey.com.

209. *The Doubting Thomas* by Carl Heinrich Bloch, courtesy of Ugerløse Kirke.

210. *Lovest Thou Me More Than These?* © David Lindsley. For more information, go to www.davidlindsley.com

213. *Go Ye Therefore and Teach* by Harry Anderson © Intellectual Reserve, Inc. Courtesy of the Museum of Church History and Art.